REFLECTIONS
FOR
DAILY PRAYER

ALAN BARTLETT
ROSALIND BROWN
STEVEN CROFT
MALCOLM GUITE
SUE HOPE
JOHN KIDDLE
JANE LEACH
JAN MCFARLANE
BARBARA MOSSE
DAVID MOXON
MARTYN PERCY
BEN QUASH
ANGELA TILBY
JANE WILLIAMS

REFLECTIONS
FOR
DAILY PRAYER

ADVENT **2011** TO
EVE OF ADVENT **2012**

Church House Publishing
Church House
Great Smith Street
London SW1P 3AZ

ISBN 978 0 7151 4230 1

Published 2011 by Church House Publishing
Copyright © The Archbishops' Council 2011

The opinions expressed in this book are those of the
authors and do not necessarily reflect the official policy of
the General Synod or The Archbishops' Council of the
Church of England.

Designed and typeset by Hugh Hillyard-Parker
Printed by CPI Bookmarque, Croydon, Surrey

Contents

About the authors

Alan Bartlett is Vicar of St Giles' in Durham City and Priest in Charge of Sherburn and Shadforth (a cluster of former pit villages). Previously on the staff of Cranmer Hall, he taught Church History, Spirituality, Anglicanism and Practical Theology, and ran the postgraduate programmes. He is married with two children.

Rosalind Brown is a Residentiary Canon and Canon Librarian at Durham Cathedral. Originally a town planner, her subsequent ordained ministry has included parish ministry while living for a few years in the USA, and training people for ordination. She written books on ministry and preaching, and is a published and prize-winning hymn writer.

Steven Croft is the Bishop of Sheffield. He was previously Warden of Cranmer Hall, and team leader of Fresh Expressions. He is the author of a number of books including *Jesus People: what next for the church?* and *The Advent Calendar*, a novel for children and adults.

Malcolm Guite is Chaplain of Girton College, Cambridge. He is also a poet and singer-songwriter, and is author of various essays and articles and a book about contemporary Christianity. He lectures widely in England and the USA on poetry and theology.

Sue Hope was in parish ministry in Sheffield for 17 years before becoming Missioner for the Diocese. She is now Priest in Charge of St Paul's Shipley and Adviser in Evangelism for the Diocese of Bradford. She is the author of *Mission-Shaped Spirituality*, and is a tertiary of the Order of the Holy Paraclete, Whitby.

John Kiddle is Mission Officer and a Residentiary Canon in the Diocese of St Albans. He has a strategic ministry helping to develop mission and discipleship in parishes and at a diocesan level. He is married with four children and a keen supporter of Watford FC.

Jane Leach is designated Principal of Wesley House Cambridge, from 1 September 2011. She teaches Pastoral Theology in the Cambridge Theological Federation and has written books on pilgrimage and pastoral supervision.

Jan McFarlane is the Archdeacon of Norwich and Director of Communications in the Diocese of Norwich. She has served as Chaplain to the Bishop of Norwich, Chaplain of Ely Cathedral and Curate in the Stafford Team Ministry. A former speech therapist, she has a lifelong interest in communications and broadcasts regularly on local radio.

Barbara Mosse is an Anglican priest and writer, and since 2006 has been Lecturer in Christian Spirituality at Sarum College, Salisbury. Alongside parish work, she has varied chaplaincy experience in prison, university, community mental health and hospital. Her book *The Treasures of Darkness* was published by Canterbury Press in 2003.

David Moxon is Bishop of Waikato, the Senior Bishop of the New Zealand Dioceses, and Archbishop and Primate of the Anglican Church in Aotearoa, New Zealand and Polynesia. He holds two Masters of Arts degrees: in Education with honours from Massey University, and in Theology from Oxford. He also has a Licenciate of Theology (Aotearoa) and a Diploma of Maori Studies from Waikato University.

Martyn Percy is Principal of Ripon College Cuddesdon and the Oxford Ministry Course. He is also Professor of Theological Education at King's College London, Professorial Research Fellow at Heythrop College London and an Honorary Canon of Salisbury Cathedral.

Ben Quash was Chaplain and Fellow of Fitzwilliam College, Cambridge, and a lecturer in the Cambridge Theological Federation from 1996 to 1999. He then returned to Peterhouse as Dean and Fellow, until he came to King's College as Professor of Christianity and the Arts in 2007.

Angela Tilby is an Anglican priest in Cambridge and was previously Vice-Principal of Westcott House, Cambridge. Prior to that, she was a senior producer at the BBC, where she made several acclaimed television programmes and series. She continues to combine parish ministry with her work as a freelance television producer, writer and broadcaster.

Jane Williams Jane Williams lectures at St Mellitus College, London and Chelmsford, and is a visiting lecturer at King's College London. She taught previously at Trinity Theological College, Bristol.

About *Reflections for Daily Prayer*

Based on the *Common Worship Lectionary* readings for Morning Prayer, these daily reflections are designed to refresh and inspire times of personal prayer. The aim is to provide rich, contemporary and engaging insights into Scripture.

Each page lists the lectionary readings for the day, with the main psalms for that day highlighted in **bold**. The Collect of the day – either the *Common Worship* collect or the shorter additional collect – is also included.

For those using this book in conjunction with a service of Morning Prayer, the following conventions apply: a psalm printed in parentheses is omitted if it has been used as the opening canticle at that office; a psalm marked with an asterisk may be shortened if desired.

A short reflection is provided on either the Old or New Testament reading. Popular writers, experienced ministers, biblical scholars and theologians will be contributing to this series. They all bring their own emphases, enthusiasms and approaches to biblical interpretation to bear.

Regular users of Morning Prayer and *Time to Pray* (from *Common Worship: Daily Prayer*) and anyone who follows the lectionary for their regular Bible reading will benefit from the rich variety of traditions represented in these stimulating and accessible pieces.

Monday 28 November

Isaiah 25.1-9

'On this mountain the Lord of hosts will make ... a feast' (v.6)

A deacon is one who waits on tables, and the first deacons of the Church were appointed to prepare and serve at the meals that the early Christians shared together. They help us to reflect on some more general things about being a servant, and especially the fact that the servant handles things – objects, food, and so on – on behalf of others.

All human beings are servants – or deacons – of God in the world. As creatures, we owe our lives to God and must handle all things on God's behalf. But this passage from Isaiah reveals that we have not yet gone nearly far enough in our thought about servanthood if we rest with this, for here we are invited to see *God* as the one who waits on *us* at table. Suddenly a run of other great biblical images comes to mind. God who spreads a table in the wilderness for Israel when they have fled Egypt: manna to eat, the grain of heaven, the bread of the angels, food in abundance. God who prepares greater things for his people's table than that: a promised land, flowing with milk and honey. And Jesus Christ who comes among us diaconally, as one who serves; who furnishes the table for us to sit at, who washes our feet. Who takes his own life, his very body and blood, and lays it on this table not for his own benefit but for that of others, in the manner of a servant.

It is an overwhelming thing to be waited on by God. But to be a deacon – which is in some way the calling of every Christian – is a calling to be *like* God. When we show ourselves unable to prepare a table, with nothing at all to put on it, God shows us how to do it, and we become good servants again in God's company.

COLLECT

Almighty God,
give us grace to cast away the works of darkness
and to put on the armour of light,
now in the time of this mortal life,
in which your Son Jesus Christ came to us in great humility;
that on the last day,
when he shall come again in his glorious majesty
    to judge the living and the dead,
we may rise to the life immortal;
through him who is alive and reigns with you,
in the unity of the Holy Spirit,
one God, now and for ever.

2

Psalms **80**, 82 *or* **5**, 6 (8)
Isaiah 26.1-13
Matthew 12.22-37

Isaiah 26.1-13

'... all that we have done, you have done for us' (v.12)

It is a standard modern assumption that the obedience of religious people to God entails the abnegation of their own will and dignity. It is jumping about in response to some imperative that comes from beyond them, like doing the hokey cokey with God as the caller. Or else, subsiding into helpless passivity, because human agency and God's agency are somehow incompatible. An action must either be God's or ours; it cannot be both.

But God's exercise of power is *not* like the descent from on high of great crushing and incomprehensible dispensations. To conclude this is to have failed really to listen and learn from that subtle and complex tradition of theological thought about the interplay of God's freedom and our freedom which has always been part of Christian wisdom. This interplay is what Luther is referring to when he says that in becoming slaves to Christ we become the most free Lords of all. Obedience to God does not take away our agency, it makes our actions the most liberated they can be; the most genuine expressions of ourselves. God's agency is the *medium* for our agency; it does not compete with it. When the poor and needy place their feet where God places his feet (which is a way of saying, 'when an action is both theirs *and* God's'), then they are empowered by this, and can even trample down city walls.

To recognize this is to share the secret of the lives of the saints, as of the people of Israel. It is to learn, with them, a lesson in how our agency and God's can be reciprocally and profoundly compatible, and a lesson in the power and beauty and freedom that such agency can unleash.

Almighty God,
as your kingdom dawns,
turn us from the darkness of sin to the
light of holiness,
that we may be ready to meet you
in our Lord and Saviour, Jesus Christ.

COLLECT

3

Wednesday 30 November

Andrew the Apostle

Psalms 47, 147.1-12
Ezekiel 47.1-12
or Ecclesiasticus 14.20-end
John 12.20-32

John 12.20-32

'Father, glorify your name' (v.28)

Jesus in his hour of darkness does not turn inwards on himself, or pity himself, or resent his circumstances. He turns towards his Father and glorifies him. He bursts out in a sort of praise of God, which has to it the quality of thanks – in Greek, *eucharistia*. 'Father, glorify your name'. It is almost, to use the word of the great Swiss Catholic theologian Hans Urs von Balthasar, *reckless*.

Thanksgiving emerges here as perhaps the most exalted form of holy utterance and the most holy kind of disposition. If Jesus is the perfect model of holiness, then that holiness is shown to be at some profound level the holy work of giving thanks to God. Could this be a central dynamic of leading a life that is worthy of our calling?

The Eucharist is the presence in our midst of Christ's grateful self-gift of himself to the Father. Gathered around the Eucharist, a common life comes to birth: a common life which we enter not as demanders but as thankful recipients. The Eucharist educates us in how to be a thankful people. But talk of being a eucharistic people can be too airy without reference to its practical dimensions. How *actually* are we eucharistic when not gathered around the altar? How *actually* do we loosen the bonds of sin in lives that are appropriately thankful?

Dietrich Bonhoeffer wrote that 'Only he who gives thanks for little things receives the big things. We prevent God from giving us the great spiritual gifts he has in store for us, because we do not give thanks for daily gifts. […] How can God entrust great things to one who will not thankfully receive from him the little things?'

COLLECT

Almighty God,
who gave such grace to your apostle Saint Andrew
that he readily obeyed the call of your Son Jesus Christ
    and brought his brother with him:
call us by your holy word,
and give us grace to follow you without delay
    and to tell the good news of your kingdom;
through Jesus Christ your Son our Lord,
who is alive and reigns with you,
in the unity of the Holy Spirit,
one God, now and for ever.

Psalms **42**, 43 *or* 14, **15**, 16
Isaiah 28.14-end
Matthew 13.1-23

Isaiah 28.14-end

'... your covenant with death will be annulled' (v.18)

Death and agriculture: they are two dominant themes in this chapter.

The first part of the passage challenges us to think of the faithless ways we try to do deals with death. Sometimes we do this in our prayers, imagining we can bargain with a higher power for *more time* on this earth, and refusing to accept the truth that it can't be 'the next guy' forever. Sometimes we do it through massive expenditure on our physical health or our personal security. More and more sophisticated technologies for buying death off in these ways keep appearing; their manufacturers know that they can always be sure of a market for them. But this passage says that without faith in God, the cornerstone-layer, our deals with death will be as inadequate to cover us as an undersized blanket.

And then we are shown a different covering: the covering of soil which God provides for seeds to grow under. This covering can be trusted; we do not need to keep mucking about with the soil, ploughing and reploughing it once the planting is done. And by extension, we can think of ourselves as like seeds, covered by God's providence. We can rest in the trust that God's gifts to us are good. His blanket of care and protection is not like our pocket-handkerchief-sized contrivances. He has a life into which he wants us to grow – one that our fear of death ought not to be allowed to hijack, because death cannot overshadow it. It is a life stronger than death. He gives us what we need, not to *avoid* death, but to grow into a life that is more enduring than it.

COLLECT

Almighty God,
give us grace to cast away the works of darkness
and to put on the armour of light,
now in the time of this mortal life,
in which your Son Jesus Christ came to us in great humility;
that on the last day,
when he shall come again in his glorious majesty
to judge the living and the dead,
we may rise to the life immortal;
through him who is alive and reigns with you,
in the unity of the Holy Spirit,
one God, now and for ever.

Isaiah 29.1-14

'... I will again do amazing things with this people' (v.14)

'The Lord gave and the Lord has taken away,' Job once cried out – affirming even in his distress that all things come from God. Could his utterance be of help in making sense of this passage, in which we find a God who is 'on both sides' – both for and against his people? This God does to his people what they, under David their king, once did to Ariel (a rarely used name for the city of Jerusalem; a name which literally means 'the lion of God'). God encamps against them. They know by this that their God is not a God blindly partisan, always fighting with them even if their cause is corrupt and their prophets' eyes shut. They must imagine how (like those they once opposed) they are more than capable of making themselves the enemies of God, and they must be chastened by this thought – as we must too. To echo C. S. Lewis, this God is not a tame lion.

But just when their speech is reduced to a voice as small as a ghost's, their whisper from the dust is overtaken by God's *roar*, and it is a roar of support and deliverance from tyranny: 'I will again do amazing things with this people'. God speaks as he once did to Job out of the whirlwind, to affirm that at the last, beyond all their affliction and apparent abandonment, and even when he encamps against them, he will still uphold their integrity. Only the God who is the source of all things can offer this absolute assurance.

COLLECT

Almighty God,
give us grace to cast away the works of darkness
and to put on the armour of light,
now in the time of this mortal life,
in which your Son Jesus Christ came to us in great humility;
that on the last day,
when he shall come again in his glorious majesty
    to judge the living and the dead,
we may rise to the life immortal;
through him who is alive and reigns with you,
in the unity of the Holy Spirit,
one God, now and for ever.

Isaiah 29.15-end

'... out of their gloom and darkness the eyes of the blind shall see'
(v.18)

The weight of imagery about eyes and looking in Shakespeare's play *King Lear* ties in with some dark themes of misrecognition and the breakdown of true and loving reciprocity between people. One of its most famous scenes contains the shocking moment in which Gloucester's eyes are put out at the instigation of Lear's two evil daughters.

The power of the eyes for good – their capacity to establish mutuality, to look with tenderness, insight and compassion – is denied by much of what is said and done in the play. The doers of bad things persistently (with various degrees of violence) seek *not to be looked at*. They cannot bear to be recognised for who they are. In such acts, they make literal what this passage from Isaiah also tells us about: evil's ancient love of darkness. Even a mostly good character, like Gloucester's disowned son Edgar, tries for a long time to avoid his father's recognition. His father did not trust his love, and now he does not trust his father's. He eventually plucks up courage to admit who he is only when his father's life has 'all but seeped away'.

What lengths we will go to to avoid other people's eyes, when actually what we most need is to be looked at with love and with understanding. Our lives are full of 'one-way looking', in which we spy on each other from dark places, or peep out from behind the security of armour. All this hiding is a sign of the power of our shame. But Isaiah 29 promises a new dawn when God's passionate desire to be in a reciprocal relationship with us – to be intimate – will lift our shame and banish all darkness.

Almighty God,
as your kingdom dawns,
turn us from the darkness of sin to the
light of holiness,
that we may be ready to meet you
in our Lord and Saviour, Jesus Christ.

COLLECT

Monday 5 December

Isaiah 30.1-18

'In returning and rest you shall be saved' (v.15)

There are two kinds of stillness in this passage. One is the stillness of inefficacy, and it is summed up in the Lord's name for Egypt: 'Rahab who sits still'. And then there is the stillness of assurance; a good sort of waiting – active, alert, hopeful. This sort of waiting is a preparation to receive God's blessing.

God's people have a collective memory of sitting still in Egypt. It was their captivity. It was the sort of enforced lack of efficacy that was the gift of 'Rahab who sat still'. We may find ourselves asking why on earth they would choose it *again*. But the longing to go back to Egypt is a perennial temptation for all those who struggle to follow the true God. The allure of the security that Egypt's wealth and power seem to offer is hard to resist.

By contrast with the flurry of superficial activity which marks the rush back to Egypt – and which is really impotence – God asks for a waiting that is full of potency, that will yield a real future, and that matches God's *own* patience: 'The Lord waits to be gracious to you ... blessed are you who trust in him.'

COLLECT

O Lord, raise up, we pray, your power
and come among us,
and with great might succour us;
that whereas, through our sins and wickedness
we are grievously hindered
in running the race that is set before us,
your bountiful grace and mercy
may speedily help and deliver us;
through Jesus Christ your Son our Lord,
to whom with you and the Holy Spirit,
be honour and glory, now and for ever.

Isaiah 30.19-end

*'... the light of the sun will be sevenfold ... when the Lord binds up
the injuries of his people' (v.26)*

Healing and burning are, for Christians, two key images of atonement
and renewal. God in Christ is the great physician who comes not to the
healthy but to the sick. But he also comes to cleanse the world, his
winnowing fork in his hand, by burning the chaff of sin.

Both themes are here in this passage, which speaks with great
tenderness of God binding up the injuries of his people, but also and
disturbingly of something that sounds rather like 'God's bonfire night':
a potent combination of festival song and ritual slaughter.

Setting the frame for both of these themes is the image of God as
teacher, and an ideal picture of our receiving all wisdom and instruction
directly from his mouth: 'This is the way, walk in it'. Dietrich Bonhoeffer
described this wonderful immediacy of relation with God as the
condition of Paradise from which we fell into the world of ethical choice
and the doomed task of trying to be our own judges. The way back to
Paradise, and to a renewal of the purest reception of God's instruction,
is a hard one that may involve fiery cleansing as well as the tending of
our wounds. It is a journey during which we humans must recognize
that the task of judgement is God's, not ours. We are relieved by this of
the responsibility for either vindicating or condemning ourselves. God's
fire threatens the self-vindicator; God's bandages unsettle the self-
condemner. This entails a transformation of our outlook and of our lives
that is both terrifying and liberating at the same time.

Almighty God,
purify our hearts and minds,
that when your Son Jesus Christ comes again as
judge and saviour
we may be ready to receive him,
who is our Lord and our God.

COLLECT

Wednesday 7 December

Psalms **62**, 63 *or* **34**
Isaiah 31
Matthew 15.1-20

Isaiah 31

'... the Assyrian shall fall by a sword, not of mortals' (v.8)

God's people are desperate for help against the Assyrians, and their inclination is to turn to Egypt and seek an alliance. It is a man-made solution – a strategic remedy, devised by the human ingenuity of the people of Judah in order to solve a frightful and pressing problem.

So is an idol. An idol is man-made, and it is devised to solve problems. Idols are things that we invent in order to answer our needs and remedy our ills. We invest them with too much dignity and authority when we begin to revere them, because really they are just extensions of ourselves. The idol-worshipper has lost the power to distinguish between what is divine spirit and what is really in the end just human.

In this passage, the Lord calls his people once again to turn from their idols of silver and their idols of gold. And the implication is that the Egyptians themselves are among the idols that must be abandoned: they are poor substitutes for God, who is the only ally worth having. The saving power with which Egypt has been invested in the minds of God's people is a fiction, an idea, a thing of 'the flesh'. A new way of looking at the world is needed in which spirit can be seen as stronger than flesh. It will make the most basic and trusted strategy of this threatened people nothing more and nothing less than faithful worship of the one true God. Its worship will be its politics. Even if the Assyrians *were* to overrun them, Judah's people would at least then be free from their thrall to idols. And without the true God as *their* object, the Assyrians' power is itself a passing shadow: flesh not spirit.

COLLECT

O Lord, raise up, we pray, your power
and come among us,
and with great might succour us;
that whereas, through our sins and wickedness
we are grievously hindered
in running the race that is set before us,
your bountiful grace and mercy
may speedily help and deliver us;
through Jesus Christ your Son our Lord,
to whom with you and the Holy Spirit,
be honour and glory, now and for ever.

Psalms 53, **54**, 60 *or* **37***
Isaiah 32
Matthew 15.21-28

Isaiah 32

'My people will abide in a peaceful habitation' (v.18)

When the city is secure, the land flourishes. When the city falls apart, the land is unfruitful. And also, conversely, when the land is barren, the city too becomes a wasteland, and only the donkeys have any joy in it. This is one of the basic convictions of this passage. We may think that city walls (the intact enclosure of the city) marks a straightforward division between city and countryside. The one shuts the other out. And that may be true of our own modern, western cities, within whose urban vastness it is easy to forget all that lies outside – even though without this 'outside' no city could survive. But the organic relationship between city and land in Isaiah's vision is clear. The walls that guarantee the peace and security of the city also ensure the well-being of the land. A city with holes in its walls could not defend and maintain a land of vines and fields and livestock. The walls of the city are a *bond* with the countryside, a *gift* to the countryside, not a slight to it. And the fruitfulness of the countryside is a strengthening of the city.

All of this, while literally true, is also a metaphor. For the intact enclosure which at the same time gives generous gifts to its environment is a symbol of human holiness and righteousness. Jesus' mother, Mary, has sometimes been compared to a walled enclosure in Christian tradition – not so much to emphasize her separateness from us, but rather her gift-giving holiness. To have a heart whose walls are not full of holes, and a community bounded firmly by righteousness, is to bestow fruit to a wider world.

Psalms 85, **86** *or* 31
Isaiah 33.1-22
Matthew 15.29-end

Isaiah 33.1-22

'Your eyes will see the king in his beauty' (v.17)

'You are what you eat', it's often said. But there is perhaps a metaphorical 'diet' that also makes us who we are, and that is the diet of things we think about, hear and see. We live in times when it is possible to look at – and listen to – any number of things, of all kinds of quality and type. And these in turn will have an effect on what our mind thinks about, turns over and absorbs.

This passage tells us that we can make choices here. We can stop our ears to tales of bloodshed, and can instead listen to the things that the Lord has done. And we can shut our eyes from looking on evil, and instead behold the king's beauty, and a spreading land, and a magnificent city: Zion, the city of festival. The beauty of both king and city are read as signs of God's own glory – good to look at.

There is an old Jewish folktale about a married couple who were convinced a demon was coming into their house at night and stealing from them. They became obsessed not just with preventing the demon's theft, but with *seeing* it, and so they set up traps, and kept vigils and put sand on the floor to see if they could at least catch its footprints. Their rabbi rebuked them for this fascination with things that were not wholesome to look at, and when at last they got what they thought they wanted (a glimpse of the demon) they lost their sight.

Is there an appropriate asceticism in our world of spectacle and easy voyeurism? And is there still a role for thinking on what is good, and true and beautiful, in order to feed our souls?

COLLECT

O Lord, raise up, we pray, your power
and come among us,
and with great might succour us;
that whereas, through our sins and wickedness
we are grievously hindered
in running the race that is set before us,
your bountiful grace and mercy
may speedily help and deliver us;
through Jesus Christ your Son our Lord,
to whom with you and the Holy Spirit,
be honour and glory, now and for ever.

Psalms **145** *or* 41, **42**, 43
Isaiah 35
Matthew 16.1-12

Isaiah 35

'The wilderness and the dry land shall be glad' (v. 1)

Where should we look for signs of God's approach? Where does he begin his great and triumphant return journey after a period of eager expectation by his longing people?

The journey begins in the middle of nowhere. In deserted space. The waste land is the first to recognize God's return. It is the desert that will see the glory of the Lord before anything else does, and it will shout for joy, even if there is no-one there to hear it.

Christians are asked never to forget that it is *margins* that are chosen by God to preach, proclaim and witness to *centres*. God's approach to the world in Christ began in a thoroughly out-of-the-way place – the womb of a virgin in a minor northern province of an occupied land. This too was a desert space that was made to shout for joy, magnifying the Lord. Mary's womb was a place that was perfectly ready for God's return because it was 'empty'. Or, perhaps, its 'emptiness' was in fact its fullness: full readiness for God.

Centres become all too cluttered with their preoccupations, their business, their self-importance. They are not good starting places for God. People of power have little time to spot the signs of God's coming. But people who know what it is to dwell in waste lands are much better equipped. This passage names some of them: those with feeble hands and fearful hearts; the blind, the deaf, the lame, and the mute.

Where are the places we think of as waste lands today? Airport lounges, sink estates, job centres, suburban sprawls? Do we pay the sort of attention to them that will equip us well to see God coming when he comes?

Almighty God,
purify our hearts and minds,
that when your Son Jesus Christ comes again as
judge and saviour
we may be ready to receive him,
who is our Lord and our God.

COLLECT

Monday 12 December

Isaiah 38.1-8, 21-22

'Set your house in order ...' (v.1)

All our neat theories go out of the window when disaster strikes.

Hezekiah contracts a terminal illness. His response is one of turmoil. Isaiah's first counsel is acceptance and to put his affairs in order – vital advice for a king who must manage the succession and handover of power. But Hezekiah is not ready to die. He holds on to the deep biblical insight which is fundamental to our human nature. Life is good. Sickness and death are bad things and to be resisted.

So Hezekiah turns to solitary prayer. He gives voice to his pain and turns to the Lord. At the same time, Isaiah advises practical help with a poultice of figs. Prayer and medicine go hand in hand.

The same emotions arise today in the face of serious illness. This passage has informed the hospice movement and those concerned with the care of the dying. When is it right to accept that life is ending? When is it right to continue the fight internally and externally? There is grace in both pathways. But Hezekiah suggests, I think, that if there is any doubt at all it is better to rally and to fight against the evils of sickness and premature death rather than accept them.

COLLECT

O Lord Jesus Christ,
who at your first coming sent your messenger
to prepare your way before you:
grant that the ministers and stewards of your mysteries
may likewise so prepare and make ready your way
by turning the hearts of the disobedient to the wisdom of the just,
that at your second coming to judge the world
we may be found an acceptable people in your sight;
for you are alive and reign with the Father
in the unity of the Holy Spirit,
one God, now and for ever.

Isaiah 38.9-20

'... like a weaver I have rolled up my life' (v.12)

Into the prose account of Hezekiah's illness, the book of Isaiah inserts this beautiful psalm. It is both a lament in time of sickness (vv.10-16) and a thanksgiving for recovery (vv.17-20). Chapters 36 to 38 of Isaiah are a duplicate of 2 Kings 18 to 20, but only the book of Isaiah has the psalm.

The lament is remarkable for its bold imagery. There are two striking pictures of death in verse 12. A life is rolled up like a shepherd's tent or cut off from the loom like a unfinished tapestry. In language reminiscent of Job, God is like a devouring lion. The psalmist is like a swallow, a crane or a dove in distress.

The thread of meaning that runs through both the lament and thanksgiving is the same as in the prose account we read yesterday: death is unambiguously a terrible thing and followed only by the shadowy existence of Sheol.

As Christians, we need to embrace the sure hope of resurrection that was unknown to the psalmist. Yet we must never treat death lightly even so. Death is never 'nothing at all'. According to Isaiah 38, death and sickness are enemies to be defeated rather than friends to be embraced.

God for whom we watch and wait,
you sent John the Baptist to prepare the way of your Son:
give us courage to speak the truth,
to hunger for justice,
and to suffer for the cause of right,
with Jesus Christ our Lord.

COLLECT

15

Wednesday 14 December

Isaiah 39

'There will be peace and security in my days' (v.8)

The story of the visit of the envoys from Babylon is pregnant with disaster. The chapter also forms a bridge between the two major sections of the book of Isaiah, normally assumed by scholars to be from two different prophets.

Hezekiah and his kingdom have survived the Assyrian crisis. Yet now, in what seems a rare moment of prosperity, the seeds are sown for the destruction of Jerusalem. More than a century will pass before this Babylon becomes the new global superpower. Yet when that happens, the king of Babylon will push south again, overwhelming the tiny buffer states around Jerusalem.

Hezekiah's sin is to drop his guard once the great crisis of his lifetime has passed. He is a leader who looks to the past but has no energy for the future. 'Peace in our time' is enough. He is like the elderly parishioners who want their church to survive long enough to serve their needs but give no thought to the future and the next generation. Prophets look forward.

In the space between 39.8 and 40.1 are 150 years of decline, pain and captivity. When the voice of Isaiah 40–55 begins to speak, the new prophet draws on the Isaiah tradition and sings again a song of comfort and of hope.

COLLECT

O Lord Jesus Christ,
who at your first coming sent your messenger
to prepare your way before you:
grant that the ministers and stewards of your mysteries
may likewise so prepare and make ready your way
by turning the hearts of the disobedient to the wisdom of the just,
that at your second coming to judge the world
we may be found an acceptable people in your sight;
for you are alive and reign with the Father
in the unity of the Holy Spirit,
one God, now and for ever.

Psalms **76**, 97 *or* 56, **57** (63*)
Zephaniah 1.1 – 2.3
Matthew 17.22-end

Zephaniah 1.1 – 2.3

'... the people who rest complacently on their dregs' (1.12)

Zephaniah is Hezekiah's great-great-grandson. He is one generation away from exile.

All around him, the prophet sees complacency. The atmosphere before the great festival ('The day of the Lord') is not unlike the two weeks before Christmas in our own day. Lots of rushing around, visiting the merchants in the different quarters of Jerusalem, planning the festivities.

The prophet's task is to speak words of challenge and judgement in a complacent and superficial world. There are eternal truths and realities beneath all the turmoil of life. All we see will ultimately come to an end. God's grace and reality endure for ever.

The heart of the challenge is at 1.12. Zephaniah describes the people as those 'who rest complacently on their dregs'. Laziness and apathy have taken a deep hold on the soul of Judah. People have stopped striving for holiness. They have stopped believing that faith makes a difference. They are less than they could be.

Zephaniah's call is to speak the word of God to awaken the conscience of the nation from torpor and idleness – the sin the saints have called *'accidie'*. Zephaniah is the enemy of apathy. Will we take up his mantle?

God for whom we watch and wait,
you sent John the Baptist to prepare the way of your Son:
give us courage to speak the truth,
to hunger for justice,
and to suffer for the cause of right,
with Jesus Christ our Lord.

COLLECT

Friday 16 December

Zephaniah 3.1-13

'... soiled, defiled, oppressing city!' (v.1)

Zephaniah's analysis of the city is bleak. Jerusalem is rotten. Ethical and political corruption is closely linked to the neglect of faith. The implication is that the renewal of faith will lead to a renewal of ethics, which in turn will lead to a renewal of community.

The anatomy of corruption is laid before us. Each branch of the nation's leadership has become distorted. They are meant to be good shepherds. Yet the judges prey on those they are meant to protect like lions and wolves. Prophets are meant to be people of truth yet have become faithless. Priests, the protectors of holiness, have profaned what is sacred.

The only remedy for the nation now is trial and judgement. For Zephaniah, this coming judgement does not mean destruction but purification. There will be a remnant of those who are faithful in the midst of the city. There will be a community that is humble and lowly, who trust in the Lord, do what is right and speak the truth.

It is no small thing to be able to name evil and describe its roots and consequences and those responsible. It is no small thing either to keep alive a vision of what is good and of what will prevail.

COLLECT

O Lord Jesus Christ,
who at your first coming sent your messenger
to prepare your way before you:
grant that the ministers and stewards of your mysteries
may likewise so prepare and make ready your way
by turning the hearts of the disobedient to the wisdom of the just,
that at your second coming to judge the world
we may be found an acceptable people in your sight;
for you are alive and reign with the Father
in the unity of the Holy Spirit,
one God, now and for ever.

Psalm **71** *or* **68**
Zephaniah 3.14-end
Matthew 18.21-end

Saturday 17 December

Zephaniah 3.14-end

'Rejoice and exult with all your heart' (v.14)

Hope is the great virtue of the Advent season. The prophets challenge us to see the world as it really is: greed, emptiness and vanity in ourselves as well as in others. Yet they also unfold for us a picture of eternal reality and of God's goodness and purpose.

Hope is the reason Zephaniah's terrible prophecy of judgement and destruction ends in song. We have seen the stark corruption of his own city and ours. Yet there is an even deeper vision of eternal reality, which is about the coming of the king of Israel, the Lord.

Like all the prophets, Zephaniah sees the coming of the King through a glass darkly. Even so, it is instructive to read his song of praise with Jesus in our minds. We are about to celebrate that God himself is in our midst, that Jesus saves the lame and gathers the outcast.

If we hold a picture of God's kingdom in our minds but lose sight of the reality of the world, we become romantics. If we hold a truthful picture of the world yet lose sight of God's kingdom, we become cynics. We must hold fast to both horizons and Zephaniah's way of hope.

God for whom we watch and wait,
you sent John the Baptist to prepare the way of your Son:
give us courage to speak the truth,
to hunger for justice,
and to suffer for the cause of right,
with Jesus Christ our Lord.

COLLECT

Monday 19 December

Psalms 144, **146**
Malachi 1.1, 6-end
Matthew 19.1-12

Malachi 1.1, 6-end

'... my name is reverenced among the nations' (v.14)

Welcome to the gym that is the last week of Advent. Meet the prophet Malachi, who will be your personal spiritual trainer for most of the week. Engage with the exercises he offers you, and you will emerge in better shape spiritually for the Christmas season.

The exercises cluster round the theme of purity. The first is about purity in worship. Malachi's own community have become lackadaisical and sloppy in the extreme. Any sick or imperfect animal can be offered on the altar (leaving the best ones to be sold in the market). Almighty God, the Lord of heaven and earth, gets the leftovers. The attitude is summed up in the powerful phrase 'you sniff at me' (v.13).

We no longer offer animals in worship. But are we bringing the best we have to offer in praise and public worship in terms of our time, our energy, the gifts we bring in leading God's people? Where have we become sloppy in our discipline or practice? Where might we be sniffing at God?

Will our worship over these next days be led by the needs of the consumer? Or will it be shaped by a sense of awe and reverence for the Lord of heaven and earth? Are we hallowing his name?

COLLECT

God our redeemer,
who prepared the Blessed Virgin Mary
to be the mother of your Son:
grant that, as she looked for his coming as our saviour,
so we may be ready to greet him
when he comes again as our judge;
who is alive and reigns with you,
in the unity of the Holy Spirit,
one God, now and for ever.

Psalms **46**, 95
Malachi 2.1-16
Matthew 19.13-15

Malachi 2.1-16

'He walked with me in integrity and uprightness' (v.6)

The second part of your workout with Malachi focuses on integrity: walking the walk. The prophet contrasts the priests of his own day with Levi of long ago. Levi is singled out for his reverence and the example of his life.

Perhaps, you may be thinking, that is a tall order for the ministers of today. Think again. The lesson is not just for those called to be ministers. In this sense, all Christians are called to be a royal priesthood, dedicated to God's service. With that priesthood comes the responsibility of goodness. Read verses 1 to 10 again and substitute 'Christian' for 'priest' and 'disciple' for 'messenger'.

One relationship in particular is singled out for special care in Malachi. The prophet is speaking of a broken covenant between Israel and God. No wonder, then, he draws attention to the breaking of the most solemn covenant in human life: the marriage bond. Christians hedge Malachi's three blunt words about divorce with all kinds of gentler qualifications, and often that is right. But sometimes, we simply need to hear them and set our lives in order again. For the first but not the last time, Malachi reminds us of the Baptist. Sort it.

What do you need to set right at the end of the Advent season?

Eternal God,
as Mary waited for the birth of your Son,
so we wait for his coming in glory;
bring us through the birth pangs of this present age
to see, with her, our great salvation
in Jesus Christ our Lord.

COLLECT

Wednesday 21 December

Malachi 2.17 – 3.12

'... a refiner's fire and ... fullers' soap' (3.2)

The word 'Malachi' means 'my messenger'. The coming messenger is in full focus here. The New Testament claims these prophecies are fulfilled in John the Baptist.

John's purpose is to call the people of God to holiness. He sets the people of God in a furnace to refine away their impurities. He sets to washing them with soap. What does this mean in practice?

Simply this: the Baptist, like the prophet, lived a life of integrity and preached the word of God in great power. There is a very high view of preaching wrapped up in this passage: the expectation that, through the word of God proclaimed, the course of nations will be changed. It has happened many times in history and can happen again.

Through all this, the daily workout continues. Today, Malachi sets out a vision of social righteousness: fair wages, support for the most needy and the stranger. Are you playing your part? Are you giving what you can and bringing in the whole tithe? In ancient Israel, the tithe was not just giving to the church but also alms for the poor.

As you plan to celebrate this Christmas, how will you bless those most in need of help? If you've not done so already, take some action today.

COLLECT

God our redeemer,
who prepared the Blessed Virgin Mary
to be the mother of your Son:
grant that, as she looked for his coming as our saviour,
so we may be ready to greet him
when he comes again as our judge;
who is alive and reigns with you,
in the unity of the Holy Spirit,
one God, now and for ever.

Malachi 3.13 – end of 4

'He will turn the hearts' (4.6)

In yesterday's reading, the people do not know what to do in the face of the prophet's preaching. They say: 'How shall we return?' (3.7). One pathway is through action. A second is through confession. As we come now to the very end of Advent, take time to make your confession to God and seek forgiveness and a new beginning.

Be specific and be practical. You may want to confess to another Christian or to a priest or to kneel in silent prayer. It may help to write a list and burn it afterwards as a sign you have been forgiven. You may want to use a set form of confession.

Take Malachi's themes as your own. Confess your lack of awe and reverence for God. Confess your lack of integrity and the neglect of key relationships. Confess your lack of commitment to social righteousness and the needs of the poor.

After your confession, dip your thumb in water and trace again the sign of the cross on your forehead: the sign that you have been baptized, washed and made new.

Malachi's final promise forms the very last words of the Old Testament. The promise is that God changes hearts. God does forgive. God renews us from within. That turning transforms individuals. That turning heals families. That turning renews whole communities.

Eternal God,
as Mary waited for the birth of your Son,
so we wait for his coming in glory;
bring us through the birth pangs of this present age
to see, with her, our great salvation
in Jesus Christ our Lord.

COLLECT

Nahum 1

'The Lord is good, a stronghold on a day of trouble' (v.7)

After the intense personal workout with Malachi, Nahum pushes out our horizon once again as we approach Christmas. The chapter is in two halves. Verses 1 to 8 are a fragment of an acrostic psalm in which each verse begins with a different letter of the Hebrew alphabet.

Nahum's psalm is uncomfortable reading and is meant to disturb us. The central section reminds us of God's great power seen in the natural world. The power of the creator is greater than the power we see in creation. This, at least, is familiar territory.

But Nathan brackets this section with two equally powerful descriptions of God's wrath (vv.2-3 and 6-8). These verses stretch us. God's awesome creative power is focused in his passion for justice and for truth. The God of Israel is not the benign and tolerant Mother Nature figure bearing everything without consequence. There will be a day of reckoning.

Three elements make it possible for us to bear this vision. The Lord is slow to anger; God's wrath is not the same as God's temper. The Lord is good; his wrath is not arbitrary but the outworking of this goodness. The third is the reminder of good news at the end of the chapter fulfilled in the birth of Jesus Christ. The way of salvation is open to all.

COLLECT

God our redeemer,
who prepared the Blessed Virgin Mary
to be the mother of your Son:
grant that, as she looked for his coming as our saviour,
so we may be ready to greet him
when he comes again as our judge;
who is alive and reigns with you,
in the unity of the Holy Spirit,
one God, now and for ever.

Saturday 24 December

Christmas Eve

Obadiah

'... you should not have gloated over your brother' (v.12)

The Old Testament is full of stories of rivalry between brothers. Jacob and Esau wrestle in the womb and are at odds throughout their lives. Joseph is sold into slavery by his brothers. The sons of David grapple for the succession. Judah and Israel are at war from generation to generation.

The background to Obadiah's prophecy is the destruction of Jerusalem and the role played by Judah's neighbour, the nation of Edom. Psalm 137 reflects the same situation. The Edomites rejoice in the destruction of their neighbours. Those who should be brothers have become enemies.

The same theme of rivalry between brothers and sisters is echoed in the New Testament in the story of Mary and Martha and the accounts of the struggles for power among the disciples. It is present in the most famous of Jesus' parables – the story of the two brothers in Luke 15.

As families gather for Christmas, it is helpful to remember not only the powerful ties that bind us, but also the destructive rivalries that can too easily pull us apart. In the midst of a prophecy about an ancient feud, Obadiah offers a simple piece of practical advice: 'As you have done, it shall be done to you' (v.15). In our families, we reap what we sow. Sow kindness this Christmas season.

COLLECT

Almighty God,
you make us glad with the yearly remembrance
of the birth of your Son Jesus Christ:
grant that, as we joyfully receive him as our redeemer,
so we may with sure confidence behold him
when he shall come to be our judge;
who is alive and reigns with you,
in the unity of the Holy Spirit,
one God, now and for ever.

Monday 26 December

Stephen, deacon, first martyr

Psalms **13**, 31.1-8, 150
Jeremiah 26.12-15
Acts 6

Acts 6

'... they chose Stephen, a man full of faith and the Holy Spirit' (v.5)

It is salutary, on the day after Christmas, to commemorate the feast day of the first Christian martyr. The seven men (including Stephen) appointed to minister at table in this chapter are traditionally understood to have been thereby ordained deacon (although the only person named as a deacon in the entire New Testament is Phoebe in Romans 16.1). From this passage, many of the hallmarks of diaconal ministry are derived: it is a practical ministry to those in need, which draws our attention to the social implications of the Eucharist; it is a ministry of teaching and preaching, which requires learning and wisdom and risk-taking in communication; it is a prophetic ministry, which ends (at least for Stephen) in death, reminding the Church of the need to be prepared to challenge authority and, if necessary, to die with Christ.

The Church traditionally teaches that service (*diakonia* in the Greek, v.2) is the character of all ministry. It does not just belong to deacons. All power exercised in Christ's name (even by bishops and presbyters) should have service as its motivation and as its reward. The role of deacons is to recall the whole Church and its ministers to the service of Christ and to keep re-presenting the image of Christ to us kneeling to wash his disciples' feet to us as a prophetic act that turns power on its head, risking death for the sake of the life of others.

Today's reading raises a question about the ways in which the Church in every generation is called to risk its own resources and ways of being for the sake of those it is called to serve.

COLLECT

Gracious Father,
who gave the first martyr Stephen
grace to pray for those who took up stones against him:
grant that in all our sufferings for the truth
we may learn to love even our enemies
and to seek forgiveness for those who desire our hurt,
looking up to heaven to him who was crucified for us,
Jesus Christ, our mediator and advocate,
who is alive and reigns with you,
in the unity of the Holy Spirit,
one God, now and for ever.

Psalms **21**, 147.13-end
Exodus 33.12-end
1 John 2.1-11

John, Apostle and Evangelist

1 John 2.1-11

'... whoever hates another believer ... walks in the darkness' (v.11)

The writings known as the letters of John are linked with the Gospel of John and with the book of Revelation. It is probably the case that, as was common in the literature of the time, the author of this letter was claiming to maintain the tradition of John's community by adopting his name, rather than claiming to be him. He uses the images of John's Gospel to establish his credentials (e.g. 'light', 'abiding') but his theme and argument is rooted in the present concerns of his community: conflict within the Church (vv.9-11) leading to schism (1 John 2.19).

Conflict within the Church (as we know to our cost) is a perennial issue, and this letter raises the difficult question of how we balance love for a brother or sister with a concern for authentic Christian teaching when there is a conflict between them. The Church is clearly told in verse 11 that to hate a brother or sister is to be blind; yet a little later, those who have left the Church are branded as liars and anti-christs.

It is easy to brand as less than Christian those with whom we strongly disagree. 'Abiding' in the truth, however, involves not only right belief, but also love for our brothers and sisters. Even as we fight for (what seems to us to be) the heart of the Church, it is important to remember that we, too, are prone to blindness and sin (v.1) and that Christ died, not just for us, but for the sins of the whole world (v.2) – even our enemies.

Merciful Lord,
cast your bright beams of light upon the Church:
that, being enlightened by the teaching
of your blessed apostle and evangelist Saint John,
we may so walk in the light of your truth
that we may at last attain to the light of everlasting life;
through Jesus Christ your incarnate Son our Lord,
who is alive and reigns with you,
in the unity of the Holy Spirit,
one God, now and for ever.

COLLECT

Wednesday 28 December

The Holy Innocents

Psalms **36**, 146
Baruch 4.21-27
or Genesis 37.13-20
Matthew 18.1-10

Matthew 18.1-10

'Take care that you do not despise one of these little ones' (v.10)

To read this text on the day we mark the Slaughter of the Innocents (Matthew 2.16) throws a particular light on the qualities that Jesus commends in children. In verse 4, the phrase Jesus uses is often translated 'become as humble as a child'. Small children, though, are rarely humble, even if their self-centredness is unselfconscious. An alternative translation suggests that those who would be great in the kingdom should consider themselves as having the status of a child or one of the other 'little ones' to which Matthew refers in this passage.

What children and Matthew's 'little ones' (the poor and outcast – or perhaps, those new to the faith) have in common is their low status in society and their vulnerability. Today, it is the vulnerability of small children that is highlighted as Herod vents his rage upon them.

One way to read this appalling episode from chapter 2 is simply to say that it is there to explain the flight into Egypt as another exodus. Jesus, like Moses, will return to save Israel. However, Matthew 18 makes it clear that the death and abuse of innocent children is no incidental matter. The deaths recorded in chapter 2 may be unavenged, but the tyranny that Herod represents is part of the sin of this world that Jesus comes to overthrow. The judgement on those who put stumbling blocks in the way of the vulnerable is made abundantly plain (vv.6-7). The implication for those living with the knowledge that they have protected the powerful rather than the vulnerable, is unequivocal.

COLLECT

Heavenly Father,
whose children suffered at the hands of Herod,
though they had done no wrong:
by the suffering of your Son
and by the innocence of our lives
frustrate all evil designs
and establish your reign of justice and peace;
through Jesus Christ your Son our Lord,
who is alive and reigns with you,
in the unity of the Holy Spirit,
one God, now and for ever.

Psalms **19**, 20
Jonah 1
Colossians 1.1-14

Colossians 1.1-14

'... so that you may lead lives worthy of the Lord' (v.10)

This opening passage of Paul's letter to the Church in Colossae contains two key images. In verses 13-14, the chief metaphor is that of the Exodus. The Greek words for 'rescue' (v.13) and 'redemption' (v.14) echo early baptismal liturgies and remind us that baptism is an Exodus from the world of darkness into the world of light.

The other metaphor in this passage speaks not of believers being transferred from one external realm to another, but of the gospel being planted within the life of each person. Here, Paul's prayer is that the faithful in Colossae may grow in faith. It is not enough to be trans-planted by faith into the kingdom of light; now growth in holiness is expected. The metaphors are organic: believers are to allow themselves to be 'filled' with wisdom (v.9); to 'grow in knowledge of God' (v.10); to be 'made strong' (v.11); and to 'bear fruit' (v.10).

The logic is typical of Paul's thought. He is praying that the Christians in Colossae will become what they are: children of light. In this way Paul holds together being made right with God (justification) and growing in holiness (sanctification). We are transferred from the kingdom of darkness into the kingdom of light simply by trusting in Christ. That, however, is only the beginning of the work that Christ wishes to complete in us. We are now to cooperate with him by allowing his faith and hope and love to expand within and among us.

COLLECT

Almighty God,
you have given us your only-begotten Son
to take our nature upon him
and as at this time to be born of a pure virgin:
grant that we, who have been born again
and made your children by adoption and grace,
may daily be renewed by your Holy Spirit;
through Jesus Christ your Son our Lord,
who is alive and reigns with you,
in the unity of the Holy Spirit,
one God, now and for ever.

Colossians 1.15-23

'... he has now reconciled in his fleshly body through death' (v.22)

The lilting language of verses 15 to 20 indicates that this is an early Christian hymn. Unlike much that passes for praise in our churches, it is not focused upon the believer's experience; rather it draws worshippers into adoration through focusing on Christ's glorious nature until they are 'lost in wonder, love and praise'. Christ is described as the 'beloved Son' (v.13) (echoing his baptism) in whom the fullness of God is pleased to dwell (v.19); as the true image of God (v.15) – the restoration of the image given to humanity in creation); the beginning (v.18) – as both the firstborn of creation and the firstborn from the dead. It is in Christ that all things (v.17) and the Church (v.18) hold together.

But what is this hymn doing in this letter? Its purpose is to remind the Colossians of two things. First, that despite his cosmic significance, Christ had a fleshly body. Secondly, that right belief is important.

For us today, these two reminders are important. Many of the growing Churches in the world tend to spiritualize Christian faith and make it other-worldly focused as if Christ had not been made flesh, had not healed the sick, had not been interested in issues of justice and community. At the same time, post-Christian society relies on Christian-derived values as if their basis in the doctrines of the faith were irrelevant.

The language of this passage reminds us of the connection between praising the one who bears the image of God and recognizing God's image in our fellow human beings.

COLLECT

Almighty God,
you have given us your only-begotten Son
to take our nature upon him
and as at this time to be born of a pure virgin:
grant that we, who have been born again
and made your children by adoption and grace,
may daily be renewed by your Holy Spirit;
through Jesus Christ your Son our Lord,
who is alive and reigns with you,
in the unity of the Holy Spirit,
one God, now and for ever.

Psalm 102
Jonah 3 – 4
Colossians 1.24 – 2.7

Colossians 1.24 – 2.7

'I am now rejoicing in my sufferings for your sake' (1.24)

This passage opens with a comment that is unparalleled in the New Testament and is difficult to interpret. What can Paul mean when he says that, in his own flesh, he is 'completing what is lacking in Christ's afflictions for the sake of his body, that is, the Church' (v.24)? Can Christ's sacrifice be effective if it is incomplete? Is it that only the one who suffers can genuinely proclaim Christ (cf. 2 Corinthians 4.10-12)? Is it only Paul as the apostle commissioned (v.25) to extend Christ's mission to the gentiles who has this role, or does it belong to all believers?

Finding meaning in suffering is a perennial human quest. For Paul, the meaning comes in offering his suffering for the sake of revealing the mystery of Christ to the gentiles. In his case (and in the case of those persecuted for their faith), it is perhaps possible to understand how, by being willing to suffer, he (and they) are making possible the proclamation of the gospel. It is perhaps also possible to see in it the chance that through this kind of Christ-like suffering, the image of God in believers is being completed.

In the case of other kinds of suffering that Christians experience, it may be difficult to see how it helps further any cause; yet, perhaps part of the mystery of Christ is that any kind of suffering (however it is caused, even sometimes by ourselves) can lead to redemptive outcomes, if it is named and freely offered to Christ in whom all things hold together (1.17).

Lord Jesus Christ,
your birth at Bethlehem
draws us to kneel in wonder at heaven touching earth:
accept our heartfelt praise
as we worship you,
our Saviour and our eternal God.

COLLECT

Monday 2 January

Psalms **18.1-30**
Ruth 1
Colossians 2.8-end

Colossians 2.8-end

'... the substance belongs to Christ' (v. 17)

It is in this passage that we get the greatest insight into the false teaching circulating in Colossae (vv.16-19) – an asceticism (regime of self denial, e.g. fasting) designed to help the believer leave behind the body and thereby witness the worship of the angels in heaven. Paul is concerned to address this by arguing that Christ is greater than the angels, for on the cross, he led the angels and other spiritual powers in triumphal procession (v.8) (though the NRSV takes the alternative view that the elemental spirits were evil and were led captive in this procession).

However, Instead of 'disarming' the rulers and powers, it makes better sense to translate this verb as referring to Christ 'stripping himself' through death (cf. v.11). This death was Christ's circumcision – who put off not a small piece of flesh in the temple, dictated by human traditions, but his whole body as a freely given offering on the cross.

Paul reminds the Colossians (and us), therefore, that no amount of self-imposed piety or asceticism can earn forgiveness (v.13). Rather, we have to stop clinging to our 'IOU to God' (v.14 'record') and accept that it has been cancelled out on the cross. God is not interested in our shame or self-abasement or other efforts to earn salvation. He wants us to join with him in the transformation of the cross and his resurrection (vv.12-13). God's forgiveness is so radical that it is hard to receive. In what ways do you find yourself still trying to earn acceptance?

COLLECT

Almighty God,
who wonderfully created us in your own image
and yet more wonderfully restored us
through your Son Jesus Christ:
grant that, as he came to share in our humanity,
so we may share the life of his divinity;
who is alive and reigns with you,
in the unity of the Holy Spirit,
one God, now and for ever.

Psalms **127**, 128, 131
Ruth 2
Colossians 3.1-11

Colossians 3.1-11

'But now you must get rid of all such things ...' (v.8)

Paul now turns his mind from the beliefs of the Colossians to the consequences of these beliefs in ethical terms. Following the baptismal imagery of the previous verses, converts need to strip off (v.9) the old self and put on (v.10) the new.

It is possible to read the list that must be 'put off' as a list of sins for individuals to refrain from – and yet, all those listed are attitudes and behaviours that affect the quality of human relationships and human community. If the old self is a self-centred individual who can take what it wants from others (fornication) or take itself out on others (anger) with impunity, by contrast, the new self is an interdependent person who belongs with other persons in the community that is being restored to the image of God (v.10).

The notion of the human race being made in the image of God is fundamental to a Judaeo-Christian way of viewing the human person. According to Genesis 1.27, when God created human beings, he created them plural. Both male and female were in God's image. For Christians, therefore, however tempting it may be to try to reflect God's glory on our own, we belong in community; like a mirror, our common life may reflect God's glory. Alternatively, the image of God may be shattered into pieces through conflict and division as we take the shards and use them to dehumanize each other, degrading the image of God in those we would enslave or declare unclean or consider less than capable of bearing God's full image.

God in Trinity,
eternal unity of perfect love:
gather the nations to be one family,
and draw us into your holy life
through the birth of Emmanuel,
our Lord Jesus Christ.

COLLECT

Wednesday 4 January

Psalm **89.1-37**
Ruth 3
Colossians 3.12 – 4.1

Colossians 3.12 – 4.1

'Above all, clothe yourselves with love' (3.14)

This passage contains a good deal of material that seems to pre-date Paul's letter. First, there are short sayings about community life and worship (3.13-17), used here to emphasize again the importance of the disciplines of common life in the body of Christ. Second, verses 3.18 to 4.1 comprise a 'household code' of instructions on how to behave at home. This is mundane stuff, and draws the Colossians' attention to the day-to-day. Our life as Christians should not be an escape into ecstatic visions, nor a retreat into a holy huddle, but should pervade even our domestic negotiations about cleaning and finances.

The passage raises the question of how Christian communities today interpret and inhabit the ethics of life in Christ. Do the details of passages like these establish the basis for right relations between people for all time? Do these passages point to key principles for relationships that need translation for new contexts? What are these key principles?

The history of the Church demonstrates that answers are not easily arrived at, yet, here, Paul offers two key ways of orienting ourselves to the endeavours of common discernment and day-to-day Christian living: we should embed our life in meditation on the Scriptures, ensuring that we listen to the discernment of each (v.16) – and, above all (even when we disagree and find each other hard to understand), we should clothe ourselves with love and a commitment to the whole body (v.15). What opportunities do you have to meditate on the Scriptures with those with whom you profoundly disagree?

COLLECT

Almighty God,
who wonderfully created us in your own image
and yet more wonderfully restored us
through your Son Jesus Christ:
grant that, as he came to share in our humanity,
so we may share the life of his divinity;
who is alive and reigns with you,
in the unity of the Holy Spirit,
one God, now and for ever.

Colossians 4.2-end

'I, Paul, write this greeting with my own hand' (v.18)

The greetings at the end of this letter are not often read aloud on Sundays, and yet they reveal some of the intimate realities of the life of the early Church. Here is a network of people who are deeply interconnected and among whom, through hardship, there is great colleagueship and affection: Tychicus is called beloved brother and fellow-servant (v.7); Onesimus is the faithful and beloved brother (v.9); Aristarchus is fellow-prisoner (v.10).

The greetings are personal and particular. These are people who know each other and are able to address each other in both their strengths and weaknesses: Epaphras needs defending (v.13); Archippus needs reminding to persevere (v.17). Also, Paul is encouraging the Colossians to have contact with other Christian communities – both those they know (Laodicea; the church meeting in Nympha's house (v.15)), and those they do not know personally (e.g. in Hierapolis v.13)

In Paul's time, the chief means of communication between Christians were letters like this that were carried in person. In our own time, there are many more means of communication open to us, but the need for Christians to be deeply interconnected remains, for the purposes of encouraging one another in faith; of helping each other persevere in the face of difficulties and in order to broaden and deepen our understanding of the Christian life so that we can live the gospel more faithfully. If you were to list the key people who help support and develop your faith, who would they be and what would you want to say to them?

God in Trinity,
eternal unity of perfect love:
gather the nations to be one family,
and draw us into your holy life
through the birth of Emmanuel,
our Lord Jesus Christ.

COLLECT

35

Friday 6 January

Epiphany

Psalms **132**, 113
Jeremiah 31.7-14
John 1.29-34

John 1.29-34

'And I myself have seen ... that this is the Son of God' (v.34)

In the Western Church, it is traditional at Epiphany to mark the visit of the magi. The origins of the word 'Epiphany', however, are from the Greek word for 'making manifest', used here in the mouth of John the Baptist (v.31). In the Eastern Church, this is the focus of Epiphany: the revealing of the Son of God in flesh. Charles Wesley captures the sense of it in his Christmas hymn, 'Let earth and heaven combine':

> He deigns in flesh to appear,
> Widest extremes to join;
> To bring our vileness near,
> And make us all divine:
> And we the life of God shall know,
> For God is manifest below.

For John, the obstacle to the unity of humanity and God is clear: the sin of the world (v.29). Yet, though the fault is not God's, God so yearns for reconciliation with his beloved creatures that it is he who makes the sacrifice: it is truly God who in the incarnation empties himself of all but love; it is truly God who at the crucifixion offers his life for the life of the world; it is truly God's life at the resurrection that cannot be destroyed by death.

Through these events, Christ's identity as Son of God (one having the same DNA as his father) is revealed (v.34); moreover, this identity is revealed to John the Baptist by the Holy Spirit (v.33). Thus, it is not only the identity of Christ that is revealed in this passage, but the full nature of God as Trinity: Father, Son and Holy Spirit.

COLLECT

O God,
who by the leading of a star
manifested your only Son to the peoples of the earth:
mercifully grant that we,
who know you now by faith,
may at last behold your glory face to face;
through Jesus Christ your Son our Lord,
who is alive and reigns with you,
in the unity of the Holy Spirit,
one God, now and for ever.

Jeremiah 23.1-8

'I will raise up for David a righteous Branch' (v.5)

Sandwiched between John's account of the baptism of Jesus (yesterday) and Matthew's account of the same event (tomorrow), here is a passage from Jeremiah that condemns the leaders of Israel and promises a righteous king.

Jeremiah's original audience was Jerusalem under siege in the sixth century BC. The blame for the enslavement of the Israelites to Babylon he laid firmly at the feet of the kings of Judah who had failed to act justly and protect the weak (Jeremiah 22.3) and who had made themselves rich at the expense of the vulnerable (Jeremiah 22.13-14). The Babylonians (Chaldeans) would be Yahweh's instrument to end corruption and oppression in Jerusalem, so that he himself could raise up a righteous ruler who would govern justly (vv.3-4).

The reference to the raising up of 'a righteous branch for David' (v.5), however, has also been interpreted as a Messianic prophecy, fulfilled in Jesus. Unlike the self-serving 'shepherds' (v.1) who still governed Israel in Jesus' day (like Herod, the collaborator with the Romans, whose magnificent palaces can still be seen today at Caesarea Maritima and near Bethlehem), the Messiah would be a just ruler who would deal wisely and even be known as 'The Lord is our righteousness' (v.6).

The Epiphany thus reveals God as a God of justice who is on the side of the oppressed, and Christ as the one leader who can stand the judgement. All other leaders are called to turn from their self-serving ways and serve the poor and the vulnerable instead.

Creator of the heavens,
who led the Magi by a star
to worship the Christ-child:
guide and sustain us,
that we may find our journey's end
in Jesus Christ our Lord.

COLLECT

Monday 9 January

Genesis 1.1-19

'Then God said, "Let there be light"' (v.3)

Epiphany, when we focus on the revelation of Jesus Christ, is a good time to be reading the stories in Genesis of the revelation of God through God's creation. Both Genesis and John's Gospel begin, 'In the beginning' and tell of what happens when God's light shines in the darkness, as God creates and then enters our world in Jesus Christ.

Genesis uses stories to tell of Hebrew beliefs about God, the world and humanity. These first verses of Genesis compress so much and differ theologically from creation stories in other cultures, where fickle gods treat humans cruelly for their own ends. In contrast, the author of Genesis makes a distinctive theological claim that everything about God is good: the God we worship is the origin of the world and of life in it, sheds light in darkness even before the creation of the sun, brings order to chaos, creates the rhythm of day and night, creates vegetation that itself generates abundance, and is the ruler of the universe. This is the God who will be revealed as the biblical stories unfold and whose purposes for the world have been good from the very beginning.

As we begin reading Genesis, we can enjoy the stories but also ask ourselves what they reveal to us of God – and thus of ourselves and God's world.

COLLECT

Eternal Father,
who at the baptism of Jesus
revealed him to be your Son,
anointing him with the Holy Spirit:
grant to us, who are born again by water and the Spirit,
that we may be faithful to our calling as your adopted children;
through Jesus Christ your Son our Lord,
who is alive and reigns with you,
in the unity of the Holy Spirit,
one God, now and for ever.

Genesis 1.20 – 2.3

*'God saw everything that he had made,
and indeed, it was very good' (1.31)*

This creation story dates from the sixth century BC, when the nation's survival was in doubt and the people were learning to trust that God was with them even in exile in Babylon. So they reminded themselves that their God created the whole world and that, although now slaves doing the bidding of others, they were made in God's image and bidden by God to care for the world. In the confusion of exile, they told of a God of order who merely spoke and worlds came to be, who doesn't ignore but sees his creation, and that humans made a good creation very good. Telling this theological story brought hope and passed on the belief that – unlike the despotic gods of their Babylonian conquerors – their almighty God was good.

As we read this story in a very different context, God is revealed as the origin of life in its glorious variety – from sea monsters to creepy-crawlies – and it is our privilege to be stewards of that creation: 'have dominion' (1.26,28) implies responsibility not exploitation. Our relationship with God is inextricably linked to our relationship with the physical world.

Note, too, that from the beginning, the rhythm of work and rest is part of the theological story. Those are significant points to ponder as we live in God's world today: are work and rest in balance in your life?

Heavenly Father,
at the Jordan you revealed Jesus as your Son:
may we recognize him as our Lord
and know ourselves to be your beloved children;
through Jesus Christ our Saviour.

COLLECT

Wednesday 11 January

Psalms 19, **20** *or* **119.105-128**
Genesis 2.4-end
Matthew 21.33-end

Genesis 2.4-end

'And the Lord God planted a garden' (v.8)

This earlier creation account (there are still more in Psalms 74.12-17 and 104, and Job 38) is very different. This source dates from the tenth century BC when the people were in the Promised Land and it describes the ideal conditions for hill farmers – God has made a fruitful land and has even planted it for them. Unlike the first account of creation, God doesn't speak the world into being but fingers creation into shape, forming things from dust and digging holes in the ground to plant trees. There is a creative partnership: God provides the life-giving water, and humans provide labour so that plants can grow; God makes animals and waits to see what humans name them. Only one thing is not good: that man is alone. So God remedies that, and thus the theology is the same as Genesis 1: God's creation is good, everything looks and tastes good, and boundaries are for our good.

However, even in these ideal conditions, human relationship with the land involves commandments and responsibilities: the Hebrew for 'to till it and to keep it' (v.15) implies 'to guard and conserve', and is also connected with keeping the law. The land is not to be worshipped (as in Canaanite fertility religions), but God is worshipped through our care of God's land and of one another. That remains true today; the answer to our prayer that we may be faithful to our calling has very earthy implications.

COLLECT

Eternal Father,
who at the baptism of Jesus
revealed him to be your Son,
anointing him with the Holy Spirit:
grant to us, who are born again by water and the Spirit,
that we may be faithful to our calling as your adopted children;
through Jesus Christ your Son our Lord,
who is alive and reigns with you,
in the unity of the Holy Spirit,
one God, now and for ever.

Psalms **21**, 24 *or* 90, **92**
Genesis 3
Matthew 22.1-14

Genesis 3

'... the Lord God called to the man ... "Where are you?"' (v.9)

The serpent appears without explanation to tempt with loaded questions that mixed truth (they didn't die) and lies (they didn't become like God). Once the woman doubted God's goodness, she saw, took, ate and gave, then they hid. In five verbs, one action led to another, until God had to protect them and all creation from the consequences. Temptation can so easily begin with doubting God, then slide into action we regret. We can fear we are missing out on something, dwell on it, act, and then hide from God.

This story explains for hill-country farmers why life is so hard in God's world. '*Adam*' (human) is linked to '*adamah*' (the ground), but human sin distorts our relationship with all creation. Now they have to toil rather than work the land in the joyful way God intended. They have gained knowledge not wisdom, and since they might live for ever, God prevents them from causing more harm by sending them from paradise. The tree of life is introduced and is to be guarded so that, when all things are restored in Jesus Christ, it will be there for the healing of the nations (Revelation 22.2).

As we pray this week that we may be faithful to our calling, we can remember that even when we spoil our relationship with God and God's world, God's good purposes continue.

Heavenly Father,
at the Jordan you revealed Jesus as your Son:
may we recognize him as our Lord
and know ourselves to be your beloved children;
through Jesus Christ our Saviour.

COLLECT

41

Friday 13 January

Psalms **67**, 72 *or* **88** (95)
Genesis 4.1-16, 25-26
Matthew 22.15-33

Genesis 4.1-16, 25-26

'... the Lord said, "What have you done?" ' (v.10)

Despite their banishment from Paradise, Eve sees her conception of her son as something wonderful achieved with God's help – 'Cain' plays on the word for 'creation'. Cain and Abel's story may be a version of older stories of the conflict between farmers and shepherds. We don't know why one offering is accepted and not another – this story predates the law's concept of blood-sacrifice – but anger and jealousy lead to murder, which further distorts the relationship between humans and creation.

Family relationships have always been complex, and we may recognize ourselves in these stories. We are created in God's image, so God holds Cain accountable for his response to misfortune: he is not powerless but can control his reactions (v.7). Just as God asked Adam and Eve 'Where are you?', now he asks Cain 'Where is your brother?'. As before, God acts both to punish and to protect rather than destroy the person who has sinned and, in the omitted verses, Cain becomes the father of city dwellers and nomads, as well as musicians and metal workers. Meanwhile, Adam and Eve have a new son, Seth. Despite our failings, God keeps searching us out and offering us new opportunities to be faithful.

COLLECT

Eternal Father,
who at the baptism of Jesus
revealed him to be your Son,
anointing him with the Holy Spirit:
grant to us, who are born again by water and the Spirit,
that we may be faithful to our calling as your adopted children;
through Jesus Christ your Son our Lord,
who is alive and reigns with you,
in the unity of the Holy Spirit,
one God, now and for ever.

Psalms 29, **33** *or* 96, **97**, 100
Genesis 6.1-10
Matthew 22.34-end

Genesis 6.1-10

'Noah walked with God' (v.9)

The curious story of the sons of God and daughters of humans draws on ancient mythologies about divine-human beings. It is another way of describing human attempts to 'be like God' (Genesis 3.22) thus rejecting their place in creation. We are linked to the ground and part of God's creation, made in God's image but not (as in some other religions) gods. God intervenes to affirm his sovereignty in giving the breath of life to humans (Genesis 2.7), limiting human life-span rather than withdrawing life altogether. In Psalm 104.29-30, this dependence on God for life is a cause for praise.

This is a transition point: God takes stock of what has happened and is pained (the same word is used of Eve in 3.16) at human sinfulness and cruelty, a theme that the prophets will repeat time and again. But one man, Noah, is righteous – unlike Cain, he has done well and resisted sin – and so the scene is set for a new beginning through the faithfulness of one man, as it will later through Abram and ultimately through Jesus Christ.

Noah is righteous and walks with God – something God yearned Adam would do in the garden (Genesis 3.8-9). We are created for fellowship and friendship with God, given responsibilities to care for God's world and live righteously in it. How can you fulfil that joyful and challenging calling today?

Heavenly Father,
at the Jordan you revealed Jesus as your Son:
may we recognize him as our Lord
and know ourselves to be your beloved children;
through Jesus Christ our Saviour.

COLLECT

Monday 16 January

Genesis 6.11 – 7.10

'Noah did this; he did all that God commanded him' (6.22)

The earth, which God had created very good (Genesis 1.31), has become corrupt and filled with violence, going its own self-destructive way. Then there is a flood that the storyteller implies is not an act of God's anger but of sorrow at a spoiled creation. God offers a new beginning and promises a covenant with Noah, who will live if he is obedient and builds the ark. Noah's righteousness is expressed in the description of him as much older than the 120-year life-span God has imposed.

The editor of Genesis has blended two versions of the story, and we need not worry about the discrepancy in numbers of animals. What is more significant is the way the Bible's flood story differs from those of other ancient cultures, where floods are capricious or malicious acts by the gods; here, it is a judgement on human sin with a view to a new beginning.

The theme of deliverance occurs again in the deliverance at the Red Sea and Isaiah's prophetic promise: 'Do not fear, for I have redeemed you ... When you pass through the waters, I will be with you; and through the rivers, they shall not overwhelm you' (Isaiah 43.1-2). As Christians, we can also see this symbolism in baptism, and this week's Collect is an appropriate and joyful prayer: in Christ our lives can be renewed.

COLLECT

Almighty God,
in Christ you make all things new:
transform the poverty of our nature by the riches of your grace,
and in the renewal of our lives
make known your heavenly glory;
through Jesus Christ your Son our Lord,
who is alive and reigns with you,
in the unity of the Holy Spirit,
one God, now and for ever.

Psalms **132**, 147.1-12 *or* **106*** (*or* 103)
Genesis 7.11-end
Matthew 24.15-28

Genesis 7.11-end

'... and the Lord shut him in' (v.16)

Archaeological records tell of extensive floods which may lie behind the flood stories of mythology. Again, we can focus on the distinctive theology in the Hebrew version of this story: God remains in control, but lets creation express its natural power. The swirling of waters coming from below and the deluge from above threaten a return to the chaos before God brought order to creation in Genesis 1.

This flood story does not allow us to see natural disasters as the capricious acts of an angry god but as a consequence of the way the earth is made. Nevertheless, the vivid descriptions of the force and extent of the flood and its devastating effect are terrible reminders of God's power, expressed vividly in Psalm 29, where the psalmist prays that God will give strength to his people and bless them with peace. When we hear of the effects of natural disasters on the lives of people it is easy to be paralysed by the extent of the resulting suffering. Our response can derive from God's who offers care and protection through the dramatic imagery of personally shutting Noah in the ark. Is there something we can do today to express our care for people who suffer from natural disasters?

Eternal Lord,
our beginning and our end:
bring us with the whole creation
to your glory, hidden through past ages
and made known
in Jesus Christ our Lord.

COLLECT

Wednesday 18 January

Genesis 8.1-14

'God remembered Noah' (v.1)

'Forty days' will appear again in the biblical stories – for example in Moses' 40 days on Mount Sinai and Jesus' 40 days in the wilderness. Essentially, it means 'a long and significant time' and usually is a time of preparation before something new happens. The 'seven days' hark back to the seventh day of rest after God created the world: new life begins after the rest of satisfaction and completion.

We are supposed to hear echoes of the creation story in the flood story – God has not abandoned his original good plans because of human sin but once again works to bring about his good purposes for the world. The wind that now blows over the earth at God's behest once swept over the face of the waters (Genesis 1.2), and there's a touching note in verse 1: God remembers the wild animals and the domestic animals with Noah – a reminder that the creation of cattle, creeping things and wild animals was good in God's eyes (Genesis 1.24-25).

In this Epiphany season when we recall the revelation of the glory of God in Jesus Christ, our prayer this week asks that God will make known his heavenly glory in the renewal of our lives. Have we considered how our care of animals might be part of this?

COLLECT

Almighty God,
in Christ you make all things new:
transform the poverty of our nature by the riches of your grace,
and in the renewal of our lives
make known your heavenly glory;
through Jesus Christ your Son our Lord,
who is alive and reigns with you,
in the unity of the Holy Spirit,
one God, now and for ever.

Psalms **76**, 148 *or* 113, **115**
Genesis 8.15 – 9.7
Matthew 25.1-13

Genesis 8.15 – 9.7

'God blessed Noah and his sons' (9.1)

God takes the initiative and sends Noah, his family and the living creatures out of the ark. Once again the animals are to be fruitful and multiply. But the human heart has not changed; God knows it is evil and further spoiling of God's creation is inevitable.

Noah is no longer passive but takes the initiative and sacrifices to God, and the smell gives God pleasure. Noah is blessed and sent to be fruitful and multiply on the earth, re-establishing God's original purposes for humans. The Hebrew words 'Noah' and 'grace' are related – God acts with grace to save Noah and, through him, others.

Despite God's sadness at human sin, God promises to continue to bless creation with the regular cycles of nature that enable life to exist, and never again to destroy every living creature. The principle of reverence for the human life is established, and the flood story ends with the re-affirmation that God created humans in his own image, echoing Genesis 1.27 and reminding us that, despite being all too aware of our sinfulness, God calls us to relationship with him and faithful living in his world. God's trust in us is remarkable – what can we do to live up to our calling?

Eternal Lord,
our beginning and our end:
bring us with the whole creation
to your glory, hidden through past ages
and made known
in Jesus Christ our Lord.

COLLECT

47

Friday 20 January

Psalms **27**, 149 *or* **139**
Genesis 9.8-19
Matthew 25.14-30

Genesis 9.8-19

'I will remember my covenant' (v.15)

A covenant puts the relationship of the partners on a legal basis. Subsequent covenants placed an individual or nation in the position of making a positive response to God's ordinance, but here nothing is asked of Noah. This is sheer grace.

This covenant, the first in the Bible, is made by God not just with Noah but with all creation and thus has an ecological dimension. The sign of the covenant, the bow in the clouds, is thought of as the rainbow, but in the Old Testament, where bows and arrows were used in battle, the word usually means 'the bow of war', so its appearance as a rainbow was reassurance that God had laid aside his bow. Significantly, when the bow was seen, it was not Noah but God who was reminded of the everlasting covenant and that his wrath had subsided, because it was God who had the power to override the covenant and destroy the earth. When Noah saw the rainbow, which would only be when it rained and he might fear that water would again destroy the earth, he would be comforted that God was not set on destruction. Sometimes, it is only when we face what causes us to fear that we see the sign of God's grace in the midst of it.

COLLECT

Almighty God,
in Christ you make all things new:
transform the poverty of our nature by the riches of your grace,
and in the renewal of our lives
make known your heavenly glory;
through Jesus Christ your Son our Lord,
who is alive and reigns with you,
in the unity of the Holy Spirit,
one God, now and for ever.

Saturday 21 January

Genesis 11.1-9

'... the Lord scattered them abroad over the face of all the earth' (v.9)

At the end of yesterday's reading, we learned that Noah's three sons peopled all the earth. Today, we hear what happened: another crisis! The phrase 'Come, let us ...' is uttered three times and shapes the story – the people make bricks, they build a city, and then the Lord confuses their language.

This story completes the cycle of stories of the beginning and takes us back to when humans and animals were first told by God to fill the earth (Genesis 1.22,28). They did this (Genesis 10.18,32) but now fear being scattered (Genesis 11.4) so resist God's purposes by building a city, in order to stay in one place. God does not judge them because they build upward to the heavens, which are the vault over creation (in their cosmology, God lives beyond the heavens and the tower with its top in the heavens is so tiny he can't see it but has to leave his home to look!). Instead, God's judgement is that they have not spread out across the earth and thus cannot care for it as he intended. So in scattering them, God pursues the well-being of all creation.

In Genesis, the people do not listen to each other or hear with understanding. At Pentecost (Acts 2), they do, and spread out across the earth proclaiming the gospel. God yearns for us to share his mission in the whole world, which means listening to God and to one another – and maybe risking our security, trusting in God's protection.

Eternal Lord,
our beginning and our end:
bring us with the whole creation
to your glory, hidden through past ages
and made known
in Jesus Christ our Lord.

COLLECT

Monday 23 January

Psalms 40, **108** *or* 123, 124, 125, **126**
Genesis 11.27 – 12.9
Matthew 26.1-16

Genesis 11.27 – 12.9

'I will bless you … so that you will be a blessing' (12.2)

The people had feared being spread abroad – would they be lost? Today, we have the resounding answer: 'no', because in far-off Ur of the Chaldeans, God calls a family. But it is a family with no future: Sarai has no child. Terah sets out but stops en route. Things are at a standstill. Then God speaks and Abram listens. In the Bible, if people don't act on what they hear, they have not listened properly. Abram acts, and the story moves from creation myths to human saga with more rounded characters with whom we can identify as they try to be faithful to God.

Despite his lack of heirs, all the families of the earth will be blessed in Abram. Nothing is impossible with God, and promise is at the heart of God's ways with the world. If we despair because we can't see how God can work in our situation, we can be encouraged by the way God used Abram's unpromising family situation to bless not just him but the whole earth. So Abram moves, putting a human face on nomadic life and challenging the prevailing idea that gods were powerful only in their own territory. All the earth is God's.

How are you listening for God? Our Collect reminds us that God is a God of miracles, so pray today for God to renew you in your weakness and make you a blessing to others.

COLLECT

Almighty God,
whose Son revealed in signs and miracles
the wonder of your saving presence:
renew your people with your heavenly grace,
and in all our weakness
sustain us by your mighty power;
through Jesus Christ your Son our Lord,
who is alive and reigns with you,
in the unity of the Holy Spirit,
one God, now and for ever.

Psalms 34, **36** *or* **132**, 133
Genesis 13.2-end
Matthew 26.17-35

Genesis 13.2-end

'Raise your eyes now, and look ...' (v.14)

Abram, a wealthy nomad, is back at Bethel ('the house of God') where he had previously worshipped (Genesis 12.8). Seeking a peaceful solution to the problem of overpopulation of livestock and people, he gives Lot the choice of where to go in the lands they have come to. Lot chooses what looks familiar and fertile, but the sting in the tail is in verse 13, as Lot will discover in time.

It is too easy to rush to the Lord's renewed promise to Abram and forget that, when Abram gave Lot the choice, he was relying on God's past promises and did not know how things would turn out. It was only after his faithful trust, and perhaps his disappointment with what was left to him, that the promises were repeated and expanded: this childless man was to have offspring like the dust of the earth. In God's purposes, Abram's calling was for the good of the whole world.

When we are faced with choices between alternatives that affect our future, it requires trust that God can work through other people's choices and will not allow us to make a mistake, as well as wisdom to know what decisions to make ourselves. Perhaps Abram's generosity to Lot can be our example of trust in God.

God of all mercy,
your Son proclaimed good news to the poor,
release to the captives,
and freedom to the oppressed:
anoint us with your Holy Spirit
and set all your people free
to praise you in Christ our Lord.

COLLECT

Wednesday 25 January

The Conversion of Paul

Psalms 66, 147.13-end
Ezekiel 3.22-end
Philippians 3.1-14

Philippians 3.1-14

'I want to know Christ ...' (v.10)

We interrupt our reading of Genesis to honour St Paul, whose conversion the Church celebrates today and who played his part in God's blessing the world as Christ was revealed through his preaching. Paul, a self-proclaimed 'Hebrew of the Hebrews', discovered through his encounter with Christ that his confidence in his human origins was worthless. Following his conversion, his passion for persecuting Christians was redirected into passion to know the power of the resurrection of Christ.

Paul wrote that everyone who believes is blessed with Abraham who believed (Galatians 3.6-9). Like Abraham, Paul abandoned his past way of life and risked all human security, trusting in God's promises, confident of the hope that God will bring life out of death. Abraham trusted God to give him an heir. Paul treated all he had relied on as rubbish in order to place his full hope in Christ Jesus. He doesn't say he gave it up *because* he trusted in Christ, but *in order to* trust in Christ: if it stood in the way of knowing Christ then it had to be abandoned.

What stands in the way of our trust in Christ? Paul's complete turnaround is an example of faithful discipleship that risks the loss of all things in the hope of gaining something more precious: knowing God in Jesus Christ. As we give thanks for Paul's conversion, we can ask ourselves what we must leave behind because it hinders our knowing Jesus Christ as Lord.

COLLECT

Almighty God,
who caused the light of the gospel
to shine throughout the world
through the preaching of your servant Saint Paul:
grant that we who celebrate his wonderful conversion
may follow him in bearing witness to your truth;
through Jesus Christ your Son our Lord,
who is alive and reigns with you,
in the unity of the Holy Spirit,
one God, now and for ever.

Thursday 26 January

Genesis 15

'Do not be afraid, Abram, I am your shield' (v.1)

It seems that God's promises to Abram are wearing a bit thin, and we can sense Abram's frustration that there is no sign of them being fulfilled. He is getting older, there's no sign of a son and heir, and he wants some certainty about it all. So he complains to God and, wonderfully, God does not tell Abram off but takes him outside for an object lesson. On a clear, starlit night in the wilderness, Abram is invited to ponder the view and, through that, take in the magnitude of God's promise to him. It has the desired effect: Abram believes and the Lord reckons that to him as righteousness (v.6) – the same right relationship with God that Noah had (Genesis 6.9).

The odd covenant ritual comes from an early tradition. After an explanation of why the promise was delayed in its fulfilment, which anticipates the time of slavery in Egypt, fire becomes the symbol of the holy presence of God, foreshadowing the burning bush that Moses saw when that slavery was about to end.

We can take comfort from God's willingness to let Abram express his questions and his fears and then give him very vivid reassurance. It is better to be honest about our doubts than just abandon our hope. That way our faith can be strengthened.

Almighty God,
whose Son revealed in signs and miracles
the wonder of your saving presence:
renew your people with your heavenly grace,
and in all our weakness
sustain us by your mighty power;
through Jesus Christ your Son our Lord,
who is alive and reigns with you,
in the unity of the Holy Spirit,
one God, now and for ever.

COLLECT

Friday 27 January

Genesis 16

'... where have you come from and where are you going?' (v.8)

Time marches on, and, frustrated, Sarai takes matters into her own hands. It was not uncommon for a wife to give her maid to her husband and claim the resulting child as her own, but things go wrong and Hagar's contempt for her childless mistress brings disaster. Abram stays out of the squabble and, on the face of it, Hagar's disappearance leaves the path clear for the Lord's original promise to be fulfilled.

But the Lord has other ideas and meets Hagar in the wilderness. The sudden burst of dialogue tells the story vividly, as Hagar is asked to account for herself and is told to go back to her work as Sarai's slave. There is promise too – she, a foreign slave woman, thus an outsider on all counts, has been heard ('Ishmael' means 'God hears') and she names God, 'El-roi', 'God of seeing'. More than that, like Abram, she is promised that her offspring will be so numerous that they cannot be counted. It is no problem to God to bless both Sarai and Hagar in this extravagant way because there is no zero sum to God's blessing. Both have to learn God's generosity.

The questions the Lord asks Hagar are worth pondering for ourselves as God meets with us today, whatever our situation. Where have you come from? And where are you going?

COLLECT

Almighty God,
whose Son revealed in signs and miracles
the wonder of your saving presence:
renew your people with your heavenly grace,
and in all our weakness
sustain us by your mighty power;
through Jesus Christ your Son our Lord,
who is alive and reigns with you,
in the unity of the Holy Spirit,
one God, now and for ever.

Saturday 28 January

Genesis 17.1-22

'I will bless her, and she shall give rise to nations' (v.16)

Names in the Bible carry meaning. The person who names something has authority over it. So, when God renames Abram ('exalted father'), 'Abraham' ('father of a multitude') and Sarai becomes Sarah (in both cases this means 'princess'), this tells us that God is about to do something through them. In the thirteen years since Ishmael was born, Abraham has staked his hopes on him as his heir. So, when God reiterates that Sarah will have a son, Abraham questions it. In chapter 15, God's promise comes in the middle of Abraham's daily life and he has a conversation with God about it; here, God announces the covenant unilaterally and Abraham hardly says a word, but instead falls over laughing. We experience God's actions in different ways at different times and the editor of Genesis includes both versions which reflect the way one source in Genesis understands God's ways with humans to be very interactive whereas in the other (also used in chapter 1) God simply speaks and things happen.

Either way, Abraham, worn out by waiting for God's word to be fulfilled, is ready to settle for blessing through Ishmael. But God has other ideas: as promised to Hagar, Ishmael will indeed be blessed, but there is still more blessing for Abraham and Sarah, because their child, whom God names Isaac ('laughter'), will be the one with whom the covenant is established.

When we are under pressure and growing weary, it is easy to settle for what we have got rather than remain open to God's promise of even more blessing in the future. Mercifully, God does not give up. So we can pray to be renewed by God's grace and sustained by God's power in our times of weakness.

God of all mercy,
your Son proclaimed good news to the poor,
release to the captives,
and freedom to the oppressed:
anoint us with your Holy Spirit
and set all your people free
to praise you in Christ our Lord.

COLLECT

Monday 30 January

Psalms **57**, 96 *or* 1, 2, 3
Genesis 18.1-15
Matthew 27.11-26

Genesis 18.1-15

'Is anything too wonderful for the Lord?' (v.14)

Now we hear the promise from chapter 17 through a human story. This time, Abraham is not silent but bursting with action, as he looks up, runs, bows down, hastens into the tent and organizes hospitality that vastly exceeds the 'little bread' he has offered. Why? Because three men have suddenly appeared in the midday heat, and oriental courtesy and hospitality are called for. Abraham does not recognize them as divine beings, or indeed that the Lord himself is among them, but they bring their amazing message, and this time it is Sarah who laughs.

Again, Abraham and Sarah are faced with the magnitude of God's grace. The question 'Is anything too wonderful for the Lord?' is one that we also can ponder when we are tempted to live parsimoniously because we cannot comprehend the extent of God's generosity and purposes to bless the whole world.

The letter to the Hebrews reminds us that sometimes we can entertain God's messengers (angels) without realizing it, while the Collect prays that the light of Christ will shine in our hearts and reveal the knowledge of God's glory in Jesus Christ. Pray that prayer for anyone you know who is discouraged by events that weaken their faith. Perhaps God will answer that prayer by sending an unrecognized angel.

COLLECT

God our creator,
who in the beginning
commanded the light to shine out of darkness:
we pray that the light of the glorious gospel of Christ
may dispel the darkness of ignorance and unbelief,
shine into the hearts of all your people,
and reveal the knowledge of your glory
    in the face of Jesus Christ your Son our Lord,
who is alive and reigns with you,
in the unity of the Holy Spirit,
one God, now and for ever.

Psalms **93**, 97 *or* **5**, 6 (8)
Genesis 18.16-end
Matthew 27.27-44

Genesis 18.16-end

'... I have chosen him ... to keep the way of the Lord by doing righteousness and justice' (v.19)

The announcement of a new beginning for Abraham and Sarah is followed immediately by the prospect of a destructive end for the city that Abraham, in his tent in the mountains, could see in the distance on the plain. The Lord deliberates about taking Abraham into his confidence and, when he does, the tables are turned, and Abraham becomes the Lord's questioner, putting God on the spot in an example of Middle Eastern bargaining. The question is not whether there will be judgement on the city, but what decides the extent of it: the wickedness of the many or the righteousness of the few?

Abraham presses hard until he receives the answer that a few innocent and righteous people are more important than many wicked people. Righteousness is the key concept here: Noah was righteous, but that quality has not been ascribed to Abraham. However, the Lord has chosen Abraham to lead his descendants in the way of righteousness and justice. So this is a testing both of God's purposes and of Abraham's commitment to, and understanding of, what it means to be righteous.

Pray today for people trying to live righteously in the midst of vice and wickedness. Can you be their advocate, as Abraham was?

God of heaven,
you send the gospel to the ends of the earth
and your messengers to every nation:
send your Holy Spirit to transform us
by the good news of everlasting life
in Jesus Christ our Lord.

COLLECT

Wednesday 1 February

Psalms **95**, 98 *or* **119.1-32**
Genesis 19.1-3, 12-29
Matthew 27.45-56

Genesis 19.1-3, 12-29

'God remembered Abraham' (v.29)

The warning note we heard about Sodom's wickedness (Genesis 13.13) proves significant. Lot has settled there and, like Abraham, welcomes the unknown visitors into his home. But things turn out differently, since their message this time is of destruction, and their attempts to save Lot's family prove difficult. This ancient story of a past catastrophic event is woven into the narrative of God's ways with the world. The story of Lot's wife may be an old tradition to explain a strange rock formation, much as we name 'Old Harry Rocks' or 'Giant's Causeway'.

Elsewhere in the Bible, the sin of Sodom is described as injustice and lack of care for widows and orphans, pride, gluttony, laziness and lack of care for the needy (Isaiah 1.10,17; Ezekiel 16.49). In contrast, there are touching references to the Lord's mercy to Lot's family (v.16) and to Abraham (v.29). We can picture Abraham, standing on the hillside looking at the smoke rising from where Sodom had been and wondering if his nephew had escaped.

The Lord remembered Abraham, as he remembered Noah during the flood (Genesis 8.1) and found Hagar in the wilderness (Genesis 16.7). From the very beginning, when God called to the man in the garden 'Where are you?', God has been seeking us out in our need.

COLLECT

God our creator,
who in the beginning
commanded the light to shine out of darkness:
we pray that the light of the glorious gospel of Christ
may dispel the darkness of ignorance and unbelief,
shine into the hearts of all your people,
and reveal the knowledge of your glory
    in the face of Jesus Christ your Son our Lord,
who is alive and reigns with you,
in the unity of the Holy Spirit,
one God, now and for ever.

Psalms **48**, 146
Exodus 13.1-16
Romans 12.1-5

**Presentation of Christ
in the Temple**

Romans 12.1-5

'... present your bodies as a living sacrifice' (v.1)

Candlemas, the Presentation of Christ, recalls Mary and Joseph presenting 40-day-old Jesus, their first-born, to the Lord (Luke 2.22-40). This reflects the law's statement that the first-born male belonged to God (Exodus 34.19) and how, at the Exodus, the Israelite first-born were saved by the sacrifice of a lamb (Exodus 12.21-32). Tomorrow, we will read an earlier challenge to Abraham to present his first-born to God.

When something is sacrificed, the donor relinquishes ownership and control to the recipient. That lies behind Paul's challenge to present ourselves as a living sacrifice to God: we are no longer our own but God's. As living sacrifices, we are gradually transformed to live as citizens of the kingdom of God, discerning the will of God. We do not do this alone but are members of the Body of Christ, something Paul explores further in 1 Corinthians 12.12-27.

Today, we pray that we may be presented to God by Christ, who was himself presented to God by Mary and Joseph. In entrusting Jesus to Mary and Joseph, God himself offered his first-born into the hands of others. It is not easy to let go of control of our lives, but our confidence lies in the goodness of God, who has already taken that risk for us. Use the Collect to offer yourself to God afresh today.

Almighty and ever-living God,
clothed in majesty,
whose beloved Son was this day presented in the Temple,
in substance of our flesh:
grant that we may be presented to you
with pure and clean hearts,
by your Son Jesus Christ our Lord,
who is alive and reigns with you,
in the unity of the Holy Spirit,
one God, now and for ever.

COLLECT

Genesis 22.1-19

'The Lord will provide' (v. 14)

At last, Isaac has been born! Abraham's faith has been tested over decades, and God has proved to be faithful. But then God tests Abraham again with a shocking request, even in a culture where children were sacrificed to pagan gods. The storyteller is concerned not with the ethics of the demand but with Abraham's willingness to trust God despite this threat to the fulfilment of the promise. '... now I know that you fear God' (v.12) is about obedience not emotion.

In powerful storytelling, verbs describe Abraham's actions, building the tension to the climax where God intervenes. Three times Abraham is called by name and three times he responds, 'Here I am'. Numerous unanswered questions occur to us: what were they both thinking as they walked together? What was Isaac's response when he realized what was happening? What did Sarah say when they got back home?

God begins as the tester (v.1) but ends as the provider (v.14), as Abraham had assured Isaac would happen. Only now does he know that for certain and so names the place 'the Lord will provide'. That deep learning was followed immediately by a renewal of the promise that all the earth would be blessed through Abraham's obedience to God's voice. God's salvific purposes are always cosmic in their scope, even if they are personal in their outworking.

COLLECT

Almighty God,
by whose grace alone we are accepted
    and called to your service:
strengthen us by your Holy Spirit
and make us worthy of our calling;
through Jesus Christ your Son our Lord,
who is alive and reigns with you,
in the unity of the Holy Spirit,
one God, now and for ever.

Saturday 4 February

Genesis 23

'... you are a mighty prince among us' (v.6)

God had promised Abraham both a name and land; in Isaac, the name is preserved, now the land is secured. Having bargained with God over Sodom, Abraham bargains with his land-owning neighbours. In a humorous story, the throw-away question, 'What is four hundred shekels of silver between friends?' begs the answer 'A lot!' Abraham is swindled, paying well over the odds, but gains a share in the land God has promised to his descendants. He is no longer a 'stranger and an alien', and Sarah is not buried in foreign soil.

So far, Genesis has told the story of God's creation of the world and intention to bring worldwide blessing, through the trauma of human failure, to a story of God working through one faithful man. Having narrowed the focus to that one man, the scene is set for the perspective to broaden out as God's blessing comes to the whole world through this one man's family. The locals call Abraham, 'a mighty prince among us' or 'a prince of God'. They are merely being polite, but, in God's way, the landless alien bears the promises of God and this deeper theological truth is picked up in Ephesians 2.19, where Christians are described as no longer strangers and aliens but citizens with the saints. As citizens, we are given our first share in our promised inheritance in the sacraments of Baptism and Eucharist or Communion.

God of our salvation,
help us to turn away from those habits
which harm our bodies
and poison our minds
and to choose again your gift of life,
revealed to us in Jesus Christ our Lord.

COLLECT

Monday 6 February

Psalms 27, **30**
Genesis 24.1-28
1 Timothy 6.1-10

1 Timothy 6.1-10

'... if we have food and clothing, we will be content with these' (v.8)

It would be easy to read this passage as a simple diatribe against money. But when we look more closely at it, we realize that Paul is writing with a deep pastoral concern for Timothy and the Church. He writes of the *oregomenoi* – those who are 'stretching themselves out', with deep hunger and unsatisfied desire, towards riches. Paul knows that trying to satisfy inner hungers with money can never work. In fact, trying to meet those inner needs with money proves to be damaging and destructive of human persons, plunging them down into debt and ruin, destroying relationships and 'piercing them with many pains'.

Instead, Paul urges his readers to cultivate contentment. He uses the word *autarkeia,* meaning 'a frame of mind viewing one's lot as "enough"'. Contentment, then, is a mind-set. It's a way of seeing. This way of seeing can be developed through contemplating our beginning and our end: we came into the world with nothing, and we certainly can't take anything with us when we go. But there's another layer of meaning to *autarkeia*. It means 'being adequate in oneself'. That's not to encourage self-satisfaction. But it's to suggest that if our inner resources are there, we need very little else – with food and clothing we've got enough. The real riches are not found with external, material things but within, with Christ, and contentment is simply the enjoyment of that hidden wealth.

COLLECT

Almighty God,
who alone can bring order
to the unruly wills and passions of sinful humanity:
give your people grace
so to love what you command
and to desire what you promise,
that, among the many changes of this world,
our hearts may surely there be fixed
where true joys are to be found;
through Jesus Christ your Son our Lord,
who is alive and reigns with you,
in the unity of the Holy Spirit,
one God, now and for ever.

1 Timothy 6.11-end

*'Fight the good fight of the faith; take hold of the eternal life
to which you were called ...' (v.12)*

It's all too tempting to try to reduce the Christian life to 'a narrow goodness' and fail to grasp what is really being offered to us. In yesterday's reading, Paul listed the pain and trouble that ensnare those for whom the pursuit of money is their goal. Today, he pleads with Timothy to 'shun all this' (v.11). But this is only the preliminary condition for something much more important. Paul urges Timothy to take hold of something, robustly, with confidence and joy. He wants him to say 'yes!' to God with everything he is. He wants him to taste eternal life, the life of God, to embrace life with God, full-bloodedly, without reservation. In short, he wants him to *live*.

And to do this, to take hold of this life, Timothy has to engage. Something is being held out to him, but he must embrace it. He can't be an armchair Christian. He has to press on through the struggle. 'Fight the good fight of the faith; take hold ...'

We, too, are invited to fight the good fight of the faith. We have to press through times of darkness and doubt. We find ourselves pushing through disappointment, through inertia and complacency. Our discipleship requires us to stretch ourselves as we reach for that which is held out to us. And the reward? *Life* in all its fullness.

Eternal God,
whose Son went among the crowds
and brought healing with his touch:
help us to show his love,
in your Church as we gather together,
and by our lives as they are transformed
into the image of Christ our Lord.

COLLECT

2 Timothy 1.1-14

'Do not be ashamed, then, of the testimony about our Lord ...' (v.8)

Timothy comes into focus in this chapter. It would appear that he had received the faith not in a dramatic conversion like Paul's, but through his family – his grandmother and his mother. It would also seem that he was a young man who lacked confidence. Nevertheless, he was the pastor of a church, and Paul's letters are full of encouragement to him to fulfil his calling. In particular, he is not to be ashamed to testify about the Lord. Later in the letter, Paul urges him to 'do the work of an evangelist' (2 Timothy 4.5).

It's sometimes tempting to think that it's only extroverts who are called to bear public witness to Christ and to share the good news. If these were things we could do in our own strength, there might be some truth in this. But, in fact, God's work can be done only in the power and strength of the indwelling Holy Spirit. And, sometimes, those who feel most vulnerable and uncertain are those whom God can use most. For when we feel weak, we lean on God for strength. We may not feel his power with us – even after prayer, we may still feel foolish, tongue-tied, awkward and stumbling. But, with his help, even our simple words may become carriers for his mighty acts.

COLLECT

Almighty God,
who alone can bring order
to the unruly wills and passions of sinful humanity:
give your people grace
so to love what you command
and to desire what you promise,
that, among the many changes of this world,
our hearts may surely there be fixed
where true joys are to be found;
through Jesus Christ your Son our Lord,
who is alive and reigns with you,
in the unity of the Holy Spirit,
one God, now and for ever.

Psalm **37***
Genesis 26.34 – 27.40
2 Timothy 1.15 – 2.13

2 Timothy 1.15 – 2.13

'Think over what I say, for the Lord will give you understanding in all things' (2.7)

Paul has been making it very clear to the young man Timothy that the truth of the gospel that he has inherited is not be tampered with – it is a precious deposit to be passed on, entrusted to others who are also competent to teach (2.2). However, although the truth of the gospel needs to be guarded (1.14), it is not a piece of dogma to be learned by rote. Nor does it have the narrow sterility of propaganda. The truth of the gospel 'Jesus Christ, raised from the dead, a descendant of David' (2.8), incarnated as it is in history, is enlivened to us by the real presence of the risen Christ, through his Spirit. Paul, in helping Timothy to grow in his ministry and understanding, does not try to control his thought processes. Like all good teachers, Paul throws out to Timothy some ideas and images – the soldier, the athlete, the farmer – and then stands back. He suggests that he meditate upon them and see what the Lord, the Spirit, says to him as he does so. He's exercising real pastoral care of Timothy but leaving him free to respond to the Lord in his own way. And he's also leaving God plenty of freedom in his dealings with the young man.

We, too, are taught at the deepest level by that same Spirit. When we take seriously the historical deposit of the gospel, anchoring ourselves into its objective reality, we then discover a glorious freedom in being able, with the Spirit, to let the gospel message play out its implications in us. It touches us personally, individually, and speaks into our own lives. That's when the word of God becomes truly living and active – in us.

Eternal God,
whose Son went among the crowds
and brought healing with his touch:
help us to show his love,
in your Church as we gather together,
and by our lives as they are transformed
into the image of Christ our Lord.

COLLECT

Friday 10 February

2 Timothy 2.14-end

'Do your best to present yourself to God as one approved by him'
(v. 15)

Timothy was under enormous pressure in the Ephesian Church. Here he was, the leader of a Christian community, and the Church was being infiltrated by false teachers. They were having an unsettling effect, causing controversy and disturbance. It's not quite clear what these teachings were, but they were possibly a form of early gnosticism – a way of viewing reality that drove a wedge between the spiritual and the material, encouraging a kind of super-spirituality and elitism.

For someone like Timothy, unsure of himself, not yet experienced in leadership, these false teachers would have posed a personal threat. He may have feared at times that they were more influential and convincing than he was, with strong and attractive personalities that his people responded to.

That's why it's heart-warming that Paul encourages him 'to present himself to God as one approved *by him*'. Whatever others say about him, his self-worth, his identity, is to be found in *God's* approval of him. Knowing God's affirmation of his ministry means he can keep on keeping on, in the work that God has given him to do.

We all get knocks to our confidence and need to return to that sense of being known and valued by God. For it's his love that is the mainspring of our life and our ministry, wherever we serve him in the world.

COLLECT

Almighty God,
who alone can bring order
to the unruly wills and passions of sinful humanity:
give your people grace
so to love what you command
and to desire what you promise,
that, among the many changes of this world,
our hearts may surely there be fixed
where true joys are to be found;
through Jesus Christ your Son our Lord,
who is alive and reigns with you,
in the unity of the Holy Spirit,
one God, now and for ever.

Psalms 41, **42**, 43
Genesis 29.1-30
2 Timothy 3

2 Timothy 3

'But as for you, continue in what you have learned and firmly believed' (v.14)

It's not surprising that the description of 'the last days' (vv.1-5) should accord with much of our contemporary society. Timothy, too, would have recognized it in Ephesus. For this is life lived without reference to God and therefore oriented around the self. It can include 'religion' (v.5), but only as an outward form rather than an inward reality. The images in this description pile up and pour out, like a great tidal river of dirty water, infecting and affecting everything. And everyone seems to be on board, sweeping downstream with the tide.

But then comes the great contrast: 'Now you ... But as for you ...' (vv.10,14). Timothy is to paddle upstream. He's got to go in the opposite direction. And it will be hard work. It's not easy paddling against the flow. To assist him, Paul acts as a mentor. He reminds Timothy of his own life. That life has various outcomes. It is soaked in the Scriptures, but it is also a *way* of life, not esoteric, but incarnated, enfleshed. It has direction, purpose, and it has produced the fruit of the Spirit – love, patience and endurance. It's marked with suffering and persecution, real persecution in real places (v.11).

Paul isn't bragging about all this. He's trying to say that this is the life of the disciple who is 'in Christ Jesus' (v.12). It's the life of Jesus himself.

Eternal God,
whose Son went among the crowds
and brought healing with his touch:
help us to show his love,
in your Church as we gather together,
and by our lives as they are transformed
into the image of Christ our Lord.

COLLECT

2 Timothy 4.1-8

*'As for me, I am already being poured out as a libation,
and the time of my departure has come.' (v.6)*

Imagine a yacht, at the quayside, ready to leave. The ropes have been uncoiled from the buoys, loosened but not yet cast off. Everything has been done for departure: all that is needed is the word from the captain. Paul, writing from his prison cell, tells Timothy that this moment has come for him. He uses the Greek word *analusews* to describe his situation: a word which means 'to loosen in order to depart'. And he says that the moment is 'at hand'. He can read the signs – he knows his time has come.

It is in this context that Paul gives Timothy his final charge: preach the word. This is the gospel imperative. To proclaim the Word – Jesus, crucified risen Lord – in words and in works. This has been the intention of his life, and he passes it on to the young disciple. And he charges Timothy to proclaim Jesus whether convenient or inconvenient, whether the time seems ripe or not, whether it is a season of 'gospel fruitfulness' or apparent barrenness. This does not mean being insensitive to the hearer or to the moment. It means being aware of the urgency of the task. It means living poised, ready, alert to the opportunities as they present day by day. It means being bold to speak and so to be identified with the cause of Christ and his kingdom.

COLLECT

Almighty God,
you have created the heavens and the earth
and made us in your own image:
teach us to discern your hand in all your works
and your likeness in all your children;
through Jesus Christ your Son our Lord,
who with you and the Holy Spirit reigns supreme over all things,
now and for ever.

Tuesday 14 February

2 Timothy 4.9-end

*'The Lord will rescue me from every evil attack
and save me for his heavenly kingdom' (v.18)*

Things have changed for Paul. Whereas others continue to be busy in the cause of the gospel, that part of his life is over. Crescens and Titus are engaged in missions, travelling just as he once did. But his life, once so full, so active, has narrowed down. From his Roman prison, he sees that a different vocation awaits him. And as he faces what is coming, he needs people. He longs for Timothy to come and see him (in fact, he may have sent Tychicus to Ephesus to free him to do so). In the solitude, he has been remembering past hurts and betrayals. Too, he's been thinking with affection of some of his possessions, and wants to communicate with particularly dear friends (v.19). Paul, with his massive intellect, his passion, his energy, his leadership, shows us here a touching vulnerability and humanity.

But two things remain constant. The message of the gospel is still to be proclaimed under these most testing of circumstances. His trial will afford him yet another opportunity. And his faith, stretched and developed through his life, is holding him steady as he looks death in the face. The pattern and shape of his life may have changed but he knows that the Lord, who has been his strength in the past (v.17), will continue to be with him and to bring him home.

Almighty God,
give us reverence for all creation
and respect for every person,
that we may mirror your likeness
in Jesus Christ our Lord.

COLLECT

Wednesday 15 February

Titus 1

'They profess to know God, but they deny him by their actions.' (v.16)

Titus was an associate of Paul whose task was to build up the young Christian communities in Crete and to establish leadership among them. But, as with Timothy in Ephesus, Titus was struggling to handle erroneous teaching that was filtering into the Church. It likely had its roots in a form of Judaism (v.10), a Jewish mysticism (v.14) that produced much idle speculation but little in the way of holiness. So Titus is urged to bend his energies towards teaching the true faith that results in character and in action. The leaders of the community, whom he is to appoint, must be exemplary, not just in the things they don't do, but in the more positive virtues of faithful living (vv.7-9).

It is the positive attitudes and actions that those outside the Church often notice first. The one whom Titus served, Jesus Christ, was immensely attractive to ordinary men and women and children – not only with his words, but also in his actions – embracing outcasts, touching lepers, welcoming children, healing the sick, freeing the tormented. His actions were a reflection of the intention of his life.

Many people like to engage in speculative chat about 'religion'. But often the words make no difference to the life lived out. Like Titus, we who profess God are called to live out that profession, in holiness and joy, wherever we are today.

COLLECT

Almighty God,
you have created the heavens and the earth
and made us in your own image:
teach us to discern your hand in all your works
and your likeness in all your children;
through Jesus Christ your Son our Lord,
who with you and the Holy Spirit reigns supreme over all things,
now and for ever.

Psalms 56, **57** (63*)
Genesis 32.3-30
Titus 2

Titus 2

'For the grace of God has appeared, bringing salvation to all' (v.11)

It is not just the leaders who are to live exemplary lives, but the whole Christian community. Age and gender and social standing do not exempt any from the need to live out in fact what is professed by faith. We do not see in this letter any challenge yet to the social order; the owning of slaves is not questioned. But the *way* in which slaves and masters (here and elsewhere in the Pauline letters) relate to each other *is* examined. It's the start of a long journey.

That same long journey – of allowing the gospel of Jesus to percolate through us and to have its full effect – is one we all must take. It means a lifetime's work. But it is primarily a work of grace. We can become 'self-controlled, upright, and godly' (v.12) only because Jesus Christ has purified us (v.14). Indeed, we do not know what true holiness looks like, apart from Christ, and human attempts to personify it always founder. Far better to soak ourselves daily in the grace of God and to allow him to *train* us (v.12) in the way that we should live. 'Training' implies 'learning', and learning suggests the possibility of mistakes. The struggle to live out our faith in this present age, while waiting for the full glory of God (v.13) has always been an authentic Christian experience.

Almighty God,
give us reverence for all creation
and respect for every person,
that we may mirror your likeness
in Jesus Christ our Lord.

COLLECT

Friday 17 February

Psalms **51**, 54
Genesis 33.1-17
Titus 3

Titus 3

*'... he saved us, not because of any works of righteousness
that we had done, but according to his mercy' (v.5)*

The point is hammered home yet more fully. Those of us who once led lives that were foolish and dissolute, driven by our own damaged hungers (v.3) must now live in a very different way. We are to live peaceably in the world, alert to those opportunities that present themselves to us to do good. We are not to run anyone down, we are to walk away from quarrelling, we are to be gentle and courteous to all people. Yes, all!

But we cannot do this by ourselves. Indeed, as we were not able even to save ourselves, so we cannot fulfil by ourselves the demands of the gospel. We have been rescued from ourselves by an act of mercy. Our old self is dead: we no longer live by our self. The waters of rebirth, of baptism (v.5), have brought us into new life, a life now lived in the power and joyful companionship of the Holy Spirit.

And this Spirit has not been given to us grudgingly. He has not been measured out according to some kind of 'progress' in faith. No, he has been *poured* out, in overwhelming abundance (v.6). The Greek word *plousios* describes opulence, wealth, riches. It's all about fullness. God loves to give his Spirit to us, whoever we are. And there are no half measures where God is concerned!

COLLECT

Almighty God,
you have created the heavens and the earth
and made us in your own image:
teach us to discern your hand in all your works
and your likeness in all your children;
through Jesus Christ your Son our Lord,
who with you and the Holy Spirit reigns supreme over all things,
now and for ever.

Psalm **68**
Genesis 35
Philemon

Philemon

*'... no longer as a slave but as more than a slave,
a beloved brother' (v.16)*

It's generally accepted that the Onesimus referred to in this letter was a former slave who had run away from Philemon and had been converted through Paul in Rome. Paul writes to Philemon asking him to take Onesimus back, no longer as a slave, but better than a slave, 'as a beloved brother' (v.16).

Slaves in the Roman Empire were not regarded as persons, but as objects, as things to be used. So Paul's attitude is revolutionary. Onesimus is to be seen 'as a man and a brother in the Lord'. We see how the gospel message is beginning to have a deep and powerful effect, calling into question not only individual morality but social institutions. There are hints, too, that Onesimus has changed, from the passivity of slavery to the activity that flows from a new self-respect (vv.11-13).

Slavery has been outlawed in our country, though is still an issue, hidden and covert. A more obvious challenge to us is that of relating to those who seem 'different', particularly to those who have been in prison, who have mental health issues or problems with drink and drugs. To really see the man or woman behind the label, to know that this is a brother or a sister, one of God's children – what does that do to us? And what does it do to our churches?

Almighty God,
give us reverence for all creation
and respect for every person,
that we may mirror your likeness
in Jesus Christ our Lord.

COLLECT

Monday 20 February

Galatians 1

'... who gave himself for our sins' (v.4)

What is the good news that Paul proclaims? One of the more remarkable facets about the New Testament is the realization that the goalposts have moved. For centuries the Israelites have been persecuted. They have prayed for deliverance from their neighbours, conquering foreign powers, imposed dictators, and now the Romans. In an occupied country, barely back from exile, the Jewish people struggle with oppression. The enemy is obvious, and the hope of liberation is to be free from all interference that comes from the outside.

Yet the gospel Paul proclaims turns the world upside down. Jesus will 'save his people from their sins'. From *their* sins. Not from their aggressive neighbours or from all-conquering empires. No. Jesus will save people from themselves: the enemy is within.

It is something of an understatement to say that this represents a seismic shift in biblical history. The enemy is within, not without. The inner life and the secrets of the heart are what God dwells upon. He is less interested in what we eat or wear. He looks on the inside.

So Paul confidently proclaims that there is no other 'good news'. This is it. Moreover, it is not comfortable to everyone who hears and receives it. But it is good – and Paul knows this. As someone who was once 'exceedingly zealous' for one faith, he now knows another life: one in Jesus Christ, 'who gave himself for our sins to set us free from the present evil age ...'.

COLLECT

Almighty Father,
whose Son was revealed in majesty
before he suffered death upon the cross:
give us grace to perceive his glory,
that we may be strengthened to suffer with him
and be changed into his likeness, from glory to glory;
who is alive and reigns with you,
in the unity of the Holy Spirit,
one God, now and for ever.

Tuesday 21 February

Galatians 2.1-10

'They asked only one thing, that we remember the poor' (v.10)

Remembering the poor may not seem much, yet in the Christian faith, true religion is judged not by its seeds, but by its fruits. Christianity is known by what is reaped, not what is sown; love, holiness and disciple-ship are found in the bounty of harvest. Faith is not judged by its origins, but by its ends. Thus, Christians have only one thing to invest: their lives. The only possession we have – ourselves – is asked to be surrendered. And we cannot truly give until we give up ourselves. And we cannot love unless we first know that we have been loved.

Today, people are crying out for exemplars of faith who are simultaneously engaged with the world and yet apart from it; in the world, yet not of it; people who are able to offer the kind of love and authenticity that are quite apart from any of the usual personal qualities that one would normally encounter.

The drive and hunger for real authenticity is what many would identify as the key location for the re-awakening of discipleship. A pie-in-the-sky piety feels elitist and disconnected; but its rejection by modern society is not a turning away from discipleship. On the contrary, I want to suggest that society remains enchanted by deep and engaged discipleship, and its capacity to transform the world.

Or as Jesus put it, 'love one another – as I have loved you'. Surely this gospel is too demanding? Brother Roger of Taizé used to reply to just that question with these words: *Il ne demande pas trop – mais il demande tout'* ('He doesn't ask too much – but he asks for everything').

Wednesday 22 February

Ash Wednesday

Daniel 9.3-6, 17-19

'... we have sinned and done wrong' (v.5)

No one likes to talk about sin; it is guilt-inducing, moralizing and anti-social to do so. Yet we ignore the concept at our peril. For we run risks of propagating general, vague morality, yet rooted in little that might offset this – moral, but no compass?

Moreover, we already know enough about our children to have grasped that acquisition has replaced aspiration; vocation given way to fulfilment. Children know what they want to have, but not what they want to be. Their heroes are no longer persons with exemplary lifestyles, but are rather individuals with conspicuous material excess.

Are we part of that generation that aspires to wealth, but not necessarily to goodness? The 'grammar of sin', or rather its absence, is a real issue for our society. And it is a more subtle problem than one might suppose. Look how easily our vapid consumerism, for example, has undermined discipline, patience and charity.

So today's uncompromising text from Daniel is a wake-up call. It is a reminder that we all stand before God and will be judged. Not on what we have amassed, but on the content, quality and character of our lives. We will be weighed – and found wanting.

The good news is that God is ready to receive all who turn to him. He is waiting. As the mystics say, God has only one weakness – his heart. It is too soft. And as Lent begins today, we turn to that heart, and away from all that keeps us from becoming the people that God intended us to be.

COLLECT

Almighty and everlasting God,
you hate nothing that you have made
and forgive the sins of all those who are penitent:
create and make in us new and contrite hearts
that we, worthily lamenting our sins
and acknowledging our wretchedness,
may receive from you, the God of all mercy,
perfect remission and forgiveness;
through Jesus Christ your Son our Lord,
who is alive and reigns with you,
in the unity of the Holy Spirit,
one God, now and for ever.

Galatians 2.11-end

'... the life I now live in the flesh' (v.20)

Peter and Paul wrestling over the gospel and contending for the truth may seem strange to us today. Yet even now, the Christian faith contains a number of competitive theories as to what its main priorities should be. However, there is a common thread that runs through them all. Out of the ashes of Good Friday, hope and new life are born. And the disciples are to be the ambassadors of the transformation found in the person of Jesus.

The resurrection, in other words, is something that does not draw disciples so much into a new sect, as it does send them out – with joy, conviction, and a desire to serve the world and the needs of others in the name of the living Christ. And this is done in love. It is not a task; it is an entire reconfiguration of one's life. You cannot command people to love. Love is for falling into. It is a state of being, as well as doing.

This does not make living the Christian life together easy, mind. As Paul knows well, the things that inspire us are not the formal rules, regulations and codes that often govern our religion. What motivates and inspires us is faith and love. And, perhaps, especially the example of others: faith 'en-fleshed'. What is set out and lived in the life of others is what can transform us, and make us into better people ourselves. One saint, in his own charge to his community, says: 'go and preach the gospel throughout all the world. If absolutely necessary, use words …'.

Holy God,
our lives are laid open before you:
rescue us from the chaos of sin
and through the death of your Son
bring us healing and make us whole
in Jesus Christ our Lord.

COLLECT

Galatians 3.1-14

'... those who believe are blessed with Abraham who believed' (v.9)

As Christians, how do we learn? Paul argues that the Christian life is not only learned through formulae or law, but also by faith. Christian wisdom, although it is rooted in Scripture and other writings, is also birthed in what we learn through practising our beliefs, and in our life of prayer. It is about walking by faith and not with sight – seeing beyond what can be seen. Paul, in appealing to Abraham, invites us to see that we might learn as much about faith through our practice as in what might be preached to us.

Ultimately, we can only teach people *about* Christianity. People have to discover it for themselves through practice. Christian wisdom is built up through the careful cultivation of reflection, practice and wisdom, with each new day building up a gradual, rich and organic repository of knowledge – stored, living wisdom – that helps us refine our discipleship and ministry as we continue to serve God. We can teach people about Jesus, but it is by faith that he is encountered.

So Paul's appeal to Abraham is no accident. By faith, Abraham stepped out into the unknown with God. By faith, Abraham's nascent belief and trust flourished, and was blessed – and so became a blessing. Paul, in drawing on Abraham, is teaching us about wisdom and the ongoing nature of partaking. Wisdom, then, is more than knowledge. It is more than committing texts, traditions or liturgies to memory. It is about walking in understanding. Moving with God, indeed, before you might know where you are going.

COLLECT

Almighty and everlasting God,
you hate nothing that you have made
and forgive the sins of all those who are penitent:
create and make in us new and contrite hearts
that we, worthily lamenting our sins
and acknowledging our wretchedness,
may receive from you, the God of all mercy,
perfect remission and forgiveness;
through Jesus Christ your Son our Lord,
who is alive and reigns with you,
in the unity of the Holy Spirit,
one God, now and for ever.

Saturday 25 February

Galatians 3.15-22

'... what was promised through faith in Jesus Christ' (v.22)

I have often remarked that if I could not be an Anglican, and had to choose another denomination, I'd be a Quaker. I have my reasons. I think silence is a greatly underestimated quality and virtue. I think that Quakerism also represents one of the more radically inventive and inclusive Christian traditions. I think that Quakers have a decent political and social edge to their gospel. The religion is unfussy, democratic, deeply thoughtful and, above all, deeply spiritual.

I also think of Sydney Carter, a favourite hymn writer, who wrote 'Lord of the Dance' – and set to a tune that is meant to be danced to. I think of the love of simplicity, and sometimes wonder how I have ended up in a denomination where everything is so complicated. Anglicans seem to be unable to avoid making a drama out of a crisis, an issue out of virtually every occurrence.

It was Bill Vanstone who once remarked that the Church of England is like a swimming pool – all the noise comes from the shallow end. It's true, isn't it? On issues of major gravity, all the noise comes from the shrill reactionary voices that grab the headlines. The voices from the deep are seldom heard – the real words we need to hear are drowned out by the splashing and the shouting.

Yet they are here today in Paul's words: covenant, mediator, promise and seed ('offspring'). The gospel is simple. But it takes a lifetime to understand what it is saying to us about being together as many, yet one, and as sinners, yet redeemed. Paul's appeal, then, is a simple one. Look to Christ, and life, in all its complexities, will fall into perspective.

Holy God,
our lives are laid open before you:
rescue us from the chaos of sin
and through the death of your Son
bring us healing and make us whole
in Jesus Christ our Lord.

COLLECT

Monday 27 February

Galatians 3.23 – 4.7

'... so that we might receive adoption as children' (4.5)

We turn today to one of the more extraordinary sequence of passages that we find in the entire New Testament. Paul boldly proclaims the radical inclusiveness of God, and tells us that in Christ, there are no divisions – by race, tribe, gender, class or heritage. In God's kingdom, we are all heirs, children of the same heavenly father. Adopted.

Some years ago, I sat on a local adoption panel, assessing the needs of children and what the adults or parents have to offer. Many of the children placed come from backgrounds of abuse – physical, sexual or other. Others come stigmatized with the knowledge that the 'stock' they have come from is no good. Their parents were no good, so they'll be no good. Yet the process of adoption for some, in a very real sense, is a kind of being born again. No, you don't get back into the womb. What you do get, though, is an affirmation that nurture is far more important than nature: we make the world we live in – the world does not make us. And the new world that Christians are born into is one of equality and one without false divisions.

For children who are adopted – including myself – this often means a second chance. It is an opportunity to become part of an entirely different family – to become part of a new community with different values and possibilities. What matters when we are adopted by God is not what has been, but what will be, and what is to come. To all Christians, Paul simply says that outsiders who receive Christ are now adopted into God's family, irrespective of their roots. And if a son or daughter of God, then they are also heirs.

COLLECT

Almighty God,
whose Son Jesus Christ fasted forty days in the wilderness,
and was tempted as we are, yet without sin:
give us grace to discipline ourselves in obedience to your Spirit;
and, as you know our weakness,
so may we know your power to save;
through Jesus Christ your Son our Lord,
who is alive and reigns with you,
in the unity of the Holy Spirit,
one God, now and for ever.

Psalms **44** *or* 87, **89.1-18**
Genesis 41.46 – 42.5
Galatians 4.8-20

Galatians 4.8-20

'I am again in the pain of childbirth until Christ is formed in you' (v.19)

There is more to Paul's notion of our adoption into the life of God than meets the eye. We are to be born again, by the Spirit – gradually recreated in the image of God. This is more than mere conversion. It is about Christ being 'formed' in us, which in turn says something profound about our humanity. We are all more than the sum of our parts, and to know this and live this is to live in the life of Christ. We are not to regard ourselves as mere keepers of rituals and traditions – or merely to be descended from a religious lineage. We are part of the dynamic life of God and are to be born again. For Christ to be formed in us is truly to realize our human nature, which in turn is to realize its divine authorship.

Paul's vision of faith, therefore, is one that is rooted in a dynamic appreciation and practice of knowing God, and of Christ being formed in us. This means that our lives, moral character, outlook, lifestyle and relationships will all be transformed by God growing into our lives, just as we grow into God.

This rich image of gestation, maturity and development is at the heart of all spiritual formation. The Christian life is not a set of principles that can be quickly learnt and swotted up on, and the exam then passed. It is a life of growth, pruning, development, commitment, wisdom, maturity, chastening and encouragement. It is, in short, learning and growing through a living relationship.

Heavenly Father,
your Son battled with the powers of darkness,
and grew closer to you in the desert:
help us to use these days to grow in wisdom and prayer
that we may witness to your saving love
in Jesus Christ our Lord.

COLLECT

Wednesday 29 February

Galatians 4.21 – 5.1

'For freedom Christ has set us free' (5.1)

Paul's somewhat playful (yet serious) excursions into nature and nurture, birth, adoption and lineage, continue in today's reading. Thomas Fuller, a seventeenth-century Anglican priest, expressed it like this:

> 'Lord, I find the genealogy of my Saviour strangely chequered,
> with four remarkable changes in four generations:
> Rehoboam begat Abijah: (A bad father begat a bad son)
> Abijah begat Asa: (A bad father and a good son)
> Asa begat Jehoshaphat: (A good father and a good son)
> Jehoshaphat begat Jehorom: (A good father and a bad son).

> I see Lord, from hence, that my Father's piety cannot be handed on:
> That is bad news for me. I see also that actual impiety is not
> hereditary; that is good news for my son!'

Many biblical commentators have pointed out that the genealogy of Jesus is full of some surprising and rather suspect stock. There are some people lurking in Jesus' 'family tree' that do not augur well for the future. Paul is saying, very plainly, that our status as children of God does not rest on our pasts, but on how we live our Christian lives now, in the light of the freedom and the promises God has bestowed upon us.

Many people today are interested in finding out more about their ancestors. But Paul wants us to think about our descendants. Having the 'faith of our fathers' is simply not enough. It must be embodied in the here and now. Good and evil were part of Christ's own ancestry. Paul is reminding us that God's grace does not run in the blood.

COLLECT

Almighty God,
whose Son Jesus Christ fasted forty days in the wilderness,
and was tempted as we are, yet without sin:
give us grace to discipline ourselves in obedience to your Spirit;
and, as you know our weakness,
so may we know your power to save;
through Jesus Christ your Son our Lord,
who is alive and reigns with you,
in the unity of the Holy Spirit,
one God, now and for ever.

Psalms **42**, 43 *or* 90, **92**
Genesis 42.18-28
Galatians 5.2-15

Galatians 5.2-15

'A little yeast leavens the whole batch of dough' (v.9)

My favourite Christmas cracker joke is: 'Why did the mushroom go to the party?' Answer: 'Because he was a fun guy'. So, in apparently one of his more innocent phrases, Paul tells us most of what we probably need to know about our discipleship: yeast.

Yeast? That microbe fungus? That discardable and forgettable material that is, oddly, the key to so much of our lives? For yeast is what ferments the wine and beer. It makes the dough rise to make the bread. It is the tiny, insignificant catalyst for our basic commodities and the formation of our communities. The leaven in the lump; the difference between bread and dough; juice and wine; refreshment and celebration.

Paul seldom quotes Jesus in his writings. But, in today's passage, the reference to yeast, and to loving one another, have clear echoes of the gospels that Paul will have known. And here he uses it to teach the Galatians about how to be the Church. Not divided over circumcision or un-circumcision – but united by 'faith working through love'.

The yeast, then, is an idea about how to be together in the world and the Church. For yeast, to fulfil its function is ultimately to be lost and dispersed into the higher purposes to which it is given. Paul, like Jesus, invites us to lose ourselves in something much bigger. But not pointlessly. Rather, in dying to our context, we activate it. We become the catalyst that brings flavour, strength, depth, potency and growth. Without yeast, there is no loaf, just dough. Literally, we die to ourselves for growth. We are the ingredient that helps to make bread for the world.

Heavenly Father,
your Son battled with the powers of darkness,
and grew closer to you in the desert:
help us to use these days to grow in wisdom and prayer
that we may witness to your saving love
in Jesus Christ our Lord.

COLLECT

Psalms **22** *or* **88** (95)
Genesis 42.29-end
Galatians 5.16-end

Galatians 5.16-end

'... the fruit of the Spirit' (v.22)

It is possible to characterize Paul's categorizations according to speed. Put simply, the 'lusts of the flesh' are about quick results, instant gratification, shortcuts, the instant sating of desire. The 'fruit of the Spirit', on the other hand, does not grow overnight. It takes time. The cultivation of joy, peace, patience, kindness, self-control, humility, gentleness and faithfulness take a lifetime. A lifetime, indeed, of wisdom, maturity, practice, humility and learning. Love that is worthy of the name may begin with a spark, but it never comes fully formed. Like a person, there is much growing to be reckoned with.

Paul's lists, then, take on a fascinating dimension: time. Anger, immorality, envy – you name it – well up in an instant. But they also quickly subside. Yet we can often spend the rest of our lives living with the results. Paul, in listing the fruits of the spirit – and comparing them to the 'fruits of the flesh' – is offering a careful and considered judgement about the Church as a community of patience and forbearance. In an age when decisions and clarity are so sought after, it is sometimes sobering to be reminded of the call to be patient and kind; to have self-control; and perhaps, who knows, to be gentle with one another, even if that means living with uncertainty and a lack of consensus.

So, let God set the pace; the bread rises in time; the wine matures only when it is ready; God's fruit takes time to come of age. It is almost as though Paul is saying to the Church: reach – but do not grasp. Hold – but do not clutch. Embrace – but do not smother. Strive – yet be patient. Hope – yet let it be. Love – yet surrender all to God. Pray purposefully – and be at peace.

COLLECT

Almighty God,
whose Son Jesus Christ fasted forty days in the wilderness,
and was tempted as we are, yet without sin:
give us grace to discipline ourselves in obedience to your Spirit;
and, as you know our weakness,
so may we know your power to save;
through Jesus Christ your Son our Lord,
who is alive and reigns with you,
in the unity of the Holy Spirit,
one God, now and for ever.

Galatians 6

'... for you reap whatever you sow' (v.7)

'Reap what you sow' is one of the more resonant biblical mantras – one that has found its way into Pentecostal hymnody, as well as many a sermon. At the heart of the phrase is a simple idea, one that echoes a frequently occurring theme of the Old Testament – the 'parents have eaten sour grapes ... and the children's teeth are set on edge'.

A society that puts work, pleasure and money at the heart of its priorities will raise a generation of individualistic, distracted and avaricious children. The development of moral character and social awareness will, alas, be secondary. Paul tells us to beware of this in the Church and in the world. Churches can foster and focus distinctive values that provide leaven in complex contexts. So faith communities often find themselves promoting forms of goodness that secular organizations might miss.

Through a simple ministry of attentiveness, hospitality, care and celebration, churches sometimes do more good for their communities than they can often know. Churches may simply offer regular lunches to the needy, or open house for tea and coffee at any time – the potency of the practice lies in the latency, and is significant. These practices say something about the possibilities for different kinds of space and time in the world – social, pastoral, spiritual. They open up a different side of the Church to the world.

The Church, in other words, is an extension of Christ's love for the world, and helps to inaugurate that new creation that is rooted in grace and hope. So, let us sow the seeds of Christ's love, patience and gentleness where we can, for the harvest reaped will come of such faith.

Heavenly Father,
your Son battled with the powers of darkness,
and grew closer to you in the desert:
help us to use these days to grow in wisdom and prayer
that we may witness to your saving love
in Jesus Christ our Lord.

COLLECT

Monday 5 March

Hebrews 1

'... he has spoken to us by a Son' (v.2)

There is no prologue or introduction to Hebrews, no greeting to those for whom the letter is intended and no named author. In making the point that God is the one who speaks, the writer simply edits himself out, allowing his message to burst upon us from the very first verse.

The message is majestic in its simplicity and scope. God spoke through the prophets to our ancestors. This means that God has always been a communicating God. He has spoken through the prophets to our ancestors in faith. But now, in these 'last days', God has spoken to us in a more intimate way, by a Son. This inaugurates a new level of God's engagement with us.

Like most people in the ancient world, those who received this letter believed in invisible powers, both evil and good. Through a skilfully crafted medley of texts, mostly from the psalms, the writer sets out to prove that the authority of the Son is final. He is not a mere angel, but a Son. He not only conveys God's will; he is the imprint of his being.

As we continue through Lent, Hebrews challenges us afresh to put God first, to listen to his voice and today, as every day, to seek his reflection in the face of Christ.

COLLECT

Almighty God,
you show to those who are in error the light of your truth,
that they may return to the way of righteousness:
grant to all those who are admitted
     into the fellowship of Christ's religion,
that they may reject those things
     that are contrary to their profession,
and follow all such things as are agreeable to the same;
through our Lord Jesus Christ,
who is alive and reigns with you,
in the unity of the Holy Spirit,
one God, now and for ever.

Psalms **50** *or* **106*** (or 103)
Genesis 44.1-17
Hebrews 2.1-9

Hebrews 2.1-9

'Jesus ... crowned with glory and honour ' (v.9)

It is easy to drift away from Christian faith. Those who received this letter were tempted to neglect their salvation and so, sometimes, are we. The writer calls us back to fundamentals. God is consistent. In the past, his message was delivered through intermediaries, and its validity was proved by the stern fact that disobedience resulted in judgement.

The salvation offered now is of a different order. In Christ, God has revealed in a new way his commitment to humanity. The author quotes the eighth psalm, a wonderful hymn of praise for the miracle of creation. God has a royal destiny in mind for human beings. We were created beneath the angels, but God's intention has always been that we should fulfil the destiny of Adam by becoming wise and gentle princes of paradise.

In the here and now, we do not fulfil this great promise. Like the Hebrews of the letter, we are easily discouraged from our destiny by suffering and temptation. What makes transformation possible is Jesus Christ. He, too, was made lower than the angels, but he has now fulfilled Adam's vocation and is indeed 'crowned with glory and honour'.

But this triumph has not been without cost. It is not in spite of, but because of, his suffering and death. What does this say to us about the cost of discipleship?

Almighty God,
by the prayer and discipline of Lent
may we enter into the mystery of Christ's sufferings,
and by following in his Way
come to share in his glory;
through Jesus Christ our Lord.

COLLECT

Psalms **35** *or* 110, **111**, 112
Genesis 44.18-end
Hebrews 2.10-end

Hebrews 2.10-end

'... the pioneer of their salvation' (v.10)

God's purpose is to bring 'many children to glory'. We are called to share in the family likeness of Jesus Christ.

The author of Hebrews urges us to contemplate the coronation of Jesus, recognizing that it is the consequence of his willingness to share our humanity to the very end, to death itself. Hebrews is noted for its stress on the humanity of Christ. Christ shares our condition, we are his brothers and sisters. This is why the author describes him as the 'pioneer' of salvation, the one who goes ahead and marks the way so that we can follow. We can trust him as our pace-setter in the race of life. As long as we keep focused on him, we will keep going towards the goal. When we lose heart, we need to recall what he has achieved for us by sharing our flesh and blood. He has made us holy, liberating us from the fear of death and so destroying the hold that death has over us.

At this point, the author introduces another image to help us understand what Christ can mean to us. His mediating role is a priestly role; he offers the sacrifice that sets us free. As a faithful priest, he knows what it is to be tested and tempted. His encouragement to us comes from his own experience.

Almighty God,
you show to those who are in error the light of your truth,
that they may return to the way of righteousness:
grant to all those who are admitted
   into the fellowship of Christ's religion,
that they may reject those things
   that are contrary to their profession,
and follow all such things as are agreeable to the same;
through our Lord Jesus Christ,
who is alive and reigns with you,
in the unity of the Holy Spirit,
one God, now and for ever.

Hebrews 3.1-6

'... we are his house' (v.6)

The author's purpose is to strengthen faith, to help those who were wavering to find stability and confidence. He does this by explaining that they are already 'partners' in a high calling; they are already brothers and sisters of the Son; they are already holy after the pattern of Jesus the 'high priest of our confession'. We begin from the fact of our Christian calling, the reality that we are marked with the cross of Christ and called to fulfil a royal destiny.

The author now introduces another theme that runs through the letter, that of the house of God, the temple. The temple is the place where God meets his people. But he is not thinking about the earthly temple in Jerusalem; Hebrews was almost certainly written after its destruction. What he is doing is tracing a pattern. Just as Moses was faithful 'in God's house' (even before the earthly temple was built), so Jesus is faithful, and even more to be trusted since he is not only God's apostle and high priest, but also his Son. His faithfulness to his vocation is not only an example for us, it provides our ultimate security. Our Christian calling is to become God's house, a place where all creation meets with God and finds its hope and its salvation.

Almighty God,
by the prayer and discipline of Lent
may we enter into the mystery of Christ's sufferings,
and by following in his Way
come to share in his glory;
through Jesus Christ our Lord.

COLLECT

Psalms 40, **41** *or* **139**
Genesis 45.16-end
Hebrews 3.7-end

Hebrews 3.7-end

'... do not harden your hearts' (v.8)

Hebrews does not only encourage; there is a note of warning that runs through the whole letter. This can sound unattractively threatening to us, but the author is simply reminding us of the experience of God's people as told in Scripture. The repeated quotation from Psalm 95 recalls the failure of God's people to trust him in the wilderness. They 'went astray in their hearts', they turned away from the living God, and it was because of their loss of confidence that they were unable to enter the Promised Land. The unbelief that the author refers to here is not the honest doubt that accompanies many faithful Christians. It is rather a gradual hardening of the heart, an attitude of reservation towards the faith that corrodes the will and turns us into half-hearted Christians, hugging our spiritual apathy to ourselves and becoming cynical in our attitudes.

Such spineless faith can deceive ourselves and others. So today, do not abandon your first love (Revelation 2.4), but hold on to the confidence that we have all been given in Christ. Try encouraging someone else (v.13) if you are feeling discouraged. Or take your rebellious thoughts to the great high priest in prayer and ask for his healing. You may find more sorrow and love in your heart than you expected.

COLLECT

Almighty God,
you show to those who are in error the light of your truth,
that they may return to the way of righteousness:
grant to all those who are admitted
    into the fellowship of Christ's religion,
that they may reject those things
    that are contrary to their profession,
and follow all such things as are agreeable to the same;
through our Lord Jesus Christ,
who is alive and reigns with you,
in the unity of the Holy Spirit,
one God, now and for ever.

Psalms 3, **25** *or* 120, **121**, 122
Genesis 46.1-7, 28-end
Hebrews 4.1-13

Saturday 10 March

Hebrews 4.1-13

'... a sabbath rest ... for the people of God' (v.9)

Today's reading continues with the warnings of scripture that it is possible to miss the grace of God, to lose out on his promises. This is an uncomfortable, but perhaps salutary, theme for us to reflect on.

God calls us to stability, to share with Christ in being his 'house' (Hebrews 3.6). This stability is described as 'rest', which is not a description of inactivity, but rather of spiritual focus. We are to be active contemplatives, grounded in the 'sabbath' rest that is the fruit of worship and mirrors God's magnificent 'rest' at the end of creation.

We cannot benefit from that rest unless we really want it. We can never enjoy it until we learn to trust. Today is the day of opportunity. There is an urgency about our response. That is not to say that we are saved by our activism, but God does expect us to make an effort. We are called to examine ourselves in the light of God's word, aware of its power to reveal the truth of our hearts, to help us to see what we really desire and to draw us closer to the rest that God desires for us. For he is the one 'to whom all hearts are open, all desires known and from whom no secrets are hidden'.

Almighty God,
by the prayer and discipline of Lent
may we enter into the mystery of Christ's sufferings,
and by following in his Way
come to share in his glory;
through Jesus Christ our Lord.

COLLECT

Psalms **5**, 7 *or* 123, 124, 125, **126**
Genesis 47.1-27
Hebrews 4.14 – 5.10

Hebrews 4.14 – 5.10

'..: he learned obedience through what he suffered' (5.8)

The writer to the Hebrews begins today's passage with a bold assertion. Christ is the great high priest whose inner sanctuary is heaven itself. Jesus is like any priest in that his personal sufferings are part of his offering to God. He prays for himself and for others, he deals gently with those who are struggling because he is aware of his own weakness. He has been through the same trials and temptations as we have, and yet, unlike us, he has not fallen short. All this should give us the ultimate confidence to trust him as we approach God with our particular needs.

Yet we misunderstand our great high priest if we assume his obedience was effortless. Even as the Son of God, he needed the discipline of prayer. He was not spared the dilemmas and ambiguities that test us every day. His human life, like ours, was a pilgrimage towards God's perfection. It is because he has persevered to the end that he manifests the eternal priesthood attributed here to Melchizedek.

The fourth-century theologian Gregory of Nazianzus insisted on the reality of Christ's humanity with the statement, 'That which he has not assumed he has not healed'. Our salvation depends not only on Christ's divine Sonship, but on the authenticity of his human struggle.

COLLECT

Almighty God,
whose most dear Son went not up to joy but first he
    suffered pain,
and entered not into glory before he was crucified:
mercifully grant that we, walking in the way of the cross,
may find it none other than the way of life and peace;
through Jesus Christ your Son our Lord,
who is alive and reigns with you,
in the unity of the Holy Spirit,
one God, now and for ever.

Hebrews 5.11 – 6.12

'... on towards perfection' (6.1)

In spite of the promises of God, the progress of the 'Hebrews' has proved disappointing. They have been taught the basics of the Christian faith, but, somehow, they have failed to build on them and are now in danger of falling away altogether. If they are unable to pull themselves together, there is a point at which they may find they have drifted beyond repentance.

This is a worrying suggestion and it is one of the reasons why there were doubts in the early Church about whether Hebrews should be regarded as genuine Scripture. But the point we should attend to is that a familiarity with the mysteries of salvation – along with a stubborn refusal to take them seriously – constitutes a toxic mixture that eventually erodes our capacity to respond to God at all. Grace is given once and for all and, if we have 'tasted the heavenly gift, and have shared in the Holy Spirit', we cannot give it back. Sluggish, half-hearted Christians bring the name of Christ into contempt and so, in the writer's vivid phrase, 'crucify again the Son of God'. This severe judgement is tempered when he recalls the fact that the Hebrews are showing evidence of Christian love in 'serving the saints'. Their situation may be dire, but it is not hopeless. They are not alone in their struggles. Nor are we.

Eternal God,
give us insight
to discern your will for us,
to give up what harms us,
and to seek the perfection we are promised
in Jesus Christ our Lord.

COLLECT

Wednesday 14 March

Hebrews 6.13-end

'... a sure and steadfast anchor of the soul' (v.19)

'Will your anchor hold in the storm of life?' That old chorus draws inspiration from this passage, where Christian hope is likened to an anchor that not only holds the soul sure and steadfast, but goes with Christ into the heavenly sanctuary to plead our cause before God. The basis of our hope is in the character of God, which is shown first in his promise to Abraham. Abraham, steadfast in the same patient endurance to which we are being called, finally obtained God's promise that he would have an heir. But his faithfulness was tested when God required him to offer Isaac in sacrifice. When he demonstrated his obedience and Isaac was saved, God reinforced his original promise with an oath, swearing by himself (Genesis 22.17) in order to confirm his purpose to Abraham's descendants in faith.

So our hope is based on two unshakeable realities: God's promise and his oath. In ancient Israel, an innocent fugitive could take sanctuary in the temple by seizing the horns of the altar. This practice is what lies behind the image of taking refuge and seizing 'the hope set before us'. Boldness in hope prepares the way for heaven, as long as we keep our eyes fixed on Jesus, our forerunner. So it comes back to us. 'Will your anchor hold ...?'

COLLECT

Almighty God,
whose most dear Son went not up to joy but first he
    suffered pain,
and entered not into glory before he was crucified:
mercifully grant that we, walking in the way of the cross,
may find it none other than the way of life and peace;
through Jesus Christ your Son our Lord,
who is alive and reigns with you,
in the unity of the Holy Spirit,
one God, now and for ever.

Psalms **56**, 57 *or* **143**, 146
Genesis 49.33 – 50.end
Hebrews 7.1-10

Hebrews 7.1-10

'... priest for ever' (v.3)

We return today to the theme of Christ's eternal priesthood and the way it is foreshadowed by the mysterious figure of Melchizedek.

Melchizedek was the priest-king of Jerusalem who blessed Abraham after his defeat of four enemy kings (Genesis 14.18-19). Melchizedek is mentioned again in the 'royal' Psalm 110, where the anointed king of Zion is declared to belong to the same eternal order of priesthood as he does. The early Christians interpreted Psalm 110 as a prophecy of Christ, and verses from it are frequently quoted in the Gospels to show how Christ fulfils the promises of Jewish scripture. The point being made in these verses is that, even though in his earthly life Christ did not come from the priestly house of Levi, his priesthood is securely founded and is, in fact, greater than Levi's. This is demonstrated by the fact that, figuratively speaking, Levi offered tithes to Christ's counterpart, Melchizedek, through his ancestor Abraham. This rather tortuous argument is intended to build confidence in the unique vocation of the Son of God to stand before the Father as our great high priest. In this role, he transcends earthly ancestry and tradition. Because he lives for ever, his priestly prayer for us cannot fail.

Eternal God,
give us insight
to discern your will for us,
to give up what harms us,
and to seek the perfection we are promised
in Jesus Christ our Lord.

COLLECT

Hebrews 7.11-end

'... a better hope' (v.19)

The argument for the supreme effectiveness of Christ's priesthood continues as the comparison between the old and the new is developed further. The old Levitical priesthood was inevitably imperfect. Its imperfection actually pointed towards 'another priest', who would be different and better, whose new powers would not be compromised by his having been part of an 'imperfect' priestly family.

The coming of Christ as high priest transforms the law requiring priests to be descended from Levi, because the life he brings is simply indestructible; its validity is proved by its total efficacy. In addition, Christ's priesthood is not ended by death, nor is it weakened by his need to offer sacrifice for his own sins before performing the sacrifices for his people. Christ as high priest simply cannot let us down. He is eternally ready to save us; 'he always lives to make intercession' for us.

The profound invitation of this chapter is to offer our prayer consciously through Christ, to see him in our mind's eye as one who stands before the Father on our behalf, taking with him into God's presence all our needs and fears and failures. He is our guarantee of God's good intent towards us, the ultimate fulfilment of God's promise to visit and redeem his people.

COLLECT

Almighty God,
whose most dear Son went not up to joy but first he
    suffered pain,
and entered not into glory before he was crucified:
mercifully grant that we, walking in the way of the cross,
may find it none other than the way of life and peace;
through Jesus Christ your Son our Lord,
who is alive and reigns with you,
in the unity of the Holy Spirit,
one God, now and for ever.

Psalms **31** *or* **147**
Exodus 1.22 – 2.10
Hebrews 8

Hebrews 8

'... a new covenant' (v.8)

We now come to the heart of the argument about Christ's high priesthood. The Jews of Jesus' time believed that the rituals of the temple imitated the worship of the angels in heaven. The author builds on that belief to establish that the earthly temple, for all its magnificence, was only 'a sketch and shadow of the heavenly sanctuary'. It is no longer needed. Jesus now ministers in the heavenly sanctuary, here described as 'the true tent', a reference back to the tent of meeting in the wilderness. The impermanence of Moses' 'tent' points forward to what is now permanent. Christ's enthronement in heaven has revealed the providential imperfection of the old and abolished it. This does not invalidate Judaism, which, during the early Christian era was radicalizing itself in the wake of the destruction of the Jerusalem temple. But it does point us to the fact that the new covenant is overwhelmingly generous and inclusive.

The ministry of Jesus to us is based on the forgiveness of sins. In the new covenant, God's commandments become intimate to God's people, written on their hearts, as Jeremiah's prophecy foretold. The new covenant is the fruit of Christ's ministry and the glorious message of this chapter is 'we have such a high priest'. There is nothing and no one beyond the reach of his prayer and his compassion.

Eternal God,
give us insight
to discern your will for us,
to give up what harms us,
and to seek the perfection we are promised
in Jesus Christ our Lord.

COLLECT

Monday 19 March

Joseph of Nazareth

Isaiah 11.1-10

'... the earth will be full of the knowledge of the Lord' (v.9)

Isaiah prophecies the coming of a descendant of David, a 'shoot from the stock of Jesse', whose kingdom will see the end of violence and a new order being inaugurated based on justice and gentleness. The king will be anointed with the Holy Spirit, and so will be 'Messiah' (the Greek translation of which is 'Christ').

This reading is given for St Joseph's day because Joseph was a distant descendent of David, and it is through Joseph that Jesus is linked to David and to his 'messianic' kingship. We know very little about Joseph other than the brief details at the beginning of the Gospels of Matthew and Luke. What we see of him there suggests that he was a faithful and trustworthy servant of God, the protector of Mary his wife and the baby Jesus, who puts their needs before his own comfort and convenience. He represents those many faithful and trustworthy servants of God whose role in history is unspectacular in terms of fame and glory, but absolutely vital for the kingdom of God.

Joseph is a good role model for us as we continue through Lent, keeping in our minds a vision of the kingdom while being ready to keep to the disciplines of prayer and obedience in the present.

COLLECT

God our Father,
who from the family of your servant David
raised up Joseph the carpenter
to be the guardian of your incarnate Son
and husband of the Blessed Virgin Mary:
give us grace to follow him
in faithful obedience to your commands;
through Jesus Christ your Son our Lord,
who is alive and reigns with you,
in the unity of the Holy Spirit,
one God, now and for ever.

Tuesday 20 March

Hebrews 9.15-end

'... without the shedding of blood there is no forgiveness of sins' (v.22)

We tend to find the idea of blood-sacrifice repellent, but the sacrificial system was based on a genuine reverence for life. It is because life is the most precious thing of all that it is offered to God. This chapter builds on this ancient assumption but changes it beyond recognition. The new covenant, like the old, is ratified by death and sacrifice, but Christ's death is a once-and-for-all offering of his life, which has the effect of dismantling the whole system. He brings about what the old system could not achieve, the removal of sin.

Christ's sacrifice is unrepeatable. It does not need to be repeated, nor could it be, because Christ, like any other human being, dies only once. The astonishing truth is that his sacrifice is sufficient to deal with the failures and sins and moral compromises of all his people. He has appeared before God on our behalf 'to remove sin by the sacrifice of himself'.

The reference to his second coming (v.28) recalls the reappearance of the high priest from the Holy of Holies on the day of atonement, demonstrating that the sacrifice has been accepted. In the words of the hymn by William Bright:

'"One offering, single and complete",
with lips and hearts we say;
but what he never can repeat
he shows forth day by day.'

Merciful Lord,
absolve your people from their offences,
that through your bountiful goodness
we may all be delivered from the chains of those sins
which by our frailty we have committed;
grant this, heavenly Father,
for Jesus Christ's sake, our blessed Lord and Saviour,
who is alive and reigns with you,
in the unity of the Holy Spirit,
one God, now and for ever.

COLLECT

Wednesday 21 March

Psalms 63, **90** *or* **119.1-32**
Exodus 4.1-23
Hebrews 10.1-18

Hebrews 10.1-18

'... he sat down at the right hand of God' (v.12)

What Christ achieved for us is final and complete, and this is emphasized by his seated posture. He is no longer standing like a temple priest to offer sacrifice every morning and evening. We live in the time between the victory and the end, waiting and praying that all that remains opposed to him is won over or defeated (compare Hebrews 10.13 with 1.13).

So what should our attitude be in this waiting time? The writer suggests, rather optimistically perhaps, that those who are cleansed once for all will cease to have any consciousness of sin (v.2) and even that we should no longer be in need of forgiveness (v.18). His perspective is that of one who is living in 'the last days'. But for us, this raises different issues. How are we to live in response to the finality of Christ's sacrifice?

The quotation from Psalm 40 suggests an answer. We are not to live in anxiety about whether or not we are acceptable to God. This anxiety might tempt us to try to appease God or bargain with him. But God takes no pleasure in such strategies. Instead, our prayer should be, 'I have come to do your will, O God'. Offering ourselves afresh in God's service is the response to all that Christ has done for us.

COLLECT

Merciful Lord,
absolve your people from their offences,
that through your bountiful goodness
we may all be delivered from the chains of those sins
which by our frailty we have committed;
grant this, heavenly Father,
for Jesus Christ's sake, our blessed Lord and Saviour,
who is alive and reigns with you,
in the unity of the Holy Spirit,
one God, now and for ever.

Hebrews 10.19-25

*'Let us hold fast to the confession of our hope
without wavering' (v.23)*

The keynote of today's reading is confidence. We can throw off anxiety and hesitation and follow Jesus into God's presence, sure that we have direct access to God. This boldness is not primarily a *feeling*. It is more a readiness to rest in the reality of what Christ has made possible. Faith, again, is not a feeling or an intellectual certainty. It is 'holding fast' to the hope that we have been given because 'he who has promised is faithful'.

Great though this confidence is, it is not to make us complacent. Confidence is corporate. We belong to the community of believers, and we should not neglect the habit of coming together in prayer and praise. This is the context in which we are able to build each other up, 'provoking one another to love and good deeds'. The common life of the Church is where we are formed as Christians and learn Christ-like habits of gentleness and virtue. Going to church is not simply a matter of choice. It is an expression of the confidence we have in Christ, a confidence to be seen and counted as Christians. Hope and faith and love increase when they are shared.

Merciful Lord,
you know our struggle to serve you:
when sin spoils our lives
and overshadows our hearts,
come to our aid
and turn us back to you again;
through Jesus Christ our Lord.

COLLECT

Friday 23 March

Psalms **102** *or* 17, **19**
Exodus 6.2-13
Hebrews 10.26-end

Hebrews 10.26-end

'It is a fearful thing to fall into the hands of the living God' (v.31)

This is perhaps the hardest passage for reflection from Hebrews, and we cannot help but be aware of the writer's somewhat threatening tone. He tells us of the dangers of continuing in sin after receiving knowledge of the truth, seeming to discount any possibility of a second repentance after conversion. There are Christians today who are haunted by the fear of God's anger, but there are perhaps as many who sit too lightly to the prospect of divine judgement.

We should not 'shrink back' from the challenge of these verses, but use this passage to reflect on what it might mean to us to 'fall into the hands of the living God'.

There is a long tradition that the love and fire of God are the same reality; how we experience them depends on the state of our heart. Christian character is not achieved in a day, and the pains and struggles of Christian life are the crucible in which we are formed to bear the love of God. 'Godly fear' is not the opposite of love, but the proper response of fallible human beings to the beauty and holiness of God. We might feel the fear but we should still go boldly on!

COLLECT

Merciful Lord,
absolve your people from their offences,
that through your bountiful goodness
we may all be delivered from the chains of those sins
which by our frailty we have committed;
grant this, heavenly Father,
for Jesus Christ's sake, our blessed Lord and Saviour,
who is alive and reigns with you,
in the unity of the Holy Spirit,
one God, now and for ever.

Hebrews 11.1-16

'... he has prepared a city for them' (v.16)

To encourage us to persevere, the writer now begins a great roll-call of faith, beginning with Abel and going on to cite some of the most heroic figures of the Old Testament and Jewish tradition. What all these individuals had in common was that they held fast to realities they could neither see nor fully experience. For them, faith meant living with confidence in the invisible realities of God's presence and providence.

What this means is that history is going somewhere, towards the city of God. It also means that our lives are going somewhere, towards the same heavenly city. We can learn from the heroes of the past and imitate them in living more lightly to the present. They realized that the blessings and sufferings of life were provisional, and were content to live as transient 'strangers and foreigners' on the earth.

The source of the contentment was their trust that God was creating a place of permanence and fulfilment beyond this life. We should take this to mean that our life on this earth is a pilgrimage, not a destination. What is important for us is that our desires are formed by the hope of heaven. Home may be a long way off, but the promise is here and now and every day we come a little nearer to glory.

Merciful Lord,
you know our struggle to serve you:
when sin spoils our lives
and overshadows our hearts,
come to our aid
and turn us back to you again;
through Jesus Christ our Lord.

COLLECT

Monday 26 March

Annunciation of Our Lord to the Blessed Virgin Mary

Psalms 111, 113
1 Samuel 2.1-10
Romans 5.12-end

Romans 5.12-end

'... one man's trespass ... one man's act of righteousness' (v.18)

This dense passage has formed part of the argument for the theology of 'original sin'. It seems to say that death and sin found their entrance into the world through the sin of Adam, and that all human beings, ever since, have been enmeshed in the fatal results of Adam's wrong choice, so that our human ability freely to choose between good and evil is now compromised.

There are good and bad theological arguments on this subject, but 'original sin' does seem to have some psychological and social truth to it. People often find themselves almost constrained to do and be less than they wish; and we are all born into webs of damaged and damaging relationships that at least partially dictate our choices.

But this is not the argument that Paul is presenting here in Romans. He does seem to say, in verse 12, that Adam opens up the possibility of sin to all of us, and we greedily and stupidly use our choices, just as Adam did. But, much more importantly, Paul is saying that God in Christ is at work to give us back our freedom. Our human choices lay burdens on all of us, but God's choice sets us free to live with God and each other, and to give and receive relationships as gifts.

As Mary says yes to God, chains begin to crumble.

COLLECT

We beseech you, O Lord,
pour your grace into our hearts,
that as we have known the incarnation of your Son Jesus Christ
    by the message of an angel,
so by his cross and passion
we may be brought to the glory of his resurrection;
through Jesus Christ your Son our Lord,
who is alive and reigns with you,
in the unity of the Holy Spirit,
one God, now and for ever.

Hebrews 11.32 – 12.2

'... let us run with perseverance the race that is set before us' (12.1)

This passage is part of Hebrews' great exhortation to faith. The author holds up the steadfast endurance of the great heroes of the Jewish people as an example to the Christian readers of the Letter. From Gideon, Samson and David, through to the more recent martyrs of the Maccabean revolt, just a couple of centuries before Christ, God's people have suffered and endured, upheld by their faith. They never assumed that, because things were going badly for them, God was not to be trusted.

Although the author argues that faith is not something visible, tangible, he also says that other people can help to make it real for us. We are 'surrounded by so great a cloud of witnesses' (12.1) who help us to make sense of our own journey of faith.

Passiontide is a sore test of faith, as Jesus moves inexorably towards the cross. We have to ask why this must always be the pattern of God's love in the world. Why must God's people struggle, why must God's Son suffer and die? Hebrews does not give us an answer, but it does give us a way of life, supported by the evidence of thousands of others who have made the choice to trust. Our faith is not just a private hope, but a passionate witness to the reality of the world. We will trust together, for the sake of all.

Most merciful God,
who by the death and resurrection of your Son Jesus Christ
delivered and saved the world:
grant that by faith in him who suffered on the cross
we may triumph in the power of his victory;
through Jesus Christ your Son our Lord,
who is alive and reigns with you,
in the unity of the Holy Spirit,
one God, now and for ever.

COLLECT

Wednesday 28 March

Psalms **55**, 124 *or* **34**
Exodus 9.1-12
Hebrews 12.3-13

Hebrews 12.3-13

'... he disciplines us for our good, in order that we may share his holiness' (v.10)

Today's passage from Hebrews needs to be approached with caution. Too many bad arguments have been constructed on the basis of a glib reading of passages like this one, with disastrous theological and pastoral consequences. It is not true to say that God deliberately inflicts suffering on people in order to teach them things, any more than it is true that parents deliberately punish their children and expect that to be seen as a sign of love.

Instead, the argument of this passage goes something like this: parents may choose never to allow their children to experience any hardship or anxiety, but, if they do, they also choose never to allow their children to grow up and take their place in the adult world.

In our Christian life, we are encouraged to face the reality of a broken and hurt world, which will break and hurt us, too, just as it did Jesus. In this world, we can either whine and give up our faith, like children having a tantrum, or we can grow up, and accept our adult, Christian role in the world.

Hebrews calls this sharing God's holiness. And that suggests that holiness is not a life set apart, but a life that shares God's love of the world, even when times are tough.

COLLECT

Most merciful God,
who by the death and resurrection of your Son Jesus Christ
delivered and saved the world:
grant that by faith in him who suffered on the cross
we may triumph in the power of his victory;
through Jesus Christ your Son our Lord,
who is alive and reigns with you,
in the unity of the Holy Spirit,
one God, now and for ever.

Hebrews 12.14-end

'But you have come ... to the city of the living God' (v.22)

There are two different understandings of religion here. One is theatrical: exhilarating and frightening in equal measures. Its essence is an exciting *experience*, with a beginning and an end. It may be a communal experience, but people leave it, awed and shaken, but not fundamentally changed.

The other is religion of daily holiness, whose mirror image is the vision of the heavenly Jerusalem, where the rejoicing hosts of heaven and earth live with God. The practices of this religion are designed to build parallels here and now with what we long for in the future.

So this religion values, above all, those virtues that build trust and fellowship. It abhors above all those vices that cause bitterness, suspicion and division.

These two pictures of religion do not have to be complete alternatives. Hebrews reminds us that our God is indeed a 'consuming fire', real, potent and all-consuming. But this God is not just a source of exciting personal experiences for us, but the God of the whole world. To serve this God is to be drawn out of ourselves, and our own interesting religious urges, into God's purposes for creation. Our faith is not just for us, but to help us build a community that will be at home in 'the city of the living God'.

Gracious Father,
you gave up your Son
out of love for the world:
lead us to ponder the mysteries of his passion,
that we may know eternal peace
through the shedding of our Saviour's blood,
Jesus Christ our Lord.

COLLECT

Hebrews 13.1-16

'Let mutual love continue' (v.1)

In the Christian world, everyday life is profound, transparent and porous. There isn't a 'sacred' sphere and a secular one: everyday actions, such as the offering of hospitality, can be a place of divine encounter, filled with light that streams out and illuminates the ordinary, making it supernatural. Nor is there the kind of spirituality or religious observance where an individual can measure their own achievement and progress; instead, the lives of other Christians, their needs and their failures, almost leak into ours: all are bound together, so that the suffering of one is the suffering of all, the success of one is the success of all.

The readers of the Letter to the Hebrews, like the rest of us, obviously found this frustrating at times. It sounds as though they were sometimes tempted to return to a more systematic kind of religious observance, 'inside the camp', where it is clearer what God does and does not have a right to expect of us.

But the writer is adamant that to be with Jesus is the only point of being a Christian. Where he is, we have to be, and we have to be there with the others who have made this choice, whatever we may think of them. This is a love affair, not a system of brownie points.

COLLECT

Most merciful God,
who by the death and resurrection of your Son Jesus Christ
delivered and saved the world:
grant that by faith in him who suffered on the cross
we may triumph in the power of his victory;
through Jesus Christ your Son our Lord,
who is alive and reigns with you,
in the unity of the Holy Spirit,
one God, now and for ever.

Psalms **23**, 127 *or* 41, **42**, 43
Exodus 11
Hebrews 13.17-end

Hebrews 13.17-end

'... may the God of peace ... make you complete in everything good'
(vv.20-21)

There is quite a touching account of the relationship between leaders and the led in today's passage from Hebrews. Although the rather hierarchical way in which it is expressed may sound odd to our ears, there are some interesting assumptions built in. Leaders are accountable for those they lead, and the led need to take some responsibility for the well-being of the leader. Both are working for the same end.

Above all, the way in which this relationship is grounded in prayer makes it clear that these are not structures embedded in any normal understanding of power or status. Instead, the writer and the readers are gifts to one another, given by the generosity of the gift-giving God. The author begs for prayer for himself, and then prays for his readers. Lifting from them any burdens his instructions have laid upon them, the writer gives them back to God. The mighty power of God, at work in Jesus, is liberating and energizing. It takes away the need for self-justification and anxiety, and gives us, in exchange, the certainty that we give God pleasure.

This is not a recipe for complacency, but for joy. This is not about us, but about God at work through Jesus Christ, and about the glory that the Father and the Son offer to one another.

Gracious Father,
you gave up your Son
out of love for the world:
lead us to ponder the mysteries of his passion,
that we may know eternal peace
through the shedding of our Saviour's blood,
Jesus Christ our Lord.

COLLECT

Monday 2 April

Monday of Holy Week

Psalm 41
Lamentations 1.1-12a
Luke 22.1-23

Luke 22.1-23

'Do this in remembrance of me' (v.19)

There are lots of echoes in today's reading from Luke.

First of all, Satan, who has been out of sight since the temptation in the wilderness in chapter 4, returns. Jesus may have resisted him, but Judas cannot. His choice does not change Jesus' fate, but it does change his own. Jesus' enemies don't really need Judas to lead them to Jesus; Judas may feel, at this moment, that he has power over Jesus, but Luke makes it clear, as Jesus gives instructions for the Passover meal, that Jesus is still in charge.

Next, as Jesus shares the meal with his followers in a house that is not his own, the echo leads us back to the manger where he was born. That didn't belong to him, either. The one who gives everything owns nothing.

Luke's readers would have recognized this supper in a large room that belonged to a well-off friend. It would have been exactly like the place where, week by week, they shared the Eucharist, repeating Jesus' words, breaking the bread together, guests of one of the better-off Christians, but all equal, nourished by the body and blood.

The words of Jesus at this supper echo through all Christian history, all of us called to this table together, all of us receiving what we have not earned and could not buy, but are given by the generosity of God.

COLLECT

Almighty and everlasting God,
who in your tender love towards the human race
   sent your Son our Saviour Jesus Christ
to take upon him our flesh
and to suffer death upon the cross:
grant that we may follow the example of his patience and
   humility,
and also be made partakers of his resurrection;
through Jesus Christ your Son our Lord,
who is alive and reigns with you,
in the unity of the Holy Spirit,
one God, now and for ever.

Psalm 27
Lamentations 3.1-18
Luke 22.[24-38] 39-53

Luke 22.[24-38] 39-53

'But this is your hour, and the power of darkness!' (v.53)

At the Last Supper, Jesus has woven his disciples together as indissolubly as words and symbols can, and provided for them out of his own sacrificial bounty. But it is clear that, while the disciples can receive, they cannot yet take responsibility for these symbols themselves. They still need to be taught about servant-leadership, and they still do not understand the cost of it.

And so Jesus prays alone in the garden, with his satiated disciples sleeping around him, unaware that soon it will be their turn to be self-giving leaders. When their time came, they would remember Jesus' bitter struggle in the garden and know that doubt and fear are not forbidden for a disciple of Christ. The leadership that Jesus called them to did not need to come effortlessly, with perfect clarity about God's call and its outcome.

Judas presumably thought he was about to exercise decisive leadership. But he was almost laughably superfluous at the one moment when he thought he was going to be in control. Only Jesus pays any attention to him, and then he is lost in the struggle between Jesus' followers and his enemies.

There are profound and unpalatable thoughts about power in today's reading, as there are throughout Holy Week. Those who think they exercise power cannot see the mighty act of God in Jesus, as he walks towards his death.

True and humble king,
hailed by the crowd as Messiah:
grant us the faith to know you and love you,
that we may be found beside you
on the way of the cross,
which is the path of glory.

COLLECT

Wednesday 4 April

Wednesday of Holy Week

Psalm 102 [or 102.1-18]
Wisdom 1.16 – 2.1; 2.12–22
or Jeremiah 11.18-20
Luke 22.54-end

Luke 22.54-end

'... he went out and wept bitterly' (v.62)

Luke's readers know all about Peter. He was a famous leader of the Church; all the stories about Jesus contain references to Peter, and so do all the stories of the earliest Christian community. They know that Peter was one of the first to recognize God's invitation to gentile Christians, like themselves, and they know that he was martyred for his faith. But they also know this story, told wherever Peter goes. They know it, paradoxically, as the thing that validates Peter's claim to authority, just as they know Paul's story as a persecutor of the faith as part of his passport to Christian leadership. Deep in the heart of the Christian story is a suspicion of Christians who believe they have earned their faith by their own merit, rather than by the free forgiveness of Jesus.

For Christians, there is no shame in failure. The only shame is in not being prepared to accept forgiveness. That is Judas' shame. 'What if' is always a dangerous question, but Jesus predicts that both Judas and Peter will betray him. If Peter can be forgiven, could Judas have been forgiven, too, if he had been brave enough, humble enough, to wait to find out?

Peter sets off, stupidly, believing he will be brave. He steps after Jesus and into his own future, while Judas slinks away to die.

COLLECT

Almighty and everlasting God,
who in your tender love towards the human race
    sent your Son our Saviour Jesus Christ
to take upon him our flesh
and to suffer death upon the cross:
grant that we may follow the example of his patience and
    humility,
and also be made partakers of his resurrection;
through Jesus Christ your Son our Lord,
who is alive and reigns with you,
in the unity of the Holy Spirit,
one God, now and for ever.

Psalms 42, 43
Leviticus 16.2-24
Luke 23.1-25

Luke 23.1-25

'So Pilate gave his verdict' (v.24)

For Pilate, this is just one more in a series of trials that he had to conduct, one more attempt to keep the peace among these quarrelsome people he was trying to govern on behalf of Rome. Pilate did his job efficiently, hearing the evidence and weighing it correctly as worthless. Luke's readers know very well that these charges are unfounded: Jesus did not advocate withholding taxes and did not claim publicly to be the Messiah. These were traps that his enemies had laid for him, but which he had adroitly side-stepped.

So Pilate would, ideally, like to discharge Jesus. He seizes instantly on the hint that Jesus should be in Herod's jurisdiction, rather than his own, but the buck cannot be passed for long. Ultimately, Pilate judges that peace is more important than justice.

Pilate, Herod and the enemies of Jesus assume that the trial and execution will be the end of the matter. But Luke's readers see the undercurrents. They see reconciliation between Pilate and Herod, brought about by Jesus. They see a criminal going free, because of Jesus, and know how many other sinners have been freed by this death. They hear the irony of the fact that the man is called 'Barabbas' – 'son of the father', when the true Son of the Father is going to death so that we may all become children of God.

God our Father,
you have invited us to share in the supper
which your Son gave to his Church
to proclaim his death until he comes:
may he nourish us by his presence,
and unite us in his love;
who is alive and reigns with you,
in the unity of the Holy Spirit,
one God, now and for ever.

Friday 6 April

Good Friday

Psalm 69
Genesis 22.1-18
John 19.38-end *or* Hebrews 10.1-10

Hebrews 10.1-10

'I have come to do your will' (v.7)

The prophets and psalmists of the Hebrew Scriptures have already begun to sow the seed of the knowledge that animal sacrifice is not really what God is interested in. These kinds of sacrifice are attempts to placate God, almost to divert God's attention from the behaviour they are trying to atone for. They acknowledge the problem, but refuse to see that the solution cannot be applied externally. What the sacrifices do not do is to change the hearts and wills of the people who offer them. But that is what God longs for.

The quotation from Psalm 40 makes the point: Jesus has come to do God's will.

And so everything changes today. Now, we know that what God offers is a relationship in which we can work with God, knowing him intimately, being part of his purposes for the world. We can't hide behind rituals and ceremonies any more; God has come close, to know and be known.

If that is frighteningly open-ended, it is also liberating. We no longer have to worry about whether our sacrifice has 'worked' to keep God satisfied, because no more sacrifices are required. All that is asked of us is that we come to God, in the company of Jesus, and say the words that he has taught us, 'I have come to do your will'.

COLLECT

Almighty Father,
look with mercy on this your family
for which our Lord Jesus Christ was content to be betrayed
and given up into the hands of sinners
and to suffer death upon the cross;
who is alive and glorified with you and the Holy Spirit,
one God, now and for ever.

Psalm 142
Hosea 6.1-6
John 2.18-22

John 2.18-22

'What sign can you show us ...?' (v.18)

During his ministry, Jesus is quite often asked for a 'sign'. The Gospels unanimously testify to Jesus' powers, primarily as a healer, but also as a miracle-worker. And yet people went on asking for a 'sign', and found that nothing they saw or heard was really convincing.

So what could really have worked for these people and the many, many others like them? What would finally convince?

The simple answer is that nothing God does is so plain that we have no choice about recognizing it. Even the resurrection can be doubted. God is extraordinarily uncoercive. Even the mightiest act will not function as a 'sign' unless we have already begun to see the character of the God to whom it bears witness.

God's greatest act is to become human, to live and to die. This ought not to be possible for 'God', on any normal definition of the word. Yet this is what God chooses to do, the mightiest sign of all, a sign of God's commitment, God's willingness to be present to us in all circumstances, God's power to transform without force but with utter creativity.

So the resurrection is a sign of the power of our God, who cannot be forced to abandon us, and whose life is unquenchable. Is that a sign? Only if this is the kind of God we long for.

COLLECT

Grant, Lord,
that we who are baptized into the death
of your Son our Saviour Jesus Christ
may continually put to death our evil desires
and be buried with him;
and that through the grave and gate of death
we may pass to our joyful resurrection;
through his merits,
who died and was buried and rose again for us,
your Son Jesus Christ our Lord.

Monday 9 April

Monday of Easter Week

Psalms 111, 117, 146
Exodus 12.1-14
1 Corinthians 15.1-11

1 Corinthians 15.1-11

'… so we proclaim and so you have come to believe' (v.11)

Some years ago I spent a fortnight in Greece in the weeks after Easter. I quite quickly grew accustomed to being greeted by both friends and strangers with the words, *Christos Anesti*, and to replying, *Alithos Anesti*.

Christ is risen! He is truly risen! At one level a simple greeting on the road, perhaps a mere custom; for me, in those two weeks, it became a meaningful expression of a common treasure. It was the recognition of a shared faith and a shared joy.

It is that faith and joy that Paul celebrates in the opening words of this great Easter chapter. Faith that is rooted in the resurrection of Jesus (v.3), an event attested by many credible eye witnesses (vv.5,6). Faith shared as good news of Christ is told and received (v.11). Joy that turned Paul's life around in his unexpected encounter with Christ (v.8). Joy in the continuing discovery of the undeserved love of God (v.10).

Easter is a celebration rooted in history and brought alive in our own encounters with the risen Christ. It's faith and it's joy. Take time to reflect on what a renewed discovery of faith and joy might bring to your life and to those you meet today. Christ is risen! He is risen indeed!

COLLECT

Lord of all life and power,
who through the mighty resurrection of your Son
overcame the old order of sin and death
to make all things new in him:
grant that we, being dead to sin
and alive to you in Jesus Christ,
may reign with him in glory;
to whom with you and the Holy Spirit
be praise and honour, glory and might,
now and in all eternity.

Psalms 112, 147.1-12
Exodus 12.14-36
1 Corinthians 15.12-19

Tuesday of Easter Week

1 Corinthians 15.12-19

'If for this life only we have hoped in Christ,
we are of all people most to be pitied' (v.19)

'There's probably no God... now stop worrying and enjoy your life'. That was the message on some buses a few years ago in a campaign organised by the British Humanist Association and others. If there is nothing after this life, we might as well enjoy ourselves now.

It's a slogan that assumes that belief in God makes you sad and anxious. Perhaps Christians are sometimes perceived as saying, 'be miserable in this life so that you can enjoy the next'. Is Paul saying something similar? Is he saying that living for Christ is so tough, so unhappy, that it's worth it only if there's 'pie in the sky when we die'?

No. His argument is that, without the resurrection of Christ, there is no real purpose in this life and no promise of the next. Easter changes both; it brings hope and life to both.

It's not that we put up with this life in order to enjoy the next. It is that we live this life in the purposeful, hope-filled light of the next. Living the resurrection life of Christ, is taking hold of a gift that is truly and fully ours, both now and beyond death. So live it today as you will in eternity.

God of glory,
by the raising of your Son
you have broken the chains of death and hell:
fill your Church with faith and hope;
for a new day has dawned
and the way to life stands open
in our Saviour Jesus Christ.

COLLECT

Wednesday 11 April

Wednesday of Easter Week

---

1 Corinthians 15.20-28

'… all will be made alive in Christ' (v.22)

Death is the great destroyer; it separates, it silences, it stops. The words of the popular poem of Henry Scott-Holland, 'Death is nothing at all' seem to fly in the face of the reality. W. H. Auden's, 'Stop all the clocks', expresses more truthfully the devastation death brings, 'I thought that love would last for ever: I was wrong'.

For Paul, the outworking of the resurrection of Christ goes on and on. Not only is it the centre of our faith and the root of hope and purpose, but it is also the pivot of history on which the destiny of all creation turns.

Without Christ, death, 'the last enemy' (v.26), is the devastating cruel victor. But, through the resurrection of Christ, death is defeated. It is still accompanied by awful pain, cruel separation and tragedy, but it marks now not separation but union, not silence but enduring melody, not an end but continuation and renewal.

Christ's resurrection is a gift, as Paul puts it, for 'all' (v.22). It's the gift of a new destiny, one in which, in the eternal union of God with all creation (v.28), love does indeed last for ever.

COLLECT

Lord of all life and power,
who through the mighty resurrection of your Son
overcame the old order of sin and death
to make all things new in him:
grant that we, being dead to sin
and alive to you in Jesus Christ,
may reign with him in glory;
to whom with you and the Holy Spirit
be praise and honour, glory and might,
now and in all eternity.

1 Corinthians 15.29-34

'Come to a sober and right mind, and sin no more' (v.34)

Paul returns to a previous theme (cf. Tuesday's reading): his life and his ministry have no meaning or purpose apart from the resurrection of Christ. What would be the point of his delight in the churches founded through his ministry (v.31)? What would be the purpose of his battles in Ephesus and elsewhere (v.32)? He – and indeed the Corinthian Christians – might as well 'eat, drink ... and die' (v.32, cf Isaiah 22.13).

But there is a point. Christ's resurrection brings for Paul a particular purpose, which is to make God known. The resurrection of Christ calls him to live God's love and to give himself to the task of sharing that life and love with others, whatever the cost.

Paul challenges the Corinthian Christians to seize that purpose. First, to grasp it with minds that know the truth of the resurrection of Christ. Secondly, to embrace it with lives that reveal to others the love and goodness of God (v.34).

So, too, for us. Easter is not simply a time of reflection and celebration, of belief and hope; it is also a time to find renewed purpose and pattern in our lives. It's a time not simply to be renewed in our faith, but to allow that resurrection faith to shape and direct our living. How might it shape yours?

God of glory,
by the raising of your Son
you have broken the chains of death and hell:
fill your Church with faith and hope;
for a new day has dawned
and the way to life stands open
in our Saviour Jesus Christ.

COLLECT

Friday 13 April

Friday of Easter Week

Psalms 115, 149
Exodus 13.17 – 14.14
1 Corinthians 15.35-50

1 Corinthians 15.35-50

'What you sow does not come to life unless it dies' (v.36)

A glance at a bulb or a seed seldom reveals anything of the beauty or the grandeur of the flower or tree that might emerge from it. The contrast is striking, yet the connection is real – the same organism in very different forms.

So Paul, in seeking to contrast, but also to connect, the reality of this life with the reality of the life to come, uses the same analogy. The contrast: perishable to imperishable, dishonour to glory, weakness to power, physical to spiritual. The connection: the one gives life to the other, the one leads, through death, to the other.

As we saw on Wednesday, death becomes the means of the transformation. The death of a seed marks the end of one form of being, but leads to something more wonderful, more life giving, more abundant. So, Paul says, does our death.

And that principle is as true in the different deaths we embrace now in this life. As we let go, as we die to fears and prides, as we embrace love and service, so those deaths become in themselves doors of transformation. What might I die to today and what transformation might I discover?

COLLECT

Lord of all life and power,
who through the mighty resurrection of your Son
overcame the old order of sin and death
to make all things new in him:
grant that we, being dead to sin
and alive to you in Jesus Christ,
may reign with him in glory;
to whom with you and the Holy Spirit
be praise and honour, glory and might,
now and in all eternity.

Psalms **116**, 150
Exodus 14.15-end
1 Corinthians 15.51-end

Saturday of Easter Week

1 Corinthians 15.51-end

'... the trumpet will sound' (v.52)

One of the glorious moments in Handel's *Messiah* is the aria 'The Trumpet Shall Sound'. The opening fanfare and confidence of the bass voice capture brilliantly the confidence and joy of the closing verses of this great chapter. If you've got a recording to hand or can get hold of one today, it's worth setting the time aside to listen to it.

The trumpet is a great Easter instrument. It announces the resurrection of Christ bursting into the world on the first Easter day. It speaks of the drama of our resurrection, not just at the end of this life, but breaking through into our lives today.

Death, the defeated enemy, has become the door to transformation, to life (vv.52,53). It has, as Paul puts it, been swallowed up in the victory of Christ (v.54). It's a victory that is the heart of our faith, the source of our hope; it brings new purpose and a new perspective. We live, we work and we love in the light of that victory (v.58).

But for Paul this is, first and foremost, a mystery (v.51). This is a glorious reality in which we can have confidence and out of which we live and love. It's a reality we take hold of by faith. In the end, and in the beginning, our response, whatever our situation today, is simply to say, 'thanks be to God'.

COLLECT

God of glory,
by the raising of your Son
you have broken the chains of death and hell:
fill your Church with faith and hope;
for a new day has dawned
and the way to life stands open
in our Saviour Jesus Christ.

Monday 16 April

Exodus 15.1-21

'I will sing to the Lord, for he has triumphed gloriously' (v.1)

Moses leads the Israelites in a jubilant song of celebration. They have escaped from the Pharaoh's army by the skin of their teeth, scrambling across sand briefly uncovered by a strong wind. They have seen the wind drop, the water return and the army swamped. After centuries of slavery, they are free. No wonder they sing.

We will, rightly, draw back from some of the sentiments in Moses' song. Perhaps our discomfort might give us cause to reflect on, and challenge, our own attitudes to the distress and suffering of others, not least those different to us or opposed to us, those we may even call our enemies.

The song of Moses, particularly in this Easter season, does however encourage us to sing; to sing to the Lord who has triumphed gloriously. The resurrection of Christ is about rescue and escape; it is about triumph and the defeat of enemies. Death defeated. Despair and anger, fear and selfishness destroyed. Life restored. Hope, love, forgiveness released. No wonder we should sing.

So why not find a time to sing today, even a silent song. Sing a song of thanks to God for his gift of life and freedom. Sing a song of hope, for those you know who in different ways live with the pain and frustration of slavery.

COLLECT

Almighty Father,
you have given your only Son to die for our sins
and to rise again for our justification:
grant us so to put away the leaven of malice and wickedness
that we may always serve you
in pureness of living and truth;
through the merits of your Son Jesus Christ our Lord,
who is alive and reigns with you,
in the unity of the Holy Spirit,
one God, now and for ever.

Psalms **8**, 20, 21 *or* **5**, 6, (8)
Exodus 15.22 – 16.10
Colossians 1.15-end

Exodus 15.22 – 16.10

'In the evening you shall know ...
and in the morning you shall see ...' (16.6,7)

After the jubilation of the crossing of the Red Sea, things seem to have deteriorated quickly for Moses and the people. The water at Marah is bitter, until God sweetens it for them with a piece of wood (15.25). The oasis of Elim gives way to the desert of Sin, and there they are hungry – so much so that they long to be back in Egypt (16.3). God promises them 'bread from heaven' (16.4). It's a test. Will they recognize the giver? God makes his presence known in a cloud of glory (16.10). Will they see?

'In the evening you shall know ... and in the morning you shall see ...' Life is often tough, it's sometimes very bitter; it may be that your life is so at the moment. Whatever is going on, however much like the wilderness it seems, there are signs of God's presence. There are ways God seeks to refresh us, to feed us, to sweeten the bitterness and to remind us he hasn't left us. The question is, do we know it, do we see it?

Take time, in the evening and in the morning, to pause and to know that God is there and to see what he is doing.

Risen Christ,
for whom no door is locked, no entrance barred:
open the doors of our hearts,
that we may seek the good of others
and walk the joyful road of sacrifice and peace,
to the praise of God the Father.

COLLECT

Psalms 16, **30** *or* 119.1-32
Exodus 16.11-end
Colossians 2.1-15

Exodus 16.11-end

'... they gathered as much as each of them needed' (v.18)

As God has promised, bread rains from heaven, adding to the seemingly abundant quails. The people called this bread, *'manna'*. 'What is this stuff?' (v.15) It may have been in fact the crystallised honeydew of an insect or possibly some sort of mushroom. Whatever it was, it fed them, and there was enough for everyone.

There is symbolism in the provision of the manna. It was a gift of God. There was enough for all. It provided for those who gathered much and for those who could gather only a little (v.18). There was enough for each day. If any tried to hoard it, it rotted and worms appeared (v.20). There was enough for rest from toil; it could be kept without spoiling for the Sabbath (v.24,25).

What might this say about all that God provides for the world? Is there enough for all? Is there enough for each day? Is there enough for rest, for the Sabbath?

How might your attitude to the 'stuff', the possessions, of your life change to reflect the generosity of God to all people? What can you do to 'gather' only as much as you need and to ensure that others can do the same?

COLLECT

Almighty Father,
you have given your only Son to die for our sins
and to rise again for our justification:
grant us so to put away the leaven of malice and wickedness
that we may always serve you
in pureness of living and truth;
through the merits of your Son Jesus Christ our Lord,
who is alive and reigns with you,
in the unity of the Holy Spirit,
one God, now and for ever.

Exodus 17

'Strike the rock, and water will come out of it' (v.6)

The difficulties continue. Despite the sweetened water at Marah, the springs of Elim, the quails and the manna in the wilderness of Sin – despite all these gifts, when they get to Rephidim and there is no water, the people argue and complain. It's understandable perhaps, deserts are tough places, but they do seem to lack a little gratitude!

God invites Moses to take his staff and to strike a rock. Water pours out. It's a powerful image; refreshing, life-giving water gushing out from what is hard and dry. The water was found there in the midst of the difficulty, not in some distant oasis.

'Strike the rock.' Sometimes the answer in the middle of a difficult or hard situation is not to search for refreshment elsewhere, but to seek – actively and determinedly – to find water right there. 'Striking the rock' may mean not giving up, it may mean going on loving and believing, it may mean seeking the best in your situation or in someone else. It certainly means prayer.

The raised hands of Moses (v.11) are often seen as a symbol of prayer. Aaron and Hur supported his weary hands as the day wore on; it is good to be reminded of those who support us in prayer and by their love. We can't do it all by ourselves.

Risen Christ,
for whom no door is locked, no entrance barred:
open the doors of our hearts,
that we may seek the good of others
and walk the joyful road of sacrifice and peace,
to the praise of God the Father.

COLLECT

Friday 20 April

Psalms 57, **61** *or* 17, **19**
Exodus 18.1-12
Colossians 3.12 – 4.1

Exodus 18.1-12

'… to eat bread with Moses' father-in-law in the presence of God'
(v.12)

In the midst of the series of trials we have reflected on this week comes this story of companionship. Moses' father-in-law, Jethro, comes to the desert to find Moses, bringing with him Moses' wife and children. It's a joyful reunion. They talk, they thank God and they eat together. As verse 12 puts it, the elders came to eat bread with Jethro in the presence of God.

Companionship is a wonderful gift. A companion is literally one with whom you share bread. If we open our eyes to see it, the presence of God is there when bread is shared in love and friendship.

Something of this is expressed (poignantly in the context of betrayal) in the Psalter of the Book of Common Prayer:

'It was even thou, my companion,
my guide, and mine own familiar friend.
We took sweet counsel together
and walked in the house of God as friends.' (Psalms 55.11)

Who are your companions? Who are those with whom you eat bread? Who are those who walk with you as friends? Thank God for the gift they are to you. Pray that you might be such a gift to others through your love and friendship. And, pray that in companionship, you may recognize the presence of God.

COLLECT

Almighty Father,
you have given your only Son to die for our sins
and to rise again for our justification:
grant us so to put away the leaven of malice and wickedness
that we may always serve you
in pureness of living and truth;
through the merits of your Son Jesus Christ our Lord,
who is alive and reigns with you,
in the unity of the Holy Spirit,
one God, now and for ever.

Exodus 18.13-end

'Now listen to me. I will give you counsel, and God be with you!'
(v.19)

Jethro proves to be more than a companion; he is a counsellor, a bringer of wisdom. Lonely in his position as leader and worn out from the responsibility, Moses finds his father-in-law to be a ready listener and someone who speaks freely and wisely.

Jethro's advice is clear and it is firm. He shows Moses the reality of his situation (vv.17,18). 'Carry on like this and you'll collapse and so will the people.' He offers Moses a practical solution (v.21). 'Find others who can share the task with you.' Moses listens and follows Jethro's advice.

It's vital for us to find people who can offer us wise counsel. Like Jethro, they may be those who can speak freely because there is some element of distance, not necessarily our close friends or people we see regularly. It's helpful to have people who listen to us; it's just as important for us to have people to whom we can listen, who will speak the truth with wisdom and clarity.

For Moses, it was a life-changing, a life-rescuing, encounter – and it can be for us too. To whom can you go for counsel? Who has God brought near to you who can speak freely and wisely?

Monday 23 April

George, martyr, patron of England

Psalms 5, 146
Joshua 1.1-9
Ephesians 6.10-20

Joshua 1.1-9

'Only be strong and very courageous ...' (v.7)

Little, if anything, is known about St George. The details of his real-life history are so scant that he was demoted to a third-class saint by the Roman Catholic Church in the early part of the twentieth century. Yet the patronage of St George survives, and his name lives on in the English psyche. Shakespeare gives Henry V the immortal lines, 'God for Harry! England and St George', shortly before the king's comprehensive defeat of the French at Agincourt. The association with conquest is, yet again, rooted in the story of the saint.

Most readers approaching this text on the Feast Day of St George might question the militaristic tone of God's promise to Joshua – that no one will be able to stand in the way of God's anointed. History, alas, has witnessed far too many leaders claiming a divine right to conquer other lands and peoples in God's name.

Yet the promise to Joshua is one tempered with caution – and a plea for mercy. God assures Joshua that he will never be forsaken, and that God will not fail him. Joshua is encouraged, therefore, to be courageous and strong. But, tellingly, he is not guaranteed victory, since God says Joshua must act within the law, and be faithful.

Indeed, faithfulness is the prerequisite for any success – sound advice to any military leader, politician ... or even a possible saint.

COLLECT

God of hosts,
who so kindled the flame of love
in the heart of your servant George
that he bore witness to the risen Lord
by his life and by his death:
give us the same faith and power of love
that we who rejoice in his triumphs
may come to share with him the fullness of the resurrection;
through Jesus Christ your Son our Lord,
who is alive and reigns with you,
in the unity of the Holy Spirit,
one God, now and for ever.

Psalms **98**, 99, 100 *or* 32, **36**
Exodus 20.1-21
Luke 1.26-38

Exodus 20.1-21

'Then God spoke all these words ...' (v.1)

The Ten Commandments. It would be hard, even in a secular culture, not find some acknowledgement and appreciation of their ongoing influence. Even when translated into film and art, the abiding image of Moses-from-the-mountain, complete with tablets in hand and revealing the will of God to the Israelites, remains utterly iconic. Even in cartoons and comedy, there is the sense that these words from God, mediated through Moses, are to be obeyed. How else does one explain comedic quips such as 'the good news is, I beat him down to ten ... the bad news is, adultery is still in' (Dave Allen).

The commandments are part of the rich and direct way in which God's will and purpose for humanity are revealed. What the commandments actually represent is a distillation of how God expects us to relate to him, and to one another. These are the rules of life so far as God is concerned; the core curriculum for human flourishing. That these commandments can be numbered on the fingers of our hands gives us some indication of God's sense of proportion. If we can simply live like this, all will be well.

There are many summaries of life and religion that are soundly descriptive. All faiths eat, pray and love – these things are at the heart of all major religions. But the Ten Commandments are not descriptive: they are prescriptive. These are God's biddings. They are not guidelines, advice or handy hints for better living. These commandments are simply to be obeyed as God's distilled wisdom for ordering human life and society.

Almighty Father,
who in your great mercy gladdened the disciples
with the sight of the risen Lord:
give us such knowledge of his presence with us,
that we may be strengthened and sustained by his risen life
and serve you continually in righteousness and truth;
through Jesus Christ your Son our Lord,
who is alive and reigns with you,
in the unity of the Holy Spirit,
one God, now and for ever.

COLLECT

129

Wednesday 25 April

Mark the Evangelist

Psalms 37.23-end, 148
Isaiah 62.6-10 *or*
Ecclesiasticus 51.13-end
Acts 12.25 – 13.13

Acts 12.25 – 13.13

'John [Mark], however, left them and returned to Jerusalem' (13.13)

The book of Acts makes no secret of how tough and demanding the work of the early Church was. Not only were there regular fall-outs in the churches themselves, but there was travelling, hardship, persecution and opposition. Moreover, success was sometimes measured not by spectacular growth, but by the faithful few. In today's passage, and for all the drama of the signs and wonders connected to Elymas, only the Governor of Paphos is moved to convert to the new faith.

In other words, the work of building the Church is slow. There are setbacks. The task of the Church is not exponential growth, but rather faith through thick and thin.

The witness of Scripture in relation to mission is sometimes uncomfortable: wait. Yes, wait. Wait for God's good time. Try and see history and destiny through God's eyes, not ours. This, of course, requires a special patience. To wait – sometimes in darkness – for his timing and light is no easy task.

We have to wait for God's goodness and completeness to gestate; for he surely feeds us even when we struggle to see the manna in his hand. So today, as we remember St Mark, we can enjoy one small detail of the story in today's reading. Preaching the gospel is not all frontline, headline and high-wire performance. The book of Acts records that Mark went back to Jerusalem after all the excitements with Elymas. He did not get to see all the new action in Perga with Paul and his companions. He went home alone, and to a desk job. He had some writing to do.

COLLECT

Almighty God,
who enlightened your holy Church
through the inspired witness of your evangelist Saint Mark:
grant that we, being firmly grounded in the truth of the gospel,
may be faithful to its teaching both in word and deed;
through Jesus Christ your Son our Lord,
who is alive and reigns with you,
in the unity of the Holy Spirit,
one God, now and for ever.

Exodus 25.1-22

'There I will meet you ...' (v.22)

The detail is extraordinary: different kinds of wood, precious stones, gold, silver and bronze. The Bible Museum of Amsterdam houses a unique scale model of the tabernacle, created in the nineteenth century by the Revd Leendert Schouten. This 1/24 scale reconstruction of the portable shrine built by the Israelites after their Exodus from Egypt was made by using all the materials mentioned in today's reading. The awning, for example, was woven from goat's wool specially imported from Syria. Even the sand which surrounds the model was brought all the way from the Sinai desert. It took Schouten two decades to make and, even today, it remains an extraordinary sight. The most moving aspect of the model, however, is the two winged creatures who sit facing each other, on the Ark of the Covenant, guarding the Ten Commandments on the two tablets of stone. 'I will meet you there, between the two creatures', is what Exodus says.

Indeed, God meets us in the spaces, in the in-between places. Just like the disciples seeking Jesus after the crucifixion, we find something of the presence of God in the space of the empty tomb. The space itself is pregnant with meaning and possibility. For the space makes us all pause. It asks us to take off our shoes, and kneel.

The detail, then, of the furnishings for the tabernacle and the Ark are rich, bewildering and beguiling. Because they are a distraction. Even with the excellent accuracy of Leendert Schouten's model, we see that this is merely the frame, so to speak, of an extraordinary portrait and landscape. The space in which God meets us is ultimately uncluttered – 'a deep, but dazzling darkness', as the poet Henry Vaughan puts it.

Almighty Father,
who in your great mercy gladdened the disciples
with the sight of the risen Lord:
give us such knowledge of his presence with us,
that we may be strengthened and sustained by his risen life
and serve you continually in righteousness and truth;
through Jesus Christ your Son our Lord,
who is alive and reigns with you,
in the unity of the Holy Spirit,
one God, now and for ever.

COLLECT

Friday 27 April

Exodus 28.1-4a, 29-38

'You shall make sacred vestments ...' (v.2)

One of my heroes is a predecessor of mine as Principal of Cuddesdon, Edward King. For King, the Christian life was one of discovery, brightness and wisdom – not doctrinaire or formulaic. Although he exercised considerable personal spiritual discipline, he was often remembered, in his early ministry, for his light touch, and for his warmth and holiness. His students remarked on the model of Anglican life he cultivated at Cuddesdon: 'a relaxed though disciplined community life – a minimum of rules without stiff formality – a true fellowship of staff and students'.

When he became Bishop of Lincoln, he is said to have remarked that 'I am glad it is John Wesley's diocese – I shall be the Bishop of the Poor'. He moved from the grand palace to the smaller medieval house next to the cathedral, and made himself accessible to the clergy and people of the city. He set aside many of the conventions that his fellow bishops took for granted. King wore old boots, lived simply, and was often seen about in pretty worn-out clothes.

The Bible takes a keen interest in what people wear, even priests like Aaron. But the Bible is keener still on what people look like on the inside. So it is ironic that King, who was a Ritualist, also wore colourful and precious vestments not seen on a bishop since the Reformation. But I suspect that King might have seen his scruffy day-wear and beautiful liturgical vestments as equally sacred. The scruffy and the ordinary, together with the beautiful and the precious, both, in their different ways, point to the God who is both with us in the manger and the stable, who reigns in heaven, presiding at the heavenly banquet.

COLLECT

Almighty Father,
who in your great mercy gladdened the disciples
    with the sight of the risen Lord:
give us such knowledge of his presence with us,
that we may be strengthened and sustained by his risen life
and serve you continually in righteousness and truth;
through Jesus Christ your Son our Lord,
who is alive and reigns with you,
in the unity of the Holy Spirit,
one God, now and for ever.

Exodus 29.1-9

'... so that they may serve me as priests' (v.1)

In one way, we could say that the detail for ordaining priests is incidental. It is not *how* the Israelites made priests that matters, but *why*. Clearly, it is so that communities have exemplars of character and virtue. The people who are ordained – set aside and consecrated for service to God and his people – need to be persons who model integrity, truth, love, holiness, wisdom and sacrifice. Their lives inspire, and simply by their living, cause others to aspire to something greater and more Godly.

Yet priests are also there to model something of the life of God to people. All Christians are called to this; it is something of what it must mean to belong to the priesthood of all believers. It is partly in this way that God lives among us – through our lives of dedication to one another. Yet it is a costly calling.

A popular story from World War Two tells of a Romanian Christian who found himself imprisoned in a concentration camp, deprived of all he needed to sustain his faith: no crucifix, Bible, icons, devotional books, corporate worship or knotted prayer beads. So he prayed in secret – that he might respond to the call of love. He found himself spending time in the camp with the sick, the starving, the diseased, the dying and the betrayers – all those who were shunned by others.

One day, as the camp drew close to liberation, an atheist – someone who had their faith shattered by the experience of war – came to see the Romanian and said, 'I see how you live here. Tell me about the God you worship'. He replied: 'He is like me'. The call to discipleship remains compellingly simple: to be like him.

> Risen Christ,
> you filled your disciples with boldness and fresh hope:
> strengthen us to proclaim your risen life
> and fill us with your peace,
> to the glory of God the Father.

COLLECT

Monday 30 April

Psalms **103** *or* **44**
Exodus 32.1-14
Luke 2.41-end

Exodus 32.1-14

'Come, make gods for us ...' (v.1)

Because worship can take many forms, so can idolatry. Few today would be tempted to make an idol in the shape of an animal, and bow down and worship. And yet our cultural blindness can often lead us to affirm or benignly bless forces that we think serve us, but to which we are actually in bondage. For example, children who are exposed to relentless advertising for their foods of choice might turn away from vegetables, fruit and balanced diets in favour of snacks and foods high in fats. The result is obesity. A relentless focus on acquisitions and commodities may lead to children knowing what they want to *have*, but not what they want to *be*, in terms of vocations and careers.

Here, of course, we may discover that less is more – that by reducing choice, we enhance our enjoyment of ourselves and one another. But to appreciate this, some aspects of capitalism might have to be checked and challenged as not only unwise, but also probably sinful. The illusion of endless choice, and sating our desires, can quickly turn our gaze away from God and the needs of others.

Moses is exasperated by what he sees – among a people who have just been delivered from one captivity only to take up another without any pressure. But he pleads with God for time. He pleads for his people, and God 'changed his mind and let them live'. One can only assume that God already knows that those who consume materialism – very much the idolatry described – will end in being consumed by it. God gives them time, even though he knows they will fail. But he also knows he will still forgive.

COLLECT

Almighty God,
whose Son Jesus Christ is the resurrection and the life:
raise us, who trust in him,
from the death of sin to the life of righteousness,
that we may seek those things which are above,
where he reigns with you
in the unity of the Holy Spirit,
one God, now and for ever.

Psalms 139, 146
Proverbs 4.10-18
James 1.1-12

Philip and James, Apostles

James 1.1-12

'... whenever you face trials of any kind, consider it nothing but joy' (v.2)

This very familiar passage was probably meant to bring a note of comfort to a group of Christians struggling to maintain their identity around the close of the first century. James, or perhaps a disciple of James by the time this was written, was attempting to give courage and hope to people who found themselves in the midst of conflict with their Jewish and pagan neighbours. Their survival as a community of faith and their individual security and safety were very much on the line. Only one thing matters in such circumstances: being true to the faith that is yours, and resisting anything else. You cannot read a book like James without keeping such circumstances in mind. James was writing to people who were defensive, and perhaps vulnerable. They needed to know that they had made the right choice, even in the midst of doubt and some very severe testing.

So, faith being tested is likened to a boat tossed in a storm. The storm, note, is unavoidable. James' readers are doubtless wondering what is going to happen to them and the people they know dear to them. It's a situation the Church knew well, and one that Jesus' disciples knew well also. The faithful are scattered; this is a time of severe testing.

The attention paid to riches and wealth, therefore, is not surprising in this context. James is drawing parallels and contrasts that invite his readers to reflect on where they place their trust. Falling back on personal wealth and resources is what most of us would do, at least sometimes, when faced with stress and hardship. Yet James is asking us to reach out and beyond to God – for wholly different rewards, that will last for ever.

Almighty Father,
whom truly to know is eternal life:
teach us to know your Son Jesus Christ
as the way, the truth, and the life;
that we may follow the steps
of your holy apostles Philip and James,
and walk steadfastly in the way that leads to your glory;
through Jesus Christ your Son our Lord,
who is alive and reigns with you,
in the unity of the Holy Spirit,
one God, now and for ever.

COLLECT

Psalms **135** *or* **119.57-80**
Exodus 33
Luke 3.15-22

Exodus 33

'... show me your ways, so that I may know you' (v.13)

'A land flowing with milk and honey' (v.3) is one of the more resonant phrases to have emerged from the Old Testament. Today, we find the Israelites poised to leave Mount Sinai, and continue their journey. Yet even as the blessing of the Promised Land is anticipated, God reminds Moses of the need for his people to prepare.

If God is to be met face to face by Moses, and on behalf of the Israelites, then preparation, obedience and readiness are required. Sins need to be set aside if God is to be truly encountered. Nothing can ultimately come between God's friendship and his pleasure in us (v.17). Yet plenty seems to hinder us – distractions, desires and sins clog up our relationships with one another, and with God. So the invitation today is to seek God's face, but by first setting aside all that hinders us from this.

Cranmer's majestic collect for purity in the Book of Common Prayer understood that a great deal of distraction, interference and sin is concealed inside us. Yet to God, all hearts are open – replete with their mixed emotions and motives. And all our desires are known too, with no secrets hidden. All of them are seen by the one who is returning. Yet the prayer continues in petition, 'cleanse the thoughts of our hearts by the inspiration of thy Holy Spirit'.

A prayer for the cleansing of desire seems an especially appropriate way to approach God. But it also captures something of the Israelites own hope. That light can pierce the darkness and salvation overcome sin. Then we shall see: face to face.

COLLECT

Almighty God,
whose Son Jesus Christ is the resurrection and the life:
raise us, who trust in him,
from the death of sin to the life of righteousness,
that we may seek those things which are above,
where he reigns with you
in the unity of the Holy Spirit,
one God, now and for ever.

Exodus 34.1-10, 27-end

'I will perform marvels' (v.10)

Two flat stones; some rules about grazing animals; a cloud that hides the voice of God; the promise of miracles; the demand for offerings. What do these messages say to us? Well, they remind us, at the very least, that messages from God are sometimes not plain – they come heavily disguised. Moreover, sometimes when they are plain, we are so fixated on what we think God *ought* to say or send, that we just don't see what is staring us in the face. We miss the obvious and fail to hear God's gentle voice of reason because we are tuned in to the sating of our desires.

Moses, then, is preparing his people to receive God afresh and is making space for him who is to come to be received once more. Plenty, then, to think about, as we try to discern the will of God in the midst what can sometimes seem like some very mixed messages.

This new time for the Israelites is, then, a season of promise. But the promises are not necessarily specific. God will perform miracles never seen before. God's messages are sometimes plain, but we are too complex and our churches too clouded to perceive them. Sometimes they are subtle, and we are too simple to perceive their wisdom.

Either way, the long journey in the desert to the Promised Land carries an important message for all Christians. It asks us to be patient, to wait, watch and listen. And to try and develop a wisdom and discernment that gets beyond the ordinary and into the supernatural. It invites us to be still and obedient, and wait for the call of God, that will surely beckon us into new places and possibilities.

Risen Christ,
faithful shepherd of your Father's sheep:
teach us to hear your voice
and to follow your command,
that all your people may be gathered into one flock,
to the glory of God the Father.

COLLECT

Friday 4 May

Exodus 35.20 – 36.7

'... what they had already brought was more than enough' (36.7)

Even in the Old Testament, faith needed some degree of financial sacrifice if it were to flourish. In today's reading, gold, silver, precious clothes and skills are all brought by the Israelites to serve God. We should remember that the opposite of growth is not maintaining the status quo – it is normally imperceptible decline. We want our churches to live and work to the praise and glory of God. But that requires intensive prayer, working together, imagination, hard work, and deep engagement with our community and our own lives. It requires sacrifice too.

Dennis Potter, the playwright, once said that 'religion is not the bandage – it is the wound'. We turn to Christ for comfort, hope and healing. But in receiving it, we are marked by the cross, which requires us to expend our own lives sacrificially in offering and gift. This means that the Church is, in a real sense, a communion; the Body of Christ. As Christians, we have a real responsibility to care for that Body, and participate with God in its growth in our spiritual lives. In giving to God, we also bless and affirm one another.

Money, of course, is not the answer to all our needs or prayers. As today's reading hints, the most rewarding part of giving is doing it together; discovering new gifts in ourselves and others that God has already bestowed. Shared stewardship leads to deeper fellowship.

That is why today's reading ends on a note that would cheer up all church treasurers: Moses sends word to the people to stop giving, 'for what they had already brought was more than enough' (36.7).

COLLECT

Almighty God,
whose Son Jesus Christ is the resurrection and the life:
raise us, who trust in him,
from the death of sin to the life of righteousness,
that we may seek those things which are above,
where he reigns with you
in the unity of the Holy Spirit,
one God, now and for ever.

Psalms **34** *or* **68**
Exodus 40.17-end
Luke 4.31-37

Exodus 40.17-end

'the cloud ... by day, and fire ... by night' (v.38)

Still in the midst of the wilderness, and yet journeying to the Promised Land, we discover that walking with God is often about learning to live with the cloud *and* the light – learning that the voice of God often comes to us in quiet ways. Our demand for a sign is, more often than not, childish. God wants us to cultivate a patience and a stillness that allow us truly to discern the depth of his presence – truly to listen.

But what is deep listening? What does it mean to follow God in the wilderness, with no apparent end in sight? First, it is about the development of a slow, patient spirituality. We live in a world where many expect instant results, instant nourishment and instant answers. But spirituality is a slow business; a marathon, not a sprint. Listening comes about by being attuned to the silent, subtle voice of God.

Secondly, deep listening comes through deep relationships. It is about a depth of attending to the other. It is not a technique, but part of a committed relationship in which there is a willingness to give of yourself, and also to receive. It is born of desire to both know and be known. So, tents are pitched; camp is broken. Day after day. Moving and relating to God, as sojourners, never ends.

Thirdly, it is about restraint. For someone to speak, someone must be silent. And for someone to speak, truly, there must be someone to listen. Being listened to fully is a deep privilege, and although we often presume that God will listen to us in prayer, it is rare, perhaps, for us to expect God to speak to us and for us to listen. Yet the whole story of the Israelites in the wilderness is about being taught to listen to the voice of God.

Risen Christ,
faithful shepherd of your Father's sheep:
teach us to hear your voice
and to follow your command,
that all your people may be gathered into one flock,
to the glory of God the Father.

COLLECT

Monday 7 May

Psalms **145** *or* **71**
Numbers 9.15-end; 10.33-end
Luke 4.38-end

Numbers 9.15-end; 10.33-end

*'As long as the cloud rested over the tabernacle,
[the Israelites] would remain in camp' (9.18)*

The Israelites are in the second year of their desert wanderings. But this literal journey is also a journey of faith, with an urgent need to keep in step with the rhythm set by God. The people's guide is a cloud: when it rests over the tabernacle, they are to stop, and when it lifts, they are to move on. But the rhythm is unpredictable: some stops are short, others of weeks' or months' duration.

The cloud is a potent symbol of the presence of God in both the Old and New Testaments (Exodus 16.10; Matthew 17.5). In *The Life of Moses*, the fourth-century spiritual master Gregory of Nyssa writes of the 'dark cloud' wrapped around Mount Sinai into which Moses enters to meet God. The image emerges again in the fourteenth-century work, *The Cloud of Unknowing*. Here, the cloud stands between humanity and the fullness of the divine reality, and the disciple is urged to reach out to God with yearning, piercing the cloud with a 'dart of longing love'.

The cloud, then, is a symbol of mystery and divine encounter. In our human striving for security, the image of the cloud invites us to trust God with the unknown, the irregular, the unexpected – with all that makes up the rich texture of our lives and journeys.

COLLECT

Almighty God,
who through your only-begotten Son Jesus Christ
have overcome death and opened to us the gate of everlasting life:
grant that, as by your grace going before us
 you put into our minds good desires,
so by your continual help
we may bring them to good effect;
through Jesus Christ our risen Lord,
who is alive and reigns with you,
in the unity of the Holy Spirit,
one God, now and for ever.

Psalms **19**, 147.1-12 *or* **73**
Numbers 11.1-33
Luke 5.1-11

Numbers 11.1-33

'I am not able to carry all this people alone' (v.14)

The honeymoon is well and truly over. The oppression of the Israelites' Egyptian captivity has been forgotten; their first halcyon days of freedom are a distant dream. The people bemoan their lot, craving the rich food they enjoyed in Egypt, begrudging the heavenly manna provided for their sustenance in the desert. This passage crackles with peevish discontent and God's responsive anger at the people's ingratitude. If the people want meat, they shall have it in abundance – until it sickens them. Even Moses is not immune to the climate of complaint as he rails against God, 'Why have you treated your servant so badly?' But God's response is merciful, and Moses receives a much-needed lesson in delegation of responsibility.

Like the Israelites, we tend to hark back to some remembered 'golden age', when life seemed carefree and any difficulties have been filtered out by our selective memories. Or we project our hopes and dreams forward in an attempt to escape the pain of the present, placing all our yearning into what might, just possibly, come to be ...

Teaching on prayer urges us to live in the present moment and, like the Israelites, we find this incredibly hard to do. But unless we first meet God *now*, in this moment with all its joys and contradictions, we will meet him nowhere.

Risen Christ,
your wounds declare your love for the world
and the wonder of your risen life:
give us compassion and courage
to risk ourselves for those we serve,
to the glory of God the Father.

COLLECT

Psalms **30**, 147.13-end *or* **77**
Numbers 12
Luke 5.12-26

Numbers 12

'Has the Lord spoken only through Moses?
Has he not spoken through us also?' (v.2)

The petulant strain of 'It's not fair!' continues. Moses has married a Cushite woman, violating the Israelites' strict laws concerning intermarriage, and Aaron and Miriam feel it right to be openly critical of him. God's response is puzzling: he defends Moses' behaviour, not on account of his status as leader, but because of his humility. The punishment for their presumption is harsh: Miriam is afflicted with leprosy and expelled from the camp for seven days, despite Moses' pleas for her healing.

We may be tempted to join the chorus of 'It's not fair!' Why Miriam? Why is she afflicted with leprosy, while the equally guilty Aaron is let off with a rebuke? Where is the justice in that?

We may find it uncomfortable that we are given no clear answer. But God is not to be held captive by human ideas of the way he should be and act. 'For my thoughts are not your thoughts, nor are your ways my ways, says the Lord' (Isaiah 55.8). 'He makes his sun rise on the evil and on the good' (Matthew 5.45). Perhaps, like Job, we are being challenged to allow God simply to be God, and to worship his ultimate mystery. 'I have uttered what I did not understand, things too wonderful for me, which I did not know' (Job 42.3).

COLLECT

Almighty God,
who through your only-begotten Son Jesus Christ
have overcome death and opened to us the gate of everlasting life:
grant that, as by your grace going before us
    you put into our minds good desires,
so by your continual help
we may bring them to good effect;
through Jesus Christ our risen Lord,
who is alive and reigns with you,
in the unity of the Holy Spirit,
one God, now and for ever.

Psalms **57**, 148 or **78.1-39***
Numbers 13.1-3,17-end
Luke 5.27-end

Numbers 13.1-3, 17-end

'So they brought ... an unfavourable report' (v.32)

In the volatile and edgy political climate of today's world, the events described in the Scripture texts over the next few days make uncomfortable reading. In today's passage, initial moves are being staked out in the plan for the Israelites' divinely ordained land-grabbing. We need to remember that theirs was a very different world to our own, with cultural and religious expectations that may well feel alien today. And their perception of God's dealings with them at this time was that conquest and victory in battle earned them his blessing and approval.

So spies are sent out secretly to assess the quality of the land and its inhabitants, to gauge the strength and numbers of the people and any weaknesses in the country's defences that could be usefully exploited in an attack. Finding a land that is agriculturally rich and well-defended, the spies return shaken by what they have seen. Fearful of undertaking an invasion, they give Moses a false report.

And it is in the spies' fear, perhaps, that the timeless teaching is to be found. When God calls us we are often fearful, unsure that we have either the will or the ability. There may be something of the 'Here am I, send him' mentality in our response, and we forget that where God calls, he also equips.

Risen Christ,
your wounds declare your love for the world
and the wonder of your risen life:
give us compassion and courage
to risk ourselves for those we serve,
to the glory of God the Father.

COLLECT

Friday 11 May

Psalms **138**, 149 *or* **55**
Numbers 14.1-25
Luke 6.1-11

Numbers 14.1-25

'... slow to anger, and abounding in steadfast love' (v.18)

The sorry story continues, and the fear that infected all the spies except Caleb and Joshua has now spread to the whole people. So perilous do they feel their plight that death in Egypt is deemed to be preferable, and they begin to make plans to return. They are not open to persuasion, and Caleb and Joshua are threatened with stoning when they offer encouragement to stay and face the challenges ahead.

The God who loves and forgives is also sorely tried by the people's faithlessness and, not for the first time, Moses mediates and asks for mercy. And God does forgive – but there are consequences. None of the people, excepting Caleb and Joshua (vv. 24,29) will live to see the land that has been promised.

The reality of a deeply loving God may be hard to hold alongside this picture of an angry and vengeful deity persuaded to compassion only by the mediation of Moses. Yet there is a deeper truth at work here, untouched by any sense of pettiness or vindictiveness. Like the Israelite people, when fear gets a grip it tends to paralyze us, and inevitably our horizons shrink. But life is not meant to be a hazardous ordeal. In order to reach our 'promised land', God calls us to a generous trust and courageous discipleship.

COLLECT

Almighty God,
who through your only-begotten Son Jesus Christ
have overcome death and opened to us the gate of everlasting life:
grant that, as by your grace going before us
    you put into our minds good desires,
so by your continual help
we may bring them to good effect;
through Jesus Christ our risen Lord,
who is alive and reigns with you,
in the unity of the Holy Spirit,
one God, now and for ever.

Psalms **146**, 150 *or* **76**, 79
Numbers 14.26-end
Luke 6.12-26

Numbers 14.26-end

'Do not go up, for the Lord is not with you' (v.42)

The Lord continues to spell out the consequences of the Israelites' lack of faith and obedience. The children, along with Caleb and Joshua, will enter the Promised Land, but they will first have to bear the weight of their elders' failure by being shepherds in the wilderness for forty years, until the last of the adults currently alive has died.

But the mourning of the people on hearing this judgement does not spring from a right motivation. They promise repentance, but they insist on going up to 'the place that the Lord has promised' (v.40) to seek the Lord's forgiveness. Moses warns them that they are going against the commands of the Lord by doing so, and that his presence will not be with them. But his warning falls on deaf ears: the inevitable happens, and the Israelites are routed by the country's inhabitants.

We tend not to bear suffering patiently, and our natural human reaction is to want to get rid of it as quickly as possible. But some painful situations, particularly those caused through our own wilfulness, are not put right so easily. When we have sinned, God's forgiveness is there for us as soon as we ask. But sometimes it will take time and patience to bring the deeper healing and greater self-knowledge that only God can give.

Risen Christ,
your wounds declare your love for the world
and the wonder of your risen life:
give us compassion and courage
to risk ourselves for those we serve,
to the glory of God the Father.

COLLECT

Monday 14 May

Matthias the Apostle

Psalms 16, 147.1-12
1 Samuel 2.27-35
Acts 2.37-end

Acts 2.37-end

*'... they broke bread ... and ate their food with glad and
generous hearts' (v.46)*

These words transport me back 23 years, to a small hill in the
Burgundian countryside and the spiritual phenomenon that is Taizé.
In that hot July week, several thousand of the young – and not so
young – of Europe and beyond had come to share for a few days in
the brothers' community life. Living conditions were primitive; food
was nourishing but basic; daily Bible study groups were stimulating
and multilingual. But above all, there was the worship: in chapel three
times a day, there was a tangible unity of prayer and worship – of
candlelight, music and silence.

Acts states that the growth of the fledgling Christian community could
not be contained. Alight with the Spirit, people were moved to
repentance and baptism in Christ's name. They committed themselves
to the apostles' teaching and fellowship, and to the breaking of bread
and shared prayer (v.42). The attractiveness and visible unity of the
believers was contagious and compelling.

Such unity may appear today to be an impossible dream. And yet – the
experience of Taizé perhaps lifts the veil for a moment and offers a
glimpse of hope; a pledge of what is possible when God's people open
themselves to the Spirit's healing and renewing power. Not just for
mountain-top experiences like Taizé, but for every day, whatever our
life situation may be.

COLLECT

Almighty God,
who in the place of the traitor Judas
chose your faithful servant Matthias
to be of the number of the Twelve:
preserve your Church from false apostles
and, by the ministry of faithful pastors and teachers,
keep us steadfast in your truth;
through Jesus Christ your Son our Lord,
who is alive and reigns with you,
in the unity of the Holy Spirit,
one God, now and for ever.

Numbers 16.36-end

*'... the censers of these sinners have become holy at the cost
of their lives' (v.38)*

Our lectionary omits the horrific events of the previous verses, where
Korah, Dathan and Abiram die for their presumption in grasping for
the priesthood. Here we witness the gruesome aftermath, as the
censers that had belonged to the three men are retrieved from the fire
that killed them. They were Levites, appointed by God to serve in his
tabernacle, but only Aaron and his family were to act as priests.
Dissatisfied with their lot and envious of Aaron, they attempted to
make themselves priests also.

And their thinking had seduced the Israelites, who then accused Moses
and Aaron of killing the Lord's people. The plague that then struck
was seen as the outworking of God's wrath, and was stopped only
when Moses made atonement – again! – on behalf of the people.

But below the surface of this shocking narrative is a message as true
today as it has ever been. In our discipleship, we are faced with the
need to deal honestly with our deepest motives. What *is* it that drives
us – a disinterested desire to follow God's leading, or the seductive
siren voice that seems to offer high esteem and personal glory? Being
human, our motives will never be unmixed, but the challenge here is
to own their confused complexity and submit them to the searing
flame of God's holy cleansing.

God our redeemer,
you have delivered us from the power of darkness
and brought us into the kingdom of your Son:
grant, that as by his death he has recalled us to life,
so by his continual presence in us he may raise us
to eternal joy;
through Jesus Christ your Son our Lord,
who is alive and reigns with you,
in the unity of the Holy Spirit,
one God, now and for ever.

COLLECT

Wednesday 16 May

Numbers 17.1-11

'... the staff of Aaron for the house of Levi had sprouted' (v.8)

The Lord moves to put an end to the grumbling of the Israelites once and for all. Moses is instructed to take one staff from each of the tribes, to inscribe each with the name of the tribe's leader, and to place them in the tent of meeting. It is the staff of Aaron for the tribe of Levi that sprouts, producing buds, blossoms and ripe almonds. Moses is instructed to display the sprouting staff visibly, as a constant warning and reminder to any who may be tempted to rebel.

Aaron was an ordinary man, but his calling – and his obedience to that call – led to a ministry of abundant blessing and fruitfulness. And the sign given was miraculous, as the hewn wood used to make the staff was no longer part of any living tree. It would have been incapable of producing growth of any kind, let alone bursting forth with bud, blossom and fruit simultaneously.

There are times when our own walk with God feels dry and barren, offering very little encouragement for our attempts to live faithfully. We may empathize with Moses and Aaron, who persisted in difficult and discouraging circumstances. But the miraculously blossoming staff of Aaron is a sign to us that where God calls he blesses and enables, however difficult our circumstances may be.

COLLECT

God our redeemer,
you have delivered us from the power of darkness
and brought us into the kingdom of your Son:
grant, that as by his death he has recalled us to life,
so by his continual presence in us he may raise us to eternal joy;
through Jesus Christ your Son our Lord,
who is alive and reigns with you,
in the unity of the Holy Spirit,
one God, now and for ever.

Hebrews 7.[11-25] 26-end

'[Jesus] is able for all time to save those who approach God through him, since he always lives to make intercession for them' (v.25)

The above verse forms the culmination of a dense passage that places the high priesthood of Jesus firmly in the line of that of Melchizedek, rather than the later development of Israel's Levitical priesthood. The fact of human mortality meant that the Israelite priesthood was a temporary measure, but Melchizedek is here presented as a mysterious figure, without beginning or end. This, too, is the pattern of Jesus (John 1.1); by his dying, rising and ascending he lives as a priest for ever.

But we may not often take time to reflect on what the implications of this stupendous fact might be. At the end of our prayers we frequently use phrases like 'through Jesus Christ our Lord', or 'in Jesus' name', without giving them much thought, but it is to this belief in Jesus as eternal intercessor that they refer.

And it is this which brings our faith most vibrantly alive, because Jesus the intercessor transcends the restrictions of time and space. Without Jesus the intercessor, we are trapped in the void between the Christ of the historical past and the Christ who promises to return sometime in the future. The Jesus who stands before his Father *now* on our behalf, bridges that deep chasm, showering us with his love and forgiveness, and offering a future full of hope.

COLLECT

Grant, we pray, almighty God,
that as we believe your only-begotten Son
our Lord Jesus Christ
to have ascended into the heavens,
so we in heart and mind may also ascend
and with him continually dwell;
who is alive and reigns with you,
in the unity of the Holy Spirit,
one God, now and for ever.

Friday 18 May

Psalms 20, **81** *or* **88** (95)
Exodus 35.30 – 36.1
Galatians 5.13-end

Galatians 5.13-end

'... through love become slaves to one another' (v.13)

In the larger part of today's reading, Paul presents us with the familiar – perhaps over-familiar – comparison of the works of the flesh and the fruit of the Spirit. But it is verse 13, cited above, that confronts us with a brain-knotting paradox. The worldly understanding of freedom believes that I am free to do what I like; the more responsible perhaps adding, 'as long as it doesn't hurt anyone else'. But this is not the kind of freedom that Paul is talking about; the freedom he refers to is that which, first and foremost, willingly puts itself at the service of others.

We may just about manage this with people we know and like – but what about our 'enemy'? How then do we keep our fear and natural self-interestedness at bay? As Paul makes abundantly clear, Christians are far from immune from this kind of defensiveness (v.15). When fearful, we tend to polarize, failing to listen to – let alone love – the other. And if any do refuse to polarize, seeking rather to hold the tension and really listen to the other, we unjustly castigate them as 'weak'.

But 'perfect love casts out fear' (1 John 4.18). God's gift of freedom calls us to hold the place of contradiction, responding to ally and opponent alike with respect and loving attention.

COLLECT

Grant, we pray, almighty God,
that as we believe your only-begotten Son our Lord Jesus Christ
to have ascended into the heavens,
so we in heart and mind may also ascend
and with him continually dwell;
who is alive and reigns with you,
in the unity of the Holy Spirit,
one God, now and for ever.

Saturday 19 May

1 Corinthians 2

*'For I decided to know nothing among you except Jesus Christ,
and him crucified' (v.2)*

These words of Paul are very familiar to us, and easily trip off the tongue. But what Paul says is easier said than done, and our behaviour as Christians, individually and corporately, often appears to betray the opposite. I find myself thinking of our proud or envious preoccupation with 'successful' churches; my sense of self-congratulation when people appreciate one of my sermons; and our over-anxious need for visible signs that we are somehow 'getting it right'.

More often than not, Paul was not given the easy reassurance that such visible signs would offer. Although the Church grew massively under his leadership, keeping the whole thing on track was an exhausting and, at times, a frustrating business. His efforts were often unappreciated and he was frequently persecuted by the authorities.

Visible signs, whether positive or negative, can be misleading and open to misinterpretation. Clearly there is an important place for God-directed energy and commitment, and a willing use of the gifts and abilities we have been given. It is also right that we should be concerned to do the best job that we can. But Paul's words here both challenge and remind us where the true source of our energy is to be found: not in any personal charisma or wisdom, but in the strength and vulnerability of the crucified Christ.

Risen Christ,
you have raised our human nature to the throne of heaven:
help us to seek and serve you,
that we may join you at the Father's side,
where you reign with the Spirit in glory,
now and for ever.

COLLECT

Monday 21 May

Psalms **93**, 96, 97 or **98**, 99, 101
Numbers 27.15-end
1 Corinthians 3

1 Corinthians 3

'For all things are yours ... all belong to you, and you belong to Christ, and Christ belongs to God' (vv.21-23)

The Corinthian church was a church fair fizzing with life (1 Corinthians 1.4-9). But in the midst of all that was good about it, there were problems. There were divisions in the church, with different groups trying to line themselves up behind different leaders. They may have been using differences of preaching style between Paul and Apollos to generate disquiet or dissatisfaction with the leadership. Paul would have none of it. This was immature behaviour for people who should by now have grown into mature Christians (vv.2b-3).

Underlying the jealousy and the quarrelling may have been a lot of anxiety. This was a church where there was life. It was growing. Things were changing rapidly. Spiritual gifts and ministries were developing. In any group, those who feel insecure often make a lot of noise just in order to make themselves heard. Everyone wants to define their place and their purpose in it. There can be power struggles and personality clashes.

Paul deals with the issue straightforwardly, then ends with a note of strong reassurance. There is no need for boasting about human leaders (v.21). Our identity is not to be found through them, but in God. And in God all things are ours. We don't have to manipulate to get our way or to get our voices heard. We belong totally in him – and in him, all is well.

COLLECT

O God the King of glory,
you have exalted your only Son Jesus Christ
with great triumph to your kingdom in heaven:
we beseech you, leave us not comfortless,
but send your Holy Spirit to strengthen us
and exalt us to the place
     where our Saviour Christ is gone before,
who is alive and reigns with you,
in the unity of the Holy Spirit,
one God, now and for ever.

1 Corinthians 12.1-13

'... no one can say "Jesus is Lord" except by the Holy Spirit' (v.3)

We don't know what led to Paul's intervention '... no one speaking by the Spirit of God ever says "Jesus be cursed"...' (v.3). It's possible that, in the exercise of prophetic speech, an immature believer took the idea of 'Jesus being made a curse for us', and got carried into heresy. In the ensuing confusion, Paul is quick to set the record straight. It's those whose lives are subject to the rule of Jesus Christ who are filled with the Holy Spirit, who are true agents of God's word.

This episode raises the question: how are we to judge whether something offered in the Church is 'from God the Spirit' or elsewhere? When we are thinking about vision and direction for the Church, how do we know whether something is a 'God-idea' or simply a 'good idea'?

That's where one of the most unnoticed gifts comes to the fore. In terms of excitement, this gift is a bit of a Cinderella. It can't compete with healing and prophecy in terms of popular interest. But it is essential for Christians, and especially for those in any kind of leadership – leading a youth group, or a men's fellowship, for example. It is the gift of discernment of spirits (v.10). It helps us sense when agendas and drives are rooted not in the Spirit, but in the individual or group psyche. A gift to pray for!

Risen, ascended Lord,
as we rejoice at your triumph,
fill your Church on earth with power and compassion,
that all who are estranged by sin
may find forgiveness and know your peace,
to the glory of God the Father.

COLLECT

Wednesday 23 May

Psalms 2, **29** or 110, **111**, 112
1 Kings 19.1-18
Matthew 3.13-end

Matthew 3.13-end

'And a voice from heaven said, "This is my Son, the Beloved, with whom I am well pleased" ' (v.17)

It is generally reckoned that the baptism of Jesus marks a pretty important point. It features in all four Gospels, though John simply refers to the descent of the Spirit. It is important because it marks the start of the public ministry of Jesus, a beginning that will eventually lead to another baptism, that of death on a cross. It also marks the *character* of his ministry: his self-offering is not for his own sake, but on behalf of others.

So we might imagine that, at this start of the ministry, the Spirit, descending from heaven, would grant him a blueprint for the job ahead. After all, there was a huge task to be accomplished. But no. The word he is given is all about who he is. He is a son. He is greatly and dearly loved. The Father takes great delight in him. In other words, it's all about his identity, who-he-is-in-God. That's what kick-starts the ministry.

All service done in the name of Christ flows from this knowledge of being loved by the Father. It's an overflow of love, which we receive for ourselves and allow to flow from us to others. And over and over again, we have to return to the same place – receiving that word from God: 'You are my son, my daughter. You are dearly and deeply loved. I take great delight in you.'

COLLECT

O God the King of glory,
you have exalted your only Son Jesus Christ
with great triumph to your kingdom in heaven:
we beseech you, leave us not comfortless,
but send your Holy Spirit to strengthen us
and exalt us to the place
    where our Saviour Christ is gone before,
who is alive and reigns with you,
in the unity of the Holy Spirit,
one God, now and for ever.

Matthew 9.35 – 10.20

*'Whatever town or village you enter, find out who in it is worthy,
and stay there until you leave' (10.11)*

This passage is, not unnaturally, packed with the principles of Christian mission. There's the starting place of prayer (9.38), and of call and equipping (10.1). There's the clarity of focus: they know to whom they are sent (10.5,6). The mission is to be conducted both in word and in deed (10.7,8). And it's freely given – no fees!

Matthew suggests, through the coupling of the names, that they are sent out two by two – Luke's account of the sending of the 72 endorses this practice (Luke 10.1). As well as the practical companionship this provides, it also serves as a demonstration of the Spirit's presence in the Body of Christ. 'For where two or three are gathered in my name, I am there among them' (Matthew 18.20). Those whom they meet taste something of the reality of *koinonia*, 'participation in the Spirit'. They are invited *in* to something. The goal of the mission is not a cerebral assent to dogma but participation in a new life.

But this mini-community is not to be a ghetto. When they arrive in a village, they are to find a way of locking their little community onto someone else's (10.11). That gives the possibility of real communication, what postmodernists call 'flow'. It also means that the missioners are dependent upon those to whom they are sent. There is mutuality, a common sharing. No missionary compounds here!

Risen, ascended Lord,
as we rejoice at your triumph,
fill your Church on earth with power and compassion,
that all who are estranged by sin
may find forgiveness and know your peace,
to the glory of God the Father.

Friday 25 May

Matthew 12.22-32

'Therefore I tell you, people will be forgiven for every sin and blasphemy, but blasphemy against the Spirit will not be forgiven' (v.31)

Many people, when they read this passage, can become exceedingly anxious. How do we know whether we have sinned against the Spirit? What does it mean?

Well, the clue lies in the context. Jesus is gaining in popular support, through the extraordinary works of healing that he is doing (vv.22,23). This is a huge challenge to the religious leadership of the day. For the power that is so evident through 'the works' endorse his words and his teaching – and that means he really is a force to be reckoned with. Jealousy, fear and anger seem to have gripped many of the Pharisaic party. Because they are convinced that 'their way is the right way', they cannot face the possibility that Jesus really is 'God's person'. And so they choose to see him – and to label him publicly – as an agent of the devil. For them, good is evil, and evil is good.

Of course, many of us will have had all kinds of distorted views of 'who Jesus is' on the journey to faith. The sin which Jesus denounces is not about the muddle and confusion of people searching for the way. It is more about the persistent denial of – the determined resistance to – the truth of Jesus when it *has* been seen. I guess we could say, it's the tragic decision to say 'no' to the offer of God's life.

COLLECT

O God the King of glory,
you have exalted your only Son Jesus Christ
with great triumph to your kingdom in heaven:
we beseech you, leave us not comfortless,
but send your Holy Spirit to strengthen us
and exalt us to the place
    where our Saviour Christ is gone before,
who is alive and reigns with you,
in the unity of the Holy Spirit,
one God, now and for ever.

Psalms 42, **43** *or* 120, **121**, 122
Micah 3.1-8
Ephesians 6.10-20

Ephesians 6.10-20

'Finally, be strong in the Lord and in the strength of his power' (v.10)

The letter to the Ephesians is marked by the maturity and grandeur of Pauline thought. Probably written towards the end of Paul's life, it points to the glory of God in Christ and to the power that is available to his children; it urges the Christian community to be united in love and in holy living. This section, starting as it does with 'Finally ...' represents the culmination towards which the letter has been inevitably moving. What is that culmination? It is the setting of the Christian pilgrimage in the geography of spiritual conflict, of struggle.

Paul is not issuing here a physical 'call to arms'. Indeed, the great mark of the early Church was its love for its enemies. No, the battle is not against 'blood and flesh' (v.12). Yet there is a battle that rages, and the context of the life of faith is to be seen as one of struggle.

And so Paul issues his final charge: 'Be strong in the Lord and in his mighty power'. Long experience has taught him that he is strong only through and in Christ. 'Dependence' is the great lesson of true power. We cannot fabricate it ourselves. Nor are we called to press an advance, but simply to stand (vv.11,12,14), clothed in his provision and trusting in his victory. It is prayer – regular, alert and persistent – that is to be our chief endeavour (vv.18-20).

Risen, ascended Lord,
as we rejoice at your triumph,
fill your Church on earth with power and compassion,
that all who are estranged by sin
may find forgiveness and know your peace,
to the glory of God the Father.

COLLECT

Monday 28 May

Joshua 1

'... for the Lord your God is with you wherever you go' (v.9)

It is generally agreed that the Israelite conquest of the land began in the thirteenth century BC. Egypt's grip on Canaan was beginning to weaken, and the Canaanites themselves were not a cohesive community. Inhabiting small city-states, they had no dynamic common faith to weld them into one coherent force.

However, it is unlikely that the conquest of the land, described in Joshua 1 to 12, happened in quite the way that the writer laid out. The evidence, both archaeological and literary, points to a more patchy conquest, probably over a long period of time. There is evidence of the three main campaigns mentioned in Joshua, but the writer telescopes the scope and success of these into a glorious series of victories, whereas the reality was probably a slower and more haphazard advance.

What, then, can we gain from this rather exaggerated account of the conquest of Canaan? It is that, however it happened, the writer is at pains to underline that, for Israel, these victories were not achieved by their own military skill or clever strategy. The land of Canaan was won by the help and presence of Yahweh, the Lord God. The history of Israel is *his* story.

Learning to look at history with the eyes of faith is a completely different way of seeing the world – *his* world. How would we write our individual history with the eyes of faith?

COLLECT

O Lord, from whom all good things come:
grant to us your humble servants,
that by your holy inspiration
we may think those things that are good,
and by your merciful guiding may perform the same;
through our Lord Jesus Christ,
who is alive and reigns with you,
in the unity of the Holy Spirit,
one God, now and for ever.

Psalms **132**, 133
Joshua 2
Luke 9.28-36

Joshua 2

'So they went, and entered the house of a prostitute whose name was Rahab, and spent the night there' (v.1)

As we have seen, the writer of Joshua is writing history through the eyes of faith. But in spite of exaggerations, what we don't get is an attempt to airbrush people who, in other ways, might have failed the religious test. This is not 'religion' reading history and approving it – it is faith, a faith that sees God's activity in and through the most unlikely and odd and characterful people. The story of the spies and the prostitute is one such story. It's a robust story, not a sanitized one. Rahab earns a place in Israel's history, a place that persists into the Christian story – see Hebrews 11 and James 2.

When history is read with the eyes of faith, it does not require glossing over the many odd and difficult and complex parts of human existence. God is not a God of the unreal but of the real. The Old Testament positively bursts with real people, characters who live with mixed motives and very 'unreligious' sort of lives. It's life in the raw. Real people are messy. Lives are untidy. We get things wrong.

No, the God who reveals himself in history is not a sanitized, plastic sort of God. He's God of the real and he's not afraid of the dark, more complex bits of our lives. He's already met them – on the cross in his Son, Jesus.

O Lord, from whom all good things come:
grant to us your humble servants,
that by your holy inspiration
we may think those things that are good,
and by your merciful guiding may perform the same;
through our Lord Jesus Christ,
who is alive and reigns with you,
in the unity of the Holy Spirit,
one God, now and for ever.

Wednesday 30 May

Psalm 119.153-end
Joshua 3
Luke 9.37-50

Joshua 3

'Follow it, so that you may know the way you should go, for you have not passed this way before' (vv.3-4)

The crossing of the Jordan marked a symbolic as well as a strategic moment. Whatever the natural cause of the stopping of the waters – possibly a landslip, a regular feature of the area – the writer's interpretation is that this is the action of Yahweh. And for Israel, Yahweh – the Lord – is now closely identified with the Ark of the Lord (v.11). This is the sacred chest and its contents, the Ten Commandments on the two tablets of stone, which represent the covenant of Yahweh to Israel. And so Joshua instructs the people to follow the Ark (v.3).

This was not the first time that the Israelites had learned to follow the signs and symbols of Yahweh. Throughout their desert wanderings, they had followed a pillar of cloud by day and a pillar of fire by night, tracking the footsteps of the Spirit (Numbers 9.15-23). Now they have, in the Ark's contents, something more tangible – the revealed word of God to his people. And they are urged to follow 'for you have not passed this way before' (v.4).

We, in our time, are also travelling a way that we have not been before. As followers of Jesus, we face complex issues and critical questions. If we are to interpret the times, we too need a deep dependence upon the word of God – that Word that is both written revelation and the real presence of Jesus.

COLLECT

O Lord, from whom all good things come:
grant to us your humble servants,
that by your holy inspiration
we may think those things that are good,
and by your merciful guiding may perform the same;
through our Lord Jesus Christ,
who is alive and reigns with you,
in the unity of the Holy Spirit,
one God, now and for ever.

Psalms 85, 150
1 Samuel 2.1-10
Mark 3.31-end

**Visit of the Blessed Virgin Mary
to Elizabeth**

1 Samuel 2.1-10

*'Hannah prayed and said, "My heart exults in the Lord;
my strength is exalted in my God"' (v.1)*

Hannah's prayer is the forerunner of Mary's 'magnificat' (Luke 1.46-55). In fact, Mary would have been familiar with Hannah's prayer, so it is not surprising that Mary's song develops Hannah's rehearsal of God's greatness and his ability to reverse the natural orders of the creation and of human organization. It is in the timing of the two songs that the difference is seen. For Hannah's prayer is offered after the event of the birth of Samuel. By contrast, Mary's song is placed before she even has the evidence of pregnancy. It's a song of faith – 'for the Mighty One has done great things for me' (Luke 1.49) – based entirely on the words of promise (Luke 1.31).

Both Hannah's prayer and Mary's magnificat tell us something very important about prayer's perspective. Both women have discovered the importance of 'magnifying' the Lord. To magnify something is to enlarge it: it becomes larger, not in itself, but in our sight. So they build up images of God and his greatness, focusing on his goodness, his power, his majesty, his ability to reorder the world. They literally enlarge their vision of God. As they do, faith levels rise.

Praising God for who he is, whether we feel like it or not, enlarges our vision. We begin to see from another perspective. We find ourselves standing in a different place. Faith rises and from that perspective, anything can happen.

Mighty God,
by whose grace Elizabeth rejoiced with Mary
and greeted her as the mother of the Lord:
look with favour on your lowly servants
that, with Mary, we may magnify your holy name
and rejoice to acclaim her Son our Saviour,
who is alive and reigns with you,
in the unity of the Holy Spirit,
one God, now and for ever.

COLLECT

Friday 1 June

Joshua 5.2-end

*'"Are you one of us, or one of our adversaries?"
He replied, "Neither ..."' (vv.13-14)*

Something of a paradox emerges here. One side concerns election, being the people of promise. The men are marked through circumcision as belonging to the Lord. The rite of circumcision is thus endorsed, not just for those who have been delivered from Egypt, but as a mark of God's continuing covenant with his people, as they enter the Promised Land. They are God's chosen people.

The other side balances this. Israel is God's chosen people. They are marked with his sign. But that does not mean that God is their own household god, a domesticated god who will automatically bless only them. He is not a tribal god, he is the God of the whole earth. He is not partisan (v.14). It is his purpose at present to give them victory. But that is not because of favouritism; it is because he is working his purpose out for the salvation of the whole world.

Living with paradox, living 'between', is one of the most exhilarating aspects of being a Christian. It is exhilarating because it stretches us beyond our natural inclinations. We are not allowed to settle for an easy accommodation of our own prejudices and interests. As we hold together things that look contradictory, God enlarges our tent. Paradox pushes out the boundaries. Our tent grows more generous. God gets more space in us – and so do other people.

COLLECT

O Lord, from whom all good things come:
grant to us your humble servants,
that by your holy inspiration
we may think those things that are good,
and by your merciful guiding may perform the same;
through our Lord Jesus Christ,
who is alive and reigns with you,
in the unity of the Holy Spirit,
one God, now and for ever.

Joshua 6.1-20

*'The Lord said to Joshua, "See, I have handed Jericho over to you,
along with its king and soldiers" ' (v.2)*

Many children are introduced to the story of the fall of Jericho with a
song whose chorus resounds 'And the walls came a-tumbling down'.
In fact, archaeological study suggests those walls had been reduced to
rubble long before Joshua and his army appeared on the scene. It is
likely that the battle for Jericho was a more modest affair and that,
once again, the writer is telescoping events. He wants to underline the
fact that it was God's strategy – not Joshua's brilliant generalship –
that delivered Jericho into their hands.

The strategy was to show Israel something as well as the people of
Jericho. For it was all about the primacy of Yahweh, his primacy in the
life of Israel. Yahweh was to go first. He was leading the assault. The
seven priests were to carry the Ark of the Covenant as the vanguard.
The people were to follow. This was to be a show of strength. But
it wasn't a show of massed armoured vehicles, of tanks of Trident
missiles – or their equivalent. Nor was it a show of strength just to the
inhabitants of Jericho. It showed Israel just where their trust must lie
– in Yahweh.

Our culture admires strength. Yet Christians believe that true strength
is found when we acknowledge our weakness and dependence on
God. It's not force of personality that brings down walls of resistance
– it's God!

O Lord, from whom all good things come:
grant to us your humble servants,
that by your holy inspiration
we may think those things that are good,
and by your merciful guiding may perform the same;
through our Lord Jesus Christ,
who is alive and reigns with you,
in the unity of the Holy Spirit,
one God, now and for ever.

COLLECT

Monday 4 June

Psalms 1, 2, 3
Joshua 7.1-15
Luke 10.25-37

Joshua 7.1-15

'Stand up! Why have you fallen upon your face?' (v.10)

There is much truth in the old adage, 'Pride goes before a fall'. Self-confidence can all too easily replace confidence in God. After the great victory at Jericho, Joshua's reputation goes before him. He heads into the next, much smaller, battle without thinking to talk to God about it first. And his men are defeated.

Joshua vents his spleen on God. How could God allow this to happen? Can't God see that, as well as Joshua looking foolish, God doesn't look too great now either? Why on earth didn't they just stay where they were, comfortable on the other side of the Jordan, content with second best? There is great honesty in Joshua's prayer. He doesn't pretend to be polite and on his best behaviour with God. He tells it as it is.

And God's reaction? 'Don't just lie there feeling sorry for yourself. Get up! We have work to do.' God recognizes that Joshua got it wrong – but recognizes too the depth of Joshua's sorrow and shame. Joshua isn't pretending that everything is all right and trying to get along just fine without God. His overwhelming sorrow opens the door to let God back in – and God has plans for them.

'Lord, I shall be very busy this day. I may forget thee, but do not thou forget me' (Sir Jacob Astley preparing for battle in the English Civil War).

COLLECT

Almighty and everlasting God,
you have given us your servants grace,
by the confession of a true faith,
to acknowledge the glory of the eternal Trinity
and in the power of the divine majesty to worship the Unity:
keep us steadfast in this faith,
that we may evermore be defended from all adversities;
through Jesus Christ your Son our Lord,
who is alive and reigns with you,
in the unity of the Holy Spirit,
one God, now and for ever.

Psalms **5**, 6, (8)
Joshua 7.16-end
Luke 10.38-end

Joshua 7.16-end

'Why did you bring trouble on us?' (v.25)

Tribe by tribe, clan by clan, family by family, household by household – all are examined and, eventually, Achan is identified as the one who stole from the spoil that should have been destroyed according to God's instructions. The theft is bad enough, but Achan's actions have a much more profound significance. Not only has he disgraced himself and his family, but his actions also have consequences for the whole community.

As a Church we are a family. When one person goes astray, it has consequences for all of us. For that reason, all of us, but perhaps Church leaders in particular, can't turn a blind eye to things that are clearly wrong. Stoning and burning are somewhat extreme, but we get the message. If we ignore words or actions that are clearly contrary to all that God wants for us, we have to be courageous and tackle those concerned head on.

In the light of Jesus' death and resurrection, confession and absolution can restore wrong relationships and offer us a means of grace. But strong and wise leadership is vital for the well-being of the Church, and leadership sometimes means having to take difficult decisions when we know, in our heart of hearts, that action must be taken for the well-being of all God's people.

Holy God,
faithful and unchanging:
enlarge our minds with the knowledge of your truth,
and draw us more deeply into the mystery of your love,
that we may truly worship you,
Father, Son and Holy Spirit,
one God, now and for ever.

COLLECT

Joshua 8.1-29

'Do not fear or be dismayed' (v.1)

This account of the defeat of Ai restores Joshua's dented reputation as a strong and wise military leader who uses not just brute force, but stealth and steady tactics to bring victory over the Israelites' enemies.

The lesson is clear for all to see. Active disobedience or sloppy inattention in our relationship with God brings unhappy results. Honest soul-searching, heartfelt confession and a will to do better brings swift forgiveness. Careful listening and the desire to stay close to God brings ultimate victory. There is no need to fear or to be dismayed. With God, we are always on the winning side, even if in the process of winning the war we lose the odd battle along the way.

But this passage says something too about patience and about strategy. Sometimes we dive straight into battle, knowing what we want the end result to be, and rushing headlong into action. Joshua waits on God and then uses a tactical approach, with crab-like movements, to achieve a far more lasting victory.

How patient are you in listening to God? Taking small and steady steps can achieve far more than going in 'all guns blazing'. How ready are you to trust in those small, steady steps?

Psalm 147
Deuteronomy 8.2-16
1 Corinthians 10.1-17

Day of Thanksgiving for the Institution of the Holy Communion (Corpus Christi)

1 Corinthians 10.1-17

"… we who are many are one body, for we all partake of the one bread' (v.17)

The words quoted above are familiar to us from our service of Holy Communion. So familiar, perhaps, that their impact can be lost on us. Paul isn't simply saying that because we all share one bread at a common meal, that makes us into one body. It's not the common action of eating together that binds us. Something much more profound lies at the heart of the 'one bread'.

'The bread that we break, is it not a sharing in the body of Christ?' asks Paul. When we share bread and wine at the Eucharist, we are active partners in Christ's death and resurrection and so become one with him – and at the same time, one with those who share that same participation with us. We become one body – and no one who shares the same bread and same cup can be separated from us without destroying that same body.

That's why unity is so crucial to the well-being of the Church, and why it should cause such profound distress when any Christian says that they have no need of their fellow Christian. This sharing in the body and blood of Christ is central to all that we are and all that we do.

What obstacle to oneness in Christ might you try to remove today?

COLLECT

Lord Jesus Christ,
we thank you that in this wonderful sacrament
you have given us the memorial of your passion:
grant us so to reverence the sacred mysteries
of your body and blood
that we may know within ourselves
and show forth in our lives
the fruits of your redemption;
for you are alive and reign with the Father
in the unity of the Holy Spirit,
one God, now and for ever.

167

Friday 8 June

Joshua 9.3-26

'And Joshua made peace with them' (v.15)

It's always painful to realize that you've been deceived, that someone you have always trusted has let you down and been less than honest with you. Or when a newcomer you hoped might become a friend and ally has been economical with the truth, leaving you high and dry. Joshua must have felt angry, embarrassed and let down when he discovered that the Gibeonites were not after all strangers from a far-off land, committed to God's cause and willing to travel for days on end to join Joshua's people, but locals, fearful for their lives and cunning in their understandable desire to avoid capture and defeat.

Joshua's embarrassment is complete when, 'all the congregation murmured against the leaders' rebuking them for their gullibility. The temptation to throw out the Gibeonites and to punish them for their deceit must have been very strong indeed.

But Joshua acts with the utmost integrity. He risks the anger of his own people in order to honour the covenant he has made with these strangers. His word is his word. He promises to let them stay and to protect them, on the understanding that they become servants and add something positive and practical to the life of the community.

Integrity, a refusal to be swayed by the crowd, the willingness to compromise, an ability to make the best of a less-than-perfect situation – all are qualities needed in our leaders, both ordained and lay, in our Church today.

COLLECT

Almighty and everlasting God,
you have given us your servants grace,
by the confession of a true faith,
to acknowledge the glory of the eternal Trinity
and in the power of the divine majesty to worship the Unity:
keep us steadfast in this faith,
that we may evermore be defended from all adversities;
through Jesus Christ your Son our Lord,
who is alive and reigns with you,
in the unity of the Holy Spirit,
one God, now and for ever.

Joshua 10.1-15

'And the sun stood still, and the moon stopped ...' (v.13)

The news of the peace treaty between Joshua and the Gibeonites was not well received in the surrounding cities. The king of Jerusalem expresses his fears to his neighbouring leaders and together they plot to overthrow Gibeon. When Joshua hears what is afoot, he is determined to honour the covenant he has made with the Gibeonites, and, putting his trust in God and God's will for his people, he leads his troops into battle.

We could spend all day discussing what actually happened with the hailstones. Whatever it was, the Israelites could only conclude that God had somehow got involved in a very practical way on their behalf. And what of the sun and the moon? How could they 'stand still'? Was it some sort of eclipse? It is impossible to know. But whatever happened, Joshua recognized that God had somehow intervened to help his people. Something had happened that could only be described in terms of the miraculous.

How willing are we to look for the miraculous? How easily do we accept that when we pray things happen which we simply don't understand? How willing are we to thank God for the manner in which he sometimes intervenes in ways which we could never have foreseen? Do we believe that God can still perform miracles? Are we willing to trust that he might?

Monday 11 June

Barnabas the Apostle

Psalms 100, 101, 117
Jeremiah 9.23-24
Acts 4.32-end

Acts 4.32-end

'Barnabas (which means "son of encouragement")' (v.36)

Barnabas leads the way when it comes to generosity and encouragement. The members of the early Church lived as one big family, sharing all they had. They took seriously the promise found in the book of Deuteronomy that there should be no poor among God's people – and they lived out that promise by asking everyone to give everything that they had to the common cause. In that way, the richer members subsidized the poorer members and no one was in any kind of need.

If only we lived with that same vision of generosity and common purpose today, there would be far less of a gap between rich and poor, between the obese and the starving, between those in security-protected, lavish homes and those who live on the streets.

In the Anglican Communion, wealthy dioceses often support poorer ones; likewise, richer parishes often subsidize poorer ones so that everyone has a parish priest, regardless of whether or not they can afford one. Thankfully, many take that charge seriously. But, sadly, many don't, and cling on to their 'reserves'. Somewhere along the line, we've lost the will to share what we have, unless that sharing doesn't cost us very much at all.

But Barnabas sells his field and gives the proceeds to the apostles. He models the kind of self-giving, abundant generosity that God shows towards us.

Why do we find it so difficult to do the same?

COLLECT

Bountiful God, giver of all gifts,
who poured your Spirit upon your servant Barnabas
and gave him grace to encourage others:
help us, by his example,
to be generous in our judgements
and unselfish in our service;
through Jesus Christ your Son our Lord,
who is alive and reigns with you,
in the unity of the Holy Spirit,
one God, now and for ever.

Tuesday 12 June

Joshua 21.43 – 22.8

'... serve him with all your heart and with all your soul' (22.5)

Back to Joshua and we jump to Chapter 21, missing out on rather a large slice of the action in the omitted chapters where, battle after battle, Joshua has gone on to conquer another 31 cities. We have skipped a number of years, but the conclusion reached is a simple one: 'Thus the Lord gave to Israel all the land that he swore to their ancestors that he would give them; and having taken possession of it, they settled there' (v.43).

The great effort is over, the land is conquered, the people can settle and rest. Peace and prosperity look certain for the foreseeable future. Perhaps Joshua knows at a very deep level that, now the immediate danger has passed, his people can relax and let down their guard, how easy it will be for them to forget the God who has made all this possible. God has brought them into the Promised Land. How soon will it be before they begin to think they don't need God any more?

It's at the most difficult times in our life that we lean most heavily on God. Our prayer in times of stress, illness or despair have an edge to them that is sometimes lost when the pressure is off. So Joshua reminds his people to remember the commandments, to walk in God's ways, to hold fast to him, to serve him with heart and soul.

How easily do we forget God when life is good?

O God,
the strength of all those who put their trust in you,
mercifully accept our prayers
and, because through the weakness of our mortal nature
we can do no good thing without you,
grant us the help of your grace,
that in the keeping of your commandments
we may please you both in will and deed;
through Jesus Christ your Son our Lord,
who is alive and reigns with you,
in the unity of the Holy Spirit,
one God, now and for ever.

COLLECT

Wednesday 13 June

Psalm **34**
Joshua 22.9-end
Luke 12.22-31

Joshua 22.9-end

'What is this treachery that you have committed?' (v.16)

Why do we find it so difficult to live in harmony with one another? What is it in human beings that causes us to seek out conflict and to be so ready to argue and fight? Joshua has just sent his people out to settle in the good land God has given them and, moments later, they are at each other's throats. Word reaches the Israelites that the eastern tribes have built an altar – and it's big. Big means threatening. What are they up to? The Israelites get ready for a fight.

We can only begin to imagine the bloodbath that would have ensued if the Israelites had gone straight into battle as a result of the rumour they had heard. But, thankfully, they decided first to send a delegation to find out what was going on. And soon an explanation – a very reasonable explanation – is delivered. The new altar isn't, after all, an act of rebellion. It is a symbol of unity, a sign of common heritage with the Israelites. The Israelites are satisfied and head back home in peace. Disaster averted.

How quickly rumours can be interpreted as truth. How swiftly we can act on something we've heard without ever questioning the reality behind the story. Today's passage teaches us something very important indeed about going to the source of a rumour and finding out for ourselves what's really happened. By so doing, a costly conflict could be avoided.

COLLECT

O God,
the strength of all those who put their trust in you,
mercifully accept our prayers
and, because through the weakness of our mortal nature
we can do no good thing without you,
grant us the help of your grace,
that in the keeping of your commandments
we may please you both in will and deed;
through Jesus Christ your Son our Lord,
who is alive and reigns with you,
in the unity of the Holy Spirit,
one God, now and for ever.

Psalm **37***
Joshua 23
Luke 12.32-40

Joshua 23

'I am now old and well advanced in years' (v.2)

Joshua's work is done. He has been faithful to his calling and God's people are now settled in the land he has given to them. It's time for Joshua to step back and rest. He gathers the leaders of Israel around him and offers them his final reflections, together with words of instruction and advice. They are to remember God's covenant and to know that God will never leave them or let them down. They are to play their part in the covenant relationship by remembering God, putting him first, and staying true to his ways. They are to remain aware of the consequences of turning their backs on God, whether deliberately or carelessly.

And the people listen. They know that Joshua's words are spoken after years of contemplating God's ways. They know that, with age, comes wisdom. Words spoken take on a whole new meaning when death approaches. There isn't time for casual speech.

We're not always good at taking the elderly seriously. We live in a society that places its value on the vigour of youth rather than the wisdom of old age. Those whose years are long, and who have reflected on their own mortality, have important truths to teach – if we will but take the time to listen.

COLLECT

God of truth,
help us to keep your law of love
and to walk in ways of wisdom,
that we may find true life
in Jesus Christ your Son.

Joshua 24.1-28

'... as for me and my household, we will serve the Lord' (v.15)

Joshua's parting shot is to throw out a challenge to his people who already were beginning to forget what God had done for them. They were starting to lose their cutting edge, and were flirting with idols and foreign gods. Joshua must have felt something close to despair when he saw how easily their faith in God would slip and slide away.

So he reminds them how far they have come. Beginning with Abraham, he recounts the story of God's people and reminds them of just how much God has done for them. Retelling our story – remembrance – is a vital element of faith. It's what we do each time we celebrate the Eucharist. We retell the story of all that God has done for us. Lest we forget.

And then he throws out the challenge. 'Choose this day whom you will serve' (v15). Who is it going to be – the foreign gods or the one true God? Make a decision.

How often do we challenge each other and ourselves about where our allegiance lies? What's it to be on Sunday – shopping and football practice – or worshipping God? What's it to be – a narrow focus on money and ambition, or a lifestyle that places God at its centre?

To follow Christ is a conscious decision – and one that we're challenged to renew from time to time, so that we can say with hand on heart, 'As for me – I will serve the Lord.'

COLLECT

O God,
the strength of all those who put their trust in you,
mercifully accept our prayers
and, because through the weakness of our mortal nature
we can do no good thing without you,
grant us the help of your grace,
that in the keeping of your commandments
we may please you both in will and deed;
through Jesus Christ your Son our Lord,
who is alive and reigns with you,
in the unity of the Holy Spirit,
one God, now and for ever.

Psalms 41, **42**, 43
Joshua 24.29-end
Luke 12.49-end

Joshua 24.29-end

'After these things Joshua son of Nun, the servant of the Lord, died'
(v.29)

Joshua's earthly life reaches an end and, his work done, he is buried in the land that God had promised to his people. The bodies of Joseph and Aaron's son Eleazar are also brought to their final resting place. There is a satisfying sense of completion. And Joshua's greatest epitaph lies in verse 31 where we're told that 'Israel served the Lord' for many years to come.

We may not know how our lives will pan out, but of one thing we can be sure. One day our bones will be laid to rest, our life complete, our work done. What will be our epitaph?

There is a spiritual exercise that can help us to set the compass. Take some time out to imagine that you are at your own funeral. Picture the scene – the music, the flowers, the faces of those who have come to say farewell. Imagine that a close family member stands up to speak. What would you like them to say? A friend or neighbour stands. What do they say? A colleague from work stands up to say a few words on behalf of those who have worked alongside you down the years. How would you best like to be remembered?

When you know how you'd like to be remembered, you can begin to live in such a way that might make it possible.

God of truth,
help us to keep your law of love
and to walk in ways of wisdom,
that we may find true life
in Jesus Christ your Son.

COLLECT

Monday 18 June

Judges 2

'... he gave them over to plunderers who plundered them' (v.14)

The book of Judges narrates the period between the entry into the Promised Land and the rise of the monarchy (1250–1020 BC). It covers the same ground as the book of Joshua, but there are important differences. In Joshua, we read about the twelve tribes of Israel as a united force, before which Yahweh (the Lord) drove out the original inhabitants of the land; in Judges, on the other hand, we see a more fragmented picture, in which not only is there real resistance, but fighting between the tribes of Israel as well.

The editors of the book of Judges (probably working in the sixth and fifth centuries BC) decry this fragmentation as a way of promoting the monarchy (18.1) and the House of Judah (1.2). The political chaos is put down to the disobedience of the Israelites, which goes in the cycles outlined here in chapter 2: Yahweh offers a leader who governs well (2.7); the Israelites obey for a while by worshipping Yahweh and not intermarrying and are consequently politically successful (2.8-9); however, then they disobey and begin to assimilate socially and culturally, turning to other gods (2.10-13); Yahweh abandons them to the consequences of their actions (2.14-15), before intervening to raise up another leader (2.16).

There are many difficult issues raised by the book of Judges for today's readers. Central is the question of land. Did (does) God give land to one group at the expense of another? Is political victory a sign of God's favour? Does God reward loyalty with prosperity? Is segregation the way to relate to other cultures and religious groups? Current events in Israel/Palestine and in other parts of the world highlight the fact that these are questions none of us can ignore.

COLLECT

Lord, you have taught us
that all our doings without love are nothing worth:
send your Holy Spirit
and pour into our hearts that most excellent gift of love,
the true bond of peace and of all virtues,
without which whoever lives is counted dead before you.
Grant this for your only Son Jesus Christ's sake,
who is alive and reigns with you,
in the unity of the Holy Spirit,
one God, now and for ever.

Psalm **48**, 50
Judges 4.1-23
Luke 13.10-21

Judges 4.1-23

'... for the Lord will sell Sisera into the hand of a woman' (v.9)

One of the difficult issues in the book of Judges for contemporary readers is the degree of violence within it. In this passage what stands out is Jael's murder of the enemy general: she is prepared to feign hospitality and then drive a tent peg into Sisera's head.

There is plenty of evidence of violence against women and of women as victims in this book. Women are raped (5.30); women are sacrificed to save men's skins (11.31); women are enslaved by the hundred (21.14). This was a fact of life in the period, and remains a fact of life in much of the world today. This passage, however, highlights the ways in which women, even in a patriarchal society, are also moral agents, capable of being called by God and needing to discern their courses of action within a complex world in which innocence is not an option.

Jael's violence may repel us – partly because it contradicts our gender stereotype that a woman's role is to offer hospitality – but it is also possible to read Jael as the deliverer of Israel for, according to Deborah, it is Yahweh who will 'sell Sisera into the hand of a woman' (4.9).

Whatever our sympathies, the book of Judges presents a complex world in which the moral choices of individuals are embedded. It is no less complex than the world in which we have to make our own moral choices. It asks us: 'What are the difficult moral choices we face in which innocence is not an option?'

Faithful Creator,
whose mercy never fails:
deepen our faithfulness to you
and to your living Word,
Jesus Christ our Lord.

COLLECT

Wednesday 20 June

Judges 5

*'Most blessed of women be Jael ...
of tent-dwelling women most blessed' (v.24)*

Chapter 5 retells the events of chapter 4, but this time in song and, as often in poetry, there are cross-references to other acts of God that help to reinforce this victory as the work of Yahweh. In particular, the location of the battle at the rushing torrent of the Kishon (5.21) and the mention of the beating of horses' hoofs (5.22) evokes the drowning of Pharaoh's chariots in the Red Sea. The song-writers are adding the victory of Barak and Deborah, and Jael's killing of Sisera, to the litany of God's mighty acts in saving and protecting Israel. The song performs something of the function that the Great Prayer of Thanksgiving performs within the Eucharist as we recite the actions of God in saving his people.

It is striking, however, that although the Exodus is an event that Christians are happy to incorporate into the Eucharistic prayer, the killing of Sisera is not. How events and heroes are selected for inclusion in the canon and the liturgy is an important gauge of values and beliefs. The book of Judges has often been source-mined for its Sunday School heroes – mostly Gideon and Samson rather than Deborah and Jael – but the more difficult issues of interpretation have been largely ignored.

This raises the question of why we read Scripture at all and what authority we give it. Is it better to read only the parts of Scripture that seem to be central to the Christian faith? Or should we persist with reading the whole and so have to face the difficult questions posed there?

COLLECT

Lord, you have taught us
that all our doings without love are nothing worth:
send your Holy Spirit
and pour into our hearts that most excellent gift of love,
the true bond of peace and of all virtues,
without which whoever lives is counted dead before you.
Grant this for your only Son Jesus Christ's sake,
who is alive and reigns with you,
in the unity of the Holy Spirit,
one God, now and for ever.

Judges 6.1-24

'I have seen the angel of the Lord face to face' (v.22)

Gideon is one of the heroes of the book of Judges. Usually, his example is cited to encourage the least to believe that they can be good servants of God (v.15). Gideon, however, is not only the youngest from the smallest clan (the Abiezrites) of the smallest tribe (Manasseh), he is also a coward who does his threshing in hiding in the wine press rather than risk a confrontation with the Midianites – a fact pointed out by the angel of the Lord, who, with heavy irony, addresses him as a 'mighty warrior' (v.12).

If the angel's approach is ironic, Gideon's response is sceptical. Having protested his lack of qualifications, he demands a sign that this messenger truly is speaking for Yahweh. Like Abraham and Sarah before him, he prepares food for his guest (Genesis 18.6-8), though it is not clear what kind of sign Gideon is expecting. Nevertheless, the consuming of the food by fire and the vanishing of the angel are common enough confirmations of Yahweh's presence (cf. 1 Kings 18.38) to convince him.

The interchangeability of 'the Lord' and the 'angel of the Lord' is a common feature of 'angel' stories in the Hebrew Scriptures, like the angel who went before the Israelites through the Red Sea (Exodus 14), the angelic visitors to Abraham (Genesis 18) and the angel who spoke to Elijah in the desert (1 Kings 19). It raises for us the question of how God communicates with us and how we recognize that it is God we are encountering.

Faithful Creator,
whose mercy never fails:
deepen our faithfulness to you
and to your living Word,
Jesus Christ our Lord.

COLLECT

Friday 22 June

Judges 6.25-end

'... the spirit of the Lord took possession of Gideon' (v.34)

Chapter 6 continues to provide evidence of Gideon's unsuitability as a deliverer for Israel. Still uncertain that it is Yahweh who is calling him, Gideon asks for another sign. Unfortunately, his first request is unlikely to prove anything. Gideon seems to realize that he is testing God's patience (6.39) when he has to devise another trial, this time asking for the more unlikely outcome of the dew avoiding the fleece.

Part of the point of Gideon's unsuitability is to emphasize how it is God who is delivering Israel from the oppression of the Midianites and not Gideon himself. The problem with the Israelites' behaviour is that they keep turning away from Yahweh and trusting in the prosperity gods of the local people. It is only when the Spirit of God takes hold of Gideon and he trusts in Yahweh that his actions are effective.

In a nutshell, this is the message of the book of Judges; it is when Israel depends on Yahweh that things go well for them. It is not that Yahweh abandons Israel (contrary to Gideon's assertion in 6.13), but that Israel keeps abandoning Yahweh (6.1). Even so, Yahweh bears with Israel as he bears with Gideon's repeated requests for signs. He allows the Israelites to experience the consequences of their faithlessness through repeated occupations, but nevertheless keeps working to fashion their salvation. He even chooses the most unlikely heroes in the hope that they will attribute their rescue to him and not to their human leaders.

COLLECT

Lord, you have taught us
that all our doings without love are nothing worth:
send your Holy Spirit
and pour into our hearts that most excellent gift of love,
the true bond of peace and of all virtues,
without which whoever lives is counted dead before you.
Grant this for your only Son Jesus Christ's sake,
who is alive and reigns with you,
in the unity of the Holy Spirit,
one God, now and for ever.

Psalm **68**
Judges 7
Luke 14.25-end

Judges 7

'With the three hundred that lapped I will deliver you' (v.7)

The question that comes to the fore in this chapter concerns how we think God works in the world. Is it through the extraordinary or through the ordinary? The battle, here, is set up to be something extraordinary – a miracle in the sense that the outcome defies the ordinary rules of the universe: a force of 300 soldiers who lap like dogs (v.7) should not cause a great army to flee. For this to happen, there must have been divine intervention (v.2). The focus of the story, as far as the editors of Judges are concerned, is to underline Yahweh's authority and provoke the Israelites to trust in Yahweh rather than in their own strength.

This focus is underlined by the use of Gideon's new name – Jerubbaal ('let Ba'al contend with me'). This he acquired having pulled down an altar to Ba'al (Judges 6.32). The point here is that, whereas the Ba'als, in their impotence, have failed to avenge themselves on Gideon, Yahweh does not need people to contend for him. Rather, he is powerful enough to achieve his own purposes, even through the most ludicrous of agents.

The implication is not that God cannot act through ordinary means, but that when he does so, people are unlikely to notice. In the Bible, demanding a sign is often an act of faithlessness (see Matthew 12.39), when holding the universe in being day by day is, in itself, a sign of God's power and self-giving love. Have you ever asked for a sign? How did you interpret the response?

Faithful Creator,
whose mercy never fails:
deepen our faithfulness to you
and to your living Word,
Jesus Christ our Lord.

COLLECT

Monday 25 June

Psalm 71
Judges 8.22-end
Luke 15.1-10

Judges 8.22-end

'... and it became a snare to Gideon and to his family' (v.27)

One of the roles that Judges plays in the canon of Scripture is to make the case for a monarchy in order to hold together the tribes of Israel; in that case, this story about Gideon is a problem. Gideon is asked to become King and for his sons to rule after him (v.22). He refuses on the grounds that Yahweh is the one who rules Israel, and Gideon should not be confused with him (v.23). At face value, this passage makes the opposite case that Israel is more likely to be faithful to Yahweh without a monarchy to idolize.

However, nothing is that simple. Two elements suggest that whatever Gideon's fine words, there were other motives in play. First, Gideon melts down the spoils of war to make an 'ephod' (v.27). Ephods feature in several guises in the Bible. At times they seem to have been undergarments (see 2 Samuel 6.14), and at other times ceremonial garments associated with prophecy (see Exodus 28). In this case, however, it is clear that, whatever Gideon's motivation in making one, it became an idolatrous object of worship and a danger to Gideon himself.

Secondly, Gideon's seventy-first son was named Abimelech (v.31), which means 'my father is king'. The name seems to suggest that, despite Gideon's refusal, he was either *de facto* king, or was made so in retrospect, to justify Abimelech's claim to rule over Israel (9.2).

Power is said to corrupt. What experience do you have of finding yourself (sometimes against your best intentions) drawn to rely on someone or something thing that is less than God?

COLLECT

Almighty God,
you have broken the tyranny of sin
and have sent the Spirit of your Son into our hearts
    whereby we call you Father:
give us grace to dedicate our freedom to your service,
that we and all creation may be brought
    to the glorious liberty of the children of God;
through Jesus Christ your Son our Lord,
who is alive and reigns with you,
in the unity of the Holy Spirit,
one God, now and for ever.

Psalm **73**
Judges 9.1-21
Luke 15.11-end

Judges 9.1-21

'So all the trees said to the bramble, "You come and reign over us"'
(v.14)

It is clear that the editors of the book of Judges are not fans of Abimelech. Shechem – where his mother came from (8.31) – was a Caananite independent city state, and it is probable that she was not an Israelite. As ever, the 'prostitution' of Israel by taking local wives and concubines is associated with the sin of idolatry (see the book of Hosea, for example). So it is unsurprising that Abimelech, the result of this union, makes a pact with the lords of Shechem to secure his succession to the throne of Israel, even using money from the temple of the Ba'als to achieve it (v.4).

From then on, Abimelech is an 'anti-hero' on the grounds that he had taken the throne by force, slaughtering all seventy of his brothers except for Jotham, the youngest, who had managed to hide (v.5). It is Jotham, then, who becomes the hero of the passage. His weapons are words, which he delivers to the rulers of Shechem in the form of a parable about the consequences of choosing Abimelech as their leader (vv.8-20). Although Jotham, as a rival claimant, is undoubtedly biased, he compares the selection of Abimelech as being like choosing a bramble when there are cedars of Lebanon available – brambles, unlike vines and figs and olive trees, are associated with wilderness and neglected gardens (cf. Isaiah 5).

He is clear that undiscerning people get the leadership they deserve (v.19). Is it the case in our society that we get the leadership we deserve?

God our saviour,
look on this wounded world
in pity and in power;
hold us fast to your promises of peace
won for us by your Son,
our Saviour Jesus Christ.

COLLECT

Judges 9.22-end

'Thus God repaid Abimelech for the crime he committed against his father' (v.56)

This section of chapter 9 reads like a morality tale. The moral of the story is that God is not mocked. Abimelech took the throne by force, but the deaths of his 70 brothers will not go unavenged (v.54). Likewise, the rulers of Shechem will not go unpunished for their support of an unworthy candidate for the throne (v.49).

As ever, there seem to be contradictions: why is Abimelech's brutality decried when the violence of other leaders is celebrated? Why is Gideon revered as a hero of Israel (Judges 9.17) when Israel clearly lapses into idolatry under his rule, whereas Abimelech is discredited for allowing such lapses (vv.24-7)? It even seems to be a good thing that the Israelite army give up and go home when Abimelech is killed (v.55) because thereby justice is served.

Sometimes, in reading the book of Judges, it seems that God is on the side of the victors and no more. At other times, there are clearly political agendas in which one dynasty is being preferred over another. Interwoven are deeper concerns about morality and justice, and the character of Yahweh and of Israel. In that sense, the avenging of the 70 sons of Gideon reveals a wrestling for the moral character of a nation, however distant that moral code seems to twenty-first-century Western ears. What are the issues at stake in the wrestling for the moral character of our own nation at the moment?

COLLECT

Almighty God,
you have broken the tyranny of sin
and have sent the Spirit of your Son into our hearts
    whereby we call you Father:
give us grace to dedicate our freedom to your service,
that we and all creation may be brought
    to the glorious liberty of the children of God;
through Jesus Christ your Son our Lord,
who is alive and reigns with you,
in the unity of the Holy Spirit,
one God, now and for ever.

Psalm **78.**1-39*
Judges 11.1-11
Luke 16.19-end

Judges 11.1-11

'... I cannot take back my vow' (v.35)

The name Jephthah means 'he opens' and it refers to Jephthah's oath (Judges 11.30) that, if Yahweh would give him the victory over the Ammonites, he would offer as a burnt offering the first thing over the threshold of his house on his return.

Jephthah's desperation to be successful over the Ammonites is understandable. His own sense of belonging and worth was riding on it, having been driven away from his father's house because he was the son of a prostitute (v.2). Military success would guarantee him citizenship and respect. In the event, however, this came at a terrible price. The first thing across the threshold after Jephthah's victory was his only beloved daughter (Judges 11.35). After a stay of execution of two months to lament the life she would not live to enjoy (Judges 11.37-8), he fulfilled the vow and sacrificed her.

Sacrifice is a core value for Christians, but the story of Jephthah raises hard questions about its motives and its consequences. Are we to conclude that oaths should be kept whatever the price? Are we to conclude that Jephthah is driven by powerfully unconscious motives that obscure and cloud his judgement? Are we to regard Jephthah's oath as a sign that he thought God would not honour the promise he had already made to him? Has this oath, in fact, anything to do with God, who did not require it and, unlike in the case of Isaac (Genesis 22), did not supply a ram as a substitute?

And for us, under what circumstances it is right to sacrifice something precious?

God our saviour,
look on this wounded world
in pity and in power;
hold us fast to your promises of peace
won for us by your Son,
our Saviour Jesus Christ.

COLLECT

185

Friday 29 June

Peter the Apostle

Psalms 71, 113
Isaiah 49.1-6
Acts 11.1-18

Acts 11.1-18

'Why did you go to uncircumcised men and eat with them?' (v.3)

It is difficult for us today to recapture the shock of this passage for the Jewish Christian community. Again and again in the book of Acts, the same story is repeated: gentile believers present themselves for baptism – and, just as the Holy Spirit descended on Jesus at his baptism (Acts 10.38), so the Holy Spirit falls upon these men from Caesarea (v.15) while they are still uncircumcised.

The evidence of the work of the Holy Spirit became the keystone of the argument for not requiring circumcision of gentile believers at the council of Jerusalem (15.8-10). For a community who for generations had associated gentiles with idolatry and an unholy assimilation, this was a radical step. It raised all kinds of theological questions about the status of the law and the covenant. It also raised practical questions that Jewish communities had never had to confront before – could they eat meat previously offered to idols? How much of the Levitical code could be discarded? Could there be different ethical codes for Jewish and gentile Christians? Could gentiles be in leadership?

The message given to Peter was unequivocal: 'The Spirit told me ... not to make a distinction between them and us' (v.12). This would mean not merely the toleration of gentile Christians, but their acceptance as equals. This would require changes of the Jewish Christians whose own norms would need adjustment in the light of the values of those coming from a different culture, and the grace, before too long, to allow the gentile Christians to shape the movement for themselves.

COLLECT

Almighty God,
who inspired your apostle Saint Peter
to confess Jesus as Christ and Son of the living God:
build up your Church upon this rock,
that in unity and peace it may proclaim one truth
and follow one Lord, your Son our Saviour Christ,
who is alive and reigns with you,
in the unity of the Holy Spirit,
one God, now and for ever.

Judges 12.1-7

'Then Jephthah gathered all the men of Gilead and fought with Ephraim' (v.4)

One debate that surrounds Jephthah is whether he was a deliverer of Israel. The classic features of a deliverer story were set out in chapter 2: Israel does evil and worships other gods; Yahweh transfers Israel to an enemy power; Israel cries out to Yahweh; Yahweh raises up a deliverer; Yahweh overcomes the enemy; the land has a rest under a judge.

At the beginning of the story of Jephthah (Judges 10.6), Israel is certainly presented as doing evil in the sight of Yahweh and, for that reason, they were sold into the hand of the Philistines and the Ammonites. This led the Israelites to cry out for help to Yahweh (Judges 10.10) and to repent of their idolatries (Judges 10.16). Jephthah is certainly the one who is raised up to deliver them – and yet, unlike other deliverers like Gideon, it was not the angel of the Lord who went to seek him out but the elders of Gilead.

This time, too, unlike Gideon, Jephthah has obvious aptitude for the task. When he is called a 'mighty warrior' (Judges 11.1, cf 6.12), there is no irony intended. But this time, too, Jephthah relies on his own strength rather than on Yahweh, making his rash promise in order to secure his victory (Judges 11.30-31).

If Jephthah is a deliverer, this is Yahweh using someone of talent but of little faith to fulfil his promises to Israel. If not, this is just another episode in the futile tribal politics that end with Israel occupying no more land than it did at the beginning of Judges. If so, perhaps there are lessons for the world to learn from that.

COLLECT

Almighty God,
you have broken the tyranny of sin
and have sent the Spirit of your Son into our hearts
whereby we call you Father:
give us grace to dedicate our freedom to your service,
that we and all creation may be brought
to the glorious liberty of the children of God;
through Jesus Christ your Son our Lord,
who is alive and reigns with you,
in the unity of the Holy Spirit,
one God, now and for ever.

Monday 2 July

Psalms **80**, 82
Judges 13.1-24
Luke 17.20-end

Judges 13.1-24

'... you shall conceive and bear a son' (v.3)

These words, in this verse, are a sign of how much God focuses the forces of new life, in order to bring deliverance into the world through a person, in this case, Samson. Samson is called to liberate Israel at a time when the whole judges system of leadership is losing its effectiveness, and the social and spiritual condition of Israel itself is disintegrating. The fresh, new, life-giving energy of God coming through in this birth will meet significant resistance – both in the minds and hearts of the people as well as the consciousness and behaviour of the leadership. Samson 'shall begin to deliver Israel from the hand of the Philistines', as mentioned in verse 5, but this liberation will be imperfect and incomplete.

So it has been throughout history. God is always coming through with grace, justice and love, and we so often meet it with half-belief, human frailty and partial vision. In Christ, who was conceived and born by God's grace, God's incarnation is whole and full. The resistance continues, but its power has been finally, fundamentally overcome within our hearts and minds.

'Nothing can separate us from the love of God in Christ Jesus' (Romans 8.39) – this is the basis of our only hope, personally, culturally and politically.

COLLECT

O God, the protector of all who trust in you,
without whom nothing is strong, nothing is holy:
increase and multiply upon us your mercy;
that with you as our ruler and guide
we may so pass through things temporal
that we lose not our hold on things eternal;
grant this, heavenly Father,
for our Lord Jesus Christ's sake,
who is alive and reigns with you,
in the unity of the Holy Spirit,
one God, now and for ever.

Psalms 92, 146
2 Samuel 15.17-21
or Ecclesiasticus 2
John 11.1-16

Thomas the Apostle

John 11.1-16

'This illness does not lead to death; rather it is for God's glory' (v.4)

The raising of Lazarus from the dead is a good text to think about on this feast day of Thomas the Apostle. Thomas doubted Jesus' risen presence from the dead and needed dramatic visceral proof. Many people doubt the Lazarus miracle as unreal or unlikely.

We come down to a fundamental choice here. Do we think that the witnesses to this event, as well as the person who wrote it down in the Gospel, were either deluded or lying? If we say they were deluded, then everything else they reported is suspect. If we say they were lying, then they cannot be trusted with any of the content of the Gospel. There is too much evidence from the local and contextual detail of John's Gospel as a whole to suggest that he and people behind the miracle got the basic facts wrong. For example, John's Gospel is correct about the number of porticos at the pool of Siloam; something about which only someone who was local and knowledgeable could be right. There is too much of great spiritual depth and intelligence in John's words to doubt his integrity as a truth-teller.

So, the data described in John about Lazarus leads us to believe that something extraordinary happened, which brought life out of the grave. This is a fundamental Christian truth in itself, and we look for signs of it everywhere, whatever shape or form it takes.

Almighty and eternal God,
who, for the firmer foundation of our faith,
allowed your holy apostle Thomas
to doubt the resurrection of your Son
till word and sight convinced him:
grant to us, who have not seen, that we also may believe
and so confess Christ as our Lord and our God;
who is alive and reigns with you,
in the unity of the Holy Spirit,
one God, now and for ever.

COLLECT

Wednesday 4 July

Psalm 119.105-128
Judges 15.1 – 16.3
Luke 18.15-30

Judges 15.1 – 16.3

'As they did to me, so I have done to them' (15.11)

This story worries us today. Samson's love-life with a prostitute, as well as the widespread slaughter he carried out upon the Philistines, seem hot-headed, immoral, abusive and immature to the Christian conscience now. In a way, this behaviour is one among many examples in the Old Testament of why Christ had to come. Using someone as a sexual object, cruelly cutting down people in large numbers and seeing it as God's power at work, belongs to an unredeemed and myopic world.

Christ came to liberate us from the power of sin and death; to renew us by the transformation of our minds. And yet within the story of Samson, we see the seeds of what will later become the glory of God in the face of Jesus Christ. There is the seed of Samson's willingness to defy the oppressor politically. Like Moses defying Pharaoh and the Egyptian empire saying 'Let my people go'. Like Amos challenging King Jeroboam for crushing the poor. And like Daniel remaining faithful under persecution to the authority and justice of God. Samson is at least seeking to enact the authority of God's will in the world.

Samson needed to be transcended by Christ and by the Christian way. Like us, he saw through a dark glass dimly, but, out of the image of God within him, there eventually came the grace and truth of the Messiah. When we reduce ourselves to primitive behaviour, we need to remember this potential.

COLLECT

O God, the protector of all who trust in you,
without whom nothing is strong, nothing is holy:
increase and multiply upon us your mercy;
that with you as our ruler and guide
we may so pass through things temporal
that we lose not our hold on things eternal;
grant this, heavenly Father,
for our Lord Jesus Christ's sake,
who is alive and reigns with you,
in the unity of the Holy Spirit,
one God, now and for ever.

Thursday 5 July

Judges 16.4-end

'Lord God, remember me and strengthen me only this once' (v.28)

This story has been depicted in movies, plays and cartoons for over 100 years now and is one of the best known of the biblical dramatic tragedies: it depicts the end of Samson and the judges in Israel.

Samson had been a figure of the pride and arrogance of Israel, his people – a man who sought to work mostly out of his own power and go it alone. He only seems to know his need of God when he comes to the end of his rope and in his dying. This is also true of the relationship between Israel and God, as we see in Deuteronomy 32.36: 'Indeed the Lord will vindicate his people, have compassion on his servants, when he sees that their power is gone.' Samson has been betrayed by his own people – and by the woman he loved. He was physically brutalized and stretched out on the two pillars of the Philistines' temple. Nevertheless, his death had the effect of overcoming the enemy and their god.

This prefigures something of the story of Jesus, except in a much more primitive and inadequate way. It does show us that deep and perennial biblical truth that God will be present within the greatest kind of human weakness and ignorance. God stays with us in our failures, captivities, exiles and death, the blood, the mess and the chaos. When something comes to an end in disaster, God's creative, life-giving hope remains undefeated.

Gracious Father,
by the obedience of Jesus
you brought salvation to our wayward world:
draw us into harmony with your will,
that we may find all things restored in him,
our Saviour Jesus Christ.

COLLECT

Friday 6 July

Judges 17

'... an idol of cast metal' (v.4)

God cannot be tamed, limited, captured or domesticated. God is free and sovereign like the breeze. Maximus the Confessor, the seventh-century monk theologian of Constantinople, put it this way: 'God is breath, for the breath of the wind is shared by all, goes everywhere, nothing shuts it in, nothing holds it prisoner.'

In this chapter of Judges, Micah tries to bottle God. However, this is not only impossible, but also disastrous. In this story, Israel has been devoted to other gods, idols, wealth and power instead of breathing in the life-giving breath of Yahweh directly. The original word for God in the Hebrew Scriptures, which was originally just written as 'YHWH', became a breath prayer in Jewish practice. People prayed the word 'YAH' while breathing out and prayed the word 'WEH' while breathing in. Because God was the author of all that lives and breathes, God's life-giving breath is a living symbol of the gift of life itself. In this way, people were being literally 'in-spired' by the life-giving air of Yahweh, as they prayed. Yahweh was as close to them as breathing, so unlike the gods of surrounding cultures, who were thought to be located in statues, bulls and natural phenomena outside a living, breathing human being.

Our chapter represents the beginning of the betrayal of the original spirituality of Yahweh. Because of this, Israel will risk death in the final chapters that follow. We are called to learn from this mistake ourselves.

COLLECT

O God, the protector of all who trust in you,
without whom nothing is strong, nothing is holy:
increase and multiply upon us your mercy;
that with you as our ruler and guide
we may so pass through things temporal
that we lose not our hold on things eternal;
grant this, heavenly Father,
for our Lord Jesus Christ's sake,
who is alive and reigns with you,
in the unity of the Holy Spirit,
one God, now and for ever.

Psalms 96, **97**, 100
Judges 18.1-20, 27-end
Luke 19.11-27

Saturday 7 July

Judges 18.1-20, 27-end

'... they maintained as their own Micah's idol that he had made' (v.31)

This is a story of idolatry, greed and power. The strange and disturbing story of Judges 17–18 asks the implicit question for Christian conscience: 'Does what we say and what we do come from a deep and true faith?' In other words, are we living out of the centre of the image of God, in our heart of hearts – or are we preoccupied with the outward show of religion?

Judges 17–18 demonstrates the spiritual conditions that later lead to a tragic social deconstruction in Chapters 19 to 21. At the heart of these preconditions seems to be that everyone was doing what was right in their own eyes, and dressing that up as holiness. However, God is not made in our image; we are made in God's image. God is not a *function* of world process, but is the *creator* of world process, as Peter Hodgson has said. We are in deep peril when we reverse these priorities, as the people did in these chapters. What does the Lord our God require of us but, as Micah said, to love kindness (not selfishness), to practise justice (not oppression), and to walk humbly with our God (not self-worship and a haughty pride)?

We are called to put what is sacred first in our lives, within our inner soul. Then everything else will find its way.

Gracious Father,
by the obedience of Jesus
you brought salvation to our wayward world:
draw us into harmony with your will,
that we may find all things restored in him,
our Saviour Jesus Christ.

COLLECT

Monday 9 July

Psalms **98**, 99, 101
I Samuel 1.1-20
Luke 19.28-40

Luke 19.28-40

'As he rode along, people kept spreading their cloaks on the road'
(v.36)

It has long been noted that the cloaks strewn in the path of Jesus, as he rode on a donkey into Jerusalem, would have been the rags of the poor. He was riding into that holy city as the champion of the suffering and the oppressed. He had shared – and would soon come to share again – the full weight of their oppression, even to death. They knew him as someone who had ministered to them in their suffering and weakness, who had endured hardship like theirs and who had welcomed them and offered them hospitality when they had found every other door closed and every other table full of other guests. Jesus was known to be a hope-bearer, the incarnation of God's love for all people without distinction or prejudice, the one who came to bring freedom rather than bondage, and joy rather than despair. And so they welcomed him as the anointed one who represented their liberation in God. Jesus was, for them, the Messiah of a kingdom that could be found everywhere and anywhere.

This procession was such a contrast to the Roman military, who would have come into Jerusalem at about the same time as Jesus, to intimidate the crowd at this annual religious festival. With Jesus, it was the blind, the prostitutes, the possessed, the disabled, the tax collectors, the Samaritans and the fishermen who were the special subject of his focus. Anyone might be included, even you and I.

COLLECT

Almighty and everlasting God,
by whose Spirit the whole body of the Church
    is governed and sanctified:
hear our prayer which we offer for all your faithful people,
that in their vocation and ministry
they may serve you in holiness and truth
to the glory of your name;
through our Lord and Saviour Jesus Christ,
who is alive and reigns with you,
in the unity of the Holy Spirit,
one God, now and for ever.

Psalm **106*** (*or* 103)
I Samuel 1.21 – 2.11
Luke 19.41-end

Luke 19.41-end

'It is written, "My house shall be a house of prayer";
but you have made it a den of robbers' (v.45)

What would happen if Jesus rode into your town?

According to Luke, a series of things take place. First, he weeps over the ignorance and prejudice that prevent people from seeing what truly makes for peace – peace within and peace without. Secondly, he goes to the most sacred religious institution and cleanses it of those who were using religion to make a profit for themselves. He drives out those whose trade in doves and temple money make the experience of God something for which you have to pay. He creates a clear new space where there was a barrier before. He quotes from Isaiah 56.7. In Isaiah, the full text is: 'my house shall be a house of prayer *for all peoples*'. This means that the sacred presence of God has no barriers of exclusion around it. God cannot be traded, brokered, or controlled in any way. God can be experienced anywhere, anytime, in a thousand different ways. Jesus challenges the mediation of God through hierarchy, money, cultural limitation and any prejudice. That is why God in Christ can save us where we are.

So the town authorities rise up and retaliate by planning to kill Christ. But, as we know, this malice ends up destroying itself and the power of death along with it. There is a clear space around you and your town, as you read these words; it is the space cleared by Christ for your healing and your liberation.

> Almighty God,
> send down upon your Church
> the riches of your Spirit,
> and kindle in all who minister the gospel
> your countless gifts of grace;
> through Jesus Christ our Lord.

COLLECT

Wednesday 11 July

Psalms 110, 111, 112
1 Samuel 2.12-26
Luke 20.1-8

Luke 20.1-8

'Tell us, by what authority are you doing these things?' (v.2)

The religious leaders in this incident seem to be as interested in their own role and status as in whatever the truth may be about Jesus' authority. Their anxiety is about the nature of his authority compared to their authority. They do not appear to have a concern for the saving grace and truth of God that was so obviously coming through the life and teaching of Jesus. They do not come close to what is happening in and around the Christ event; they fret only about a new form of authority in the precincts of their own temple.

Jesus, however, looks to what is happening in terms of the work of the kingdom wherever and in whatever form it manifests itself. So he does not engage with the specifically hierarchical concerns of the gatekeepers of the temple, who were the chief priests and teachers of the law and the elders. Rather, he answers their question with a deeper question, so characteristic of the brilliance and wisdom of Jesus. He shifts the conversation from patriarchal paranoia to what is being done among the people, which is hope-bearing, truth-telling and a redeeming grace in action. This tells us that we, too, should centre ourselves in 'the happening' of the kingdom of God as it comes in, rather than in the self-interest and hierarchies of our institutions. The institutions are like scaffolding; the building-up of the people in grace and truth are like the edification of a living temple.

COLLECT

Almighty and everlasting God,
by whose Spirit the whole body of the Church
    is governed and sanctified:
hear our prayer which we offer for all your faithful people,
that in their vocation and ministry
they may serve you in holiness and truth
to the glory of your name;
through our Lord and Saviour Jesus Christ,
who is alive and reigns with you,
in the unity of the Holy Spirit,
one God, now and for ever.

Psalms 113, 115
1 Samuel 2.27-end
Luke 20.9-19

Luke 20.9-19

'What then will the owner of the vineyard do to them?' (v.15)

Tenants who have been given oversight as vintners in a vineyard make plans to take over the viticulture completely and, in fact, plot against the owner. This is very like the song of the vineyard in Isaiah, which Jesus may well have had in mind. The people who followed Jesus would easily think of the chief priest and the scribes in their rejection of Jesus, God, the owner's unique representative in this world in which we have been called to grow the new wine of the kingdom of God. However, this parable gets to the heart of all humanity's prideful obsessions to colonize God's creation with a self-serving agenda. So often the good wine of the kingdom of God – the fruit of the spirit, righteousness and justice – is overtaken by a lustful ambition. Instead, we are called to a humble and covenantal relationship with the true creator and owner of all things.

Our sinful impulses start out in a small way as in this parable. At first, these tenants simply wanted to keep the produce of the vineyard for themselves. They were not initially thinking of murder, because the first of the owner's servants was simply assaulted. But the slippery slope of greed led to subversion, which resulted in violence, which culminated in death. And so the vineyard is lost.

We must always test our hearts: how closely do we walk with God in Christ on the daily pathways we take at work, with the things for which we work?

Almighty God,
send down upon your Church
the riches of your Spirit,
and kindle in all who minister the gospel
your countless gifts of grace;
through Jesus Christ our Lord.

COLLECT

Friday 13 July

Psalm **139**
I Samuel 3.1 – 4.1a
Luke 20.20-26

Luke 20.20-26

'Show me a denarius. Whose head and whose title does it bear?'
(v.24)

Once again we see the brilliance and wisdom of Jesus. He answers a question with a deeper question that gets to the heart of the matter. He is saying we have an allegiance to God, which is so much deeper and higher and wider than any other duty. No allegiance to our nation can manipulate our allegiance to God, the sovereign of the universe. For example, it is extremely dangerous to hear a politician claim that God is on our side. This is essentially rendering to Caesar the things of God. We have a strong responsibility to support our government and country when duly elected by the people. As Jesus says, we are called to pay taxes, and should do so. This is not the same thing as treating Caesar as if he were God, which is what the Roman empire at the time of Jesus often tried to enforce.

We can never say 'my country, right or wrong'. We are called to say 'God is my sovereign; God is my way, my truth, my life'. Every human authority is ultimately under this cosmic and universal truth. This enables Christians to be prophetic, to be change-agents in the context of our political limitations and weaknesses.

Some politicians hold their finger up to the wind to test the breeze. Christians seeking the kingdom of God on earth are called to witness to the wind of God as it blows and to be the agents of its moving and billowing.

COLLECT

Almighty and everlasting God,
by whose Spirit the whole body of the Church
    is governed and sanctified:
hear our prayer which we offer for all your faithful people,
that in their vocation and ministry
they may serve you in holiness and truth
to the glory of your name;
through our Lord and Saviour Jesus Christ,
who is alive and reigns with you,
in the unity of the Holy Spirit,
one God, now and for ever.

Luke 20.27-40

'... they are like angels and are children of God' (v.36)

Who can say what heaven is like? It would be like asking a fish to describe the Milky Way. What we do know is that the word 'heaven' in Hebrew means 'with God'. Whatever God is like, whatever is the intimate and transcendent nature and being of God, then heaven is like that. We do know what God is like from the revelation of the sacred Scriptures. God is love. God is good, God is just, God is holy, God is everywhere. Therefore, heaven, as the reality of being in the being of God, has these characteristics as its essence. Any attempt to go beyond this revelation is speculation.

Jesus is well within these realities when he talks about the nature of marriage in heaven. He simply transcends the Sadducees' small-minded and legalistic question about heavenly realities and conditions with a remarkable image of freedom in resurrection, of the primacy of life over death and of the beautiful image of God's eternal love for God's children.

It has been said that death for a Christian is simply the extinguishing of a candle at the dawn because a greater light has come. Our life with its warmth and light, as well as its vulnerability and shadow, is to be utterly transformed, completely illumined in that resurrection light like a rising sun shining upon us. How then should we be afraid to die, to fall into the hands that made all things? The anxiety of the Sadducees is irrelevant.

Almighty God,
send down upon your Church
the riches of your Spirit,
and kindle in all who minister the gospel
your countless gifts of grace;
through Jesus Christ our Lord.

COLLECT

Monday 16 July

Luke 20.41 – 21.4

'Beware of the scribes' (20.46)

What does a hero look like? In an age of 'get rich quick' celebrity, this is not an easy question for the Church to answer. The language of 'lordship' or 'kingship', when applied to Christ, seems both antiquated and hierarchical. What does it mean for Christ to be 'David's Lord', a hero?

It doesn't mean being one of the pompous public élite, described in verse 47; rather, it means being a hero by risking deep unpopularity, by challenging the social conventions of the élite. Part of Jesus' criticism was that the scribes did not deserve public honour because, in reality, they were greedy hypocrites. Our churches are not composed of such greedy hypocrites. But what messages do we convey with our elaborate hierarchical processions? How would we cope in the chapter house of a cathedral if someone objected to the carefully planned choreography? Where would Jesus stand in one of our processions?

Being a hero means spotting hidden love and sacrifice, no matter how humble its location. The phrase, 'little old lady', trips demeaningly off people's lips too often. Some of them give and pray magnificently and secretly. Who would Jesus honour in our parish churches?

We follow an uncomfortable hero. But perhaps that's why we followed him in the first place.

COLLECT

Merciful God,
you have prepared for those who love you
such good things as pass our understanding:
pour into our hearts such love toward you
that we, loving you in all things and above all things,
may obtain your promises,
which exceed all that we can desire;
through Jesus Christ your Son our Lord,
who is alive and reigns with you,
in the unity of the Holy Spirit,
one God, now and for ever.

Psalms **132**, 133
1 Samuel 6.1-16
Luke 21.5-19

Luke 21.5-19

'… not a hair of your head will perish' (v.18)

I've heard the following cliché in many prayer meetings: 'Lord, we pray for our persecuted brothers and sisters in … we just thank you that we have freedom to gather in your name, but send us the time of trial when we will be really tested for you…'

I don't want to see our Church persecuted. Persecution involves real flesh-and-blood human beings having their bodies broken. Rightly, we honour our martyrs, but the Church has, at its best, been wary of those who seek martyrdom.

Martyrdom costs lives. But did you notice the odd juxtaposition: 'they will put some of you to death' (v.16) and 'not a hair of your head will perish' (v.18). What might this mean? Does it suggest – as elsewhere in Jesus' teaching – that death is not the worst thing that can happen to a Christian? So should we rather say, 'martyrdom costs bodies but not lives'?

We live in an anxious Church. Perhaps we should read a passage like this and reflect on our good providence that we live in a, relatively, peaceful place. But even more, should we read a passage like this and think, 'Jesus, Luke and the early Christians talked like this because they faced these realities, but did not lose their peace-filled faith'? And so be less anxious and more thankful?

Creator God,
you made us all in your image:
may we discern you in all that we see,
and serve you in all that we do;
through Jesus Christ our Lord.

COLLECT

Wednesday 18 July

Luke 21.20-28

'... "the Son of Man coming in a cloud" with power and great glory'
(v.27)

Here we are deep in apocalyptic. Biblical scholars have taught us to be honest that Jesus, too, was an apocalyptic prophet, who described the present and his sense of the future in these vivid images, however uncomfortable this may sound to us. Apocalyptic sits uneasily with the calm Anglican church! But sometimes only this violent imagery conveys the desperation and horror of a situation and the longing for release and justice.

Ancient warfare was conducted without the benefits of the Geneva Convention. Defeat would often mean summary execution, public torture, sexual abuse, slavery – this is what Jerusalem suffered at the hands of the Romans. The risk and reality of this dreadful fate lies behind these words. You can feel Jesus' anguish. There is, I think, some sense of the perplexing providence of God – God had given Jerusalem freedom, but the choices they made brought suffering. Even more tangible is a sense of impending tragedy. God's heart breaks for Jerusalem. Some historians argue that these words were well understood in the Christian community and that they left before the final siege. But the New Testament is haunted by the spectacle of Jerusalem burning.

It is into this most broken world that the glory of the Son of Man comes. Again, honesty forces us to note that for many Christians this was, and is, a literal conviction – 'Christ will come again in glory'. But Christ did not return in 70 AD. What does his glory look like in a broken world? Can we see it in the smile of a Sudanese child – child of years of civil war – loved, fed and attending her new school?

COLLECT

Merciful God,
you have prepared for those who love you
such good things as pass our understanding:
pour into our hearts such love toward you
that we, loving you in all things and above all things,
may obtain your promises,
which exceed all that we can desire;
through Jesus Christ your Son our Lord,
who is alive and reigns with you,
in the unity of the Holy Spirit,
one God, now and for ever.

Luke 21.29-end

'…the kingdom of God is near' (v.31)

Today, we hit one of biblical criticism's old chestnuts. Jesus appears to say, here and elsewhere, that the kingdom would come – the Son of Man would return – before some of his contemporaries ('this generation', v.32) had died. I've heard many thoughtful (and some specious!) attempts to explain these words. My own modest conclusion is that Jesus probably did say something like this but, in a straightforward, literal sense, it didn't happen.

This is not the place for lengthy exploration, but I am left with two thoughts. The first is the sense that Christ's 'return' is always imminent. This could feel like a strait-jacket – better not be tipsy when he returns! Or we could take it as a call to action. We live in hard times for the Church. Ministry is often a struggle. The language of 'spiritual warfare' resonates with my experience of parish life. So I hear Christ saying: 'Don't be distracted. Be at "action stations", ready to respond energetically to whatever comes at you.'

More deeply, it feels like the kingdom is close again. Out of the current struggles of the Church in the West, a new Church will be born to serve the kingdom in new ways. For this task, we need to pray to see clearly and to be ready to move swiftly.

Creator God,
you made us all in your image:
may we discern you in all that we see,
and serve you in all that we do;
through Jesus Christ our Lord.

COLLECT

203

Friday 20 July

Luke 22.1-13

'... a man carrying a jar of water will meet you;
follow him into the house he enters' (v.10)

With our sacred paintings and stained glass windows, it is easy to miss the sheer danger of Jesus' world. He is a marked man and a public figure. The mood in Jerusalem is febrile. The authorities want him dead, but cannot simply kill him.

I love John le Carré's novels, especially those set in the Cold War. There is something about the secrecy in the midst of normality, and the moral ambiguities, that captures my imagination.

This passage feels like something from a le Carré novel to me. Jesus is being betrayed by a disappointed colleague. Jesus is playing hide and seek with the authorities. He has arranged a place for a final rendezvous and sends some of his comrades to set up the meeting by means of secret code words and mysterious contacts.

Too far-fetched? Perhaps. But every Holy Week I struggle to hang on to the simple humanity of Jesus. How did he feel, as he spoke in public by day and went to hide by night? How did he feel, knowing that the authorities hated him enough to want to kill him? How did he feel, sensing that one of his friends was to betray him? How did he feel, knowing that this was the climax, that his people would be set free, but that it would cost him everything?

All we can do is watch and wonder.

COLLECT

Merciful God,
you have prepared for those who love you
such good things as pass our understanding:
pour into our hearts such love toward you
that we, loving you in all things and above all things,
may obtain your promises,
which exceed all that we can desire;
through Jesus Christ your Son our Lord,
who is alive and reigns with you,
in the unity of the Holy Spirit,
one God, now and for ever.

Luke 22.14-23

'... the one who betrays me is with me, and his hand is on the table' (v.21)

There were many shocks when I was training for ordination. I still remember the shock of discovering that we do not know exactly the Words of Institution at the Last Supper. (Write out the words in the Synoptic Gospels and in Corinthians and see where they differ and where they are the same – there seems to be some variation in the transmission of the tradition, even if the essence is very clear.) Of all the words they should have remembered, I thought arrogantly and naively, those early Christians should have remembered these.

But that was not how it was. They did not know the future. They did not know that these words needed to be preserved. Anyway, their concepts of 'preservation' are different from ours. So we work with what was recorded in the New Testament. And as is often the case, the Church has done a good job of systematizing the words and presenting a beautiful compilation that takes us back to the Last Supper and makes Jesus present to us now. We have 'enough'.

And yet Christians have killed each other about the meaning of these words. Are there greater blasphemies than that? Especially because we do only have a 'good enough' knowledge of them. The Church as systematizer can also be very dangerous.

We need to be wary of the Church. We need also to value the Church. The Eucharist profoundly helps us to do both. It is Christ's gift of himself to and through the Church, but it is not the Church's gift.

One of the recipients of Christ at this first Eucharist betrayed him. How might we distort, control, betray him in our Eucharists?

Creator God,
you made us all in your image:
may we discern you in all that we see,
and serve you in all that we do;
through Jesus Christ our Lord.

COLLECT

Monday 23 July

Luke 22.24-30

'… I am among you as one who serves' (v.27)

Jesus is so powerfully counter-cultural, especially for the Church. Our secular and ecclesiastical rulers don't lord it over us the way an ancient despot did – thank God for democratic revolutions! – but so much of the symbolism of the Church shrieks hierarchy. Especially in the Anglican Church, we have preserved the trappings of medieval Christendom. I write from Durham, the Land of the Prince Bishops. Brothers and sisters, I don't think Jesus would have lived in a palace! It may be that among the liberations of post-Christendom will be freedom from the trappings of empire and the attractiveness that comes from being more visibly Christ-like. That was part of what captivated people in Jesus' day, and we should not be surprised that his words ring hollow on our lips if we live differently.

But servant-hood is not 'doormat'-hood. '… I am among you as one who serves' are dangerous words. As a vicar, I take my share of moving the chairs, but I also have a family, and a need to rest and be refreshed, and it is not good for others to treat me like a doormat. I see many of our church members being overworked, not least by their fellow church members – all shrouded in the language of 'Christian service'. I find the promises of Jesus to his disciples – that they will reign with him – uncongenial, archaic. But they do speak of dignity. A dignity to be honoured, even in a life of service.

COLLECT

Lord of all power and might,
the author and giver of all good things:
graft in our hearts the love of your name,
increase in us true religion,
nourish us with all goodness,
and of your great mercy keep us in the same;
through Jesus Christ your Son our Lord,
who is alive and reigns with you,
in the unity of the Holy Spirit,
one God, now and for ever.

Psalms **5**, 6 (8)
1 Samuel 10.17-end
Luke 22.31-38

Luke 22.31-38

'... when once you have turned back,
strengthen your brothers [and sisters]' (v.32)

We all fail. We often fall badly short of Christ. And while the Church, like any human institution, has to have rules, so that those who have failed in certain sorts of ways are not allowed to return to leadership, others of us do have to repent and return.

People love Peter. When we are reading the Passion Gospel, there is always a surge of emotion at the moment of his betrayal of Christ. *'Me too.'* And yet, of course, we know that he will be restored, even after this most bitter of failures.

The Church lives in the real world. I wonder if that is what lies behind Jesus' strange words, changing his earlier teaching and telling his disciples to hang on to their equipment, even the swords. We don't do ministry with prayer alone. Another part of living in the 'real world' is that we have fallible leaders – 'Peters'. Honest recognition of our own failings keeps self-righteousness and self-deception at bay, and compassion close. Christ is in us and with us, but we are not Christ.

And I love the fact that, even after this shattering experience of failure and restoration, Peter is still not perfect. He has his squabbles and most poignantly, in the *Quo Vadis* legend, he almost let Christ be crucified again. Christ was firm and yet gentle with him. As he is with us.

Generous God,
you give us gifts and make them grow:
though our faith is small as mustard seed,
make it grow to your glory
and the flourishing of your kingdom;
through Jesus Christ our Lord.

COLLECT

207

Wednesday 25 July

James the Apostle

Psalms 7, 29, 117
2 Kings 1.9-15
Luke 9.46-56

Luke 9.46-56

'... for the least among all of you is the greatest' (v.48)

'What sort of leader are you?' is the question that leaps out from passage after passage in Luke. Today, we celebrate St James. Yet again, the disciples have been arguing about 'who is the greatest?' We read these stories and smile. How could they have been so stupid and arrogant? We, of course, never compete about who is the most important or who sets the boundaries or who is right ...

Luke has put these stories together so thoughtfully. The answer to the question of 'who is the most important?' is 'none of you', because the question is nonsense to the Christian. Jesus compares himself to a child, along with a slave, the person with the fewest rights in the ancient world.

The answer to the question about 'who sets the boundaries?' is 'not you'. James wants to decide who is in and who is out. Jesus says, 'I take that decision'.

The answer to the question about 'who is right?', is 'that is not for you to decide'. Jesus actually rebukes James for wanting to punish even wrong-doers (and the Samaritans were surely wrong not to welcome Jesus).

This is a terrifying model of leadership because it exposes both so many of our motives – actually, it is about 'me' not the issue in question – and requires us to leave the authority with God in Christ; who appears a little unpredictable for our tastes ...

COLLECT

Merciful God,
whose holy apostle Saint James,
leaving his father and all that he had,
was obedient to the calling of your Son Jesus Christ
and followed him even to death:
help us, forsaking the false attractions of the world,
to be ready at all times to answer your call without delay;
through Jesus Christ your Son our Lord,
who is alive and reigns with you,
in the unity of the Holy Spirit,
one God, now and for ever.

Thursday 26 July

Luke 22.47-62

'the Lord turned and looked at Peter' (v.61)

I wonder what colour eyes Jesus had? Probably not the clear blue eyes of my old Sunday School pictures. But I would have loved to have looked into them – I hope.

Judas comes to betray Jesus with a kiss. Both a routine and an intimate gesture. And Jesus says: 'Would you betray the Son of Man with a kiss?' Their eyes would have met. Deep hurt in Jesus' eyes. Could Judas bear to look back into them?

The authorities come to arrest him, by night, mob-handed, with violence. And Jesus looks them in the eye and says: 'This is your hour, the power of darkness.' Could they bear to look back into his eyes?

Peter runs away and then denies Jesus. As Jesus is led out of the high priest's house, across the flickering light of the courtyard, he looks Peter in the eye. He does not need to say anything.

Jesus' eyes. Eyes are the windows of, and to, the soul. Even if we don't know what colour eyes he had, I bet you have a favourite picture of Jesus: an icon, a classic painting, even a Sunday School card. Today, why not make some time to look at it, to look into those eyes and let them look back into yours? What is Jesus saying to you today?

COLLECT

Lord of all power and might,
the author and giver of all good things:
graft in our hearts the love of your name,
increase in us true religion,
nourish us with all goodness,
and of your great mercy keep us in the same;
through Jesus Christ your Son our Lord,
who is alive and reigns with you,
in the unity of the Holy Spirit,
one God, now and for ever.

Friday 27 July

Psalms 17, 19
I Samuel 13.5-18
Luke 22.63-end

Luke 22.63-end

'... blindfolded' (v.64)

Now it is getting ugly. Picture Abu Ghraib: photographs of prisoners being mocked, humiliated, abused, beaten. Picture Jesus in the middle of that. Blindfolded too. The authorities stand by, waiting for the results of the softening-up process. And they get what they want, an admission from Jesus that he is the 'Son of God'. But they are the ones who can't see. They have the blindfolds on. Because this is the Son of God standing before them.

Son of God and also Son of Man. Is that partly why they don't see? There have been theological 'fireworks' – miracles, profound teaching, a compelling integrated life – but what they are actually seeing is a battered human body and a young man who challenged their status, but who has lost. Clearly something had frightened them, but they had not let themselves see. 'This is not the Messiah. It can't be. It's all too uncomfortable. He's not divine in the way we had expected.'

Is one of the problems with God that we go with such strong expectations that we are unable to see God as God really is? What does God look like? We need to remind ourselves, as Christians, both that we do not know – 'no one has ever seen God' (1 John 4.12) – and that we do know: God looks like the Son of Man.

And the Son of Man was seen in places like Abu Ghraib.

COLLECT

Lord of all power and might,
the author and giver of all good things:
graft in our hearts the love of your name,
increase in us true religion,
nourish us with all goodness,
and of your great mercy keep us in the same;
through Jesus Christ your Son our Lord,
who is alive and reigns with you,
in the unity of the Holy Spirit,
one God, now and for ever.

Psalms 20, 21, **23**
1 Samuel 13.19 – 14.15
Luke 23.1-12

Luke 23.1-12

'I find no basis for an accusation against this man' (v.4)

I have Buddhists in my family and have gladly gone with them to their temples. I have spent time and talked seriously with Hindus and Muslims and Jews. I have enjoyed and learned from these relationships. But I am a Christian. And I am a Christian because of Jesus and because of the doctrine of the Incarnation. God is not distant from us.

There are many terrible things that human beings experience – and the passion narrative cannot be used as a sort of comparative suffering ('it was worse for Jesus than anyone else') – but Jesus' passion was a terrible experience. He did suffer very badly – physically, emotionally, psychologically, spiritually. And there is a peculiar pain in suffering innocently. Jesus did not deserve what happened to him. He was a very good man, and he was innocent of the charges brought against him. Pilate knew this, but out of cowardice had him tortured to death anyway.

But this is God standing before us and with us. Not competing with our suffering, but sharing it and redeeming it.

So much of our learning about God is done not through words or concepts but through images and experiences. For Christians, one of our most precious images of God is Christ on the cross: God with us in our sufferings. We can simply and physically hold on to this. This is why I am a Christian.

> Generous God,
> you give us gifts and make them grow:
> though our faith is small as mustard seed,
> make it grow to your glory
> and the flourishing of your kingdom;
> through Jesus Christ our Lord.

COLLECT

Monday 30 July

Luke 23.13-25

'... he has done nothing to deserve death' (v.15)

I am writing these reflections looking out at the winter snow, but think I will be back from summer holiday when they are published – bronzed and chilled. So it is disturbing and unusually painful to read this story away from Easter, when I am braced for it.

That has had the consequence of making elements of this story feel very contemporary. The casual brutality of the treatment of Jesus is shocking. Pilate thinks Jesus has been accused of 'perverting' the people, literally 'turning them away' from the proper authorities. Jesus has been bounced between different military authorities, beaten up, abused and sleep-deprived. This is a political show trial with a battered prisoner before the 'court'. Even if Pilate had let Jesus go, as innocent, Jesus would have been professionally flogged just to remind him not to be troublesome. There is the 'urgency' of the crowd. For whatever reason, the crowd want Jesus dead. They are baying for his blood. This is ugly 'mob rule'. And Pilate caves in and hands Jesus over to the will of the mob. The only saving grace is that Jesus' death is at the hands of professional torturers, not the amateur mob.

Luke wants to make it very clear that Jesus of Nazareth was not a threat to Rome. But beyond this considered presentation of political innocence, there is still the bleeding face of an innocent man: Emmanuel, 'God with us'.

Almighty Lord and everlasting God,
we beseech you to direct, sanctify and govern
    both our hearts and bodies
in the ways of your laws
    and the works of your commandments;
that through your most mighty protection, both here and ever,
we may be preserved in body and soul;
through our Lord and Saviour Jesus Christ,
who is alive and reigns with you,
in the unity of the Holy Spirit,
one God, now and for ever.

Luke 23.26-43

'… today you will be with me in Paradise' (v.43)

Along with the shock of discovering uncertainty about the Words of Institution was the shock of realizing that the accounts of the crucifixion differ. We, the Church, have done such a good job of harmonizing the accounts that many Christians don't realize that they are different. I guess if we asked the average Christian to recount from memory what Jesus said on the cross, we would hear a combination of 'My God, my God, why have you forsaken me?', 'It is finished', and 'Father forgive them'. In truth, this is not a bad theology of the cross!

But harmonizing can mean flattening. So we need to read Luke straight and on his own, if we are to hear his theology of the cross. And it is surely linked to the parable of the Prodigal Son and the extravagant 'welcome home' to the repentant sinner: at-one-ment bursting to get out from the patient generous heart of God, not begrudging, legal or calculated. Neither the Prodigal Son, even less the penitent thief on the cross, has done anything good to deserve salvation. And salvation is immediate. The Prodigal Son was instantly welcomed with fine clothes and jewellery and a party. So, too, the penitent thief on the cross is straight away to Paradise, back to the Garden of Eden with Christ.

This is truly the God who welcomes us and who welcomes all those with whom we work.

Lord God,
your Son left the riches of heaven
and became poor for our sake:
when we prosper save us from pride,
when we are needy save us from despair,
that we may trust in you alone;
through Jesus Christ our Lord.

COLLECT

Wednesday 1 August

Luke 23.44-56a

'…the sun's light failed' (v.45)

The morning I wrote this, we had thunder, lightning and snow. It was a disturbing combination. Even with all our scientific meteorological know-how, the sky is still full of moods for us. I vividly remember the last major eclipse of the sun in Western Europe. I was on holiday in France and as the sun disappeared, we were left in an eerie light. It just felt very strange. The world was out of joint.

And so it is surely right that the sun disappears as the Son dies. The world is out of joint if this innocent good man, the Son of Man and Son of God, cannot be welcomed, but has to die to save the world. Jesus' death is the triumph of eerie darkness. His family and friends were devastated. No wonder they remembered that eerie darkness.

We sometimes find ourselves in these places of eerie darkness. And, often, we cannot hurry our journey out of them. Nature, life, God, all have to take their course. We may just have to watch and wait for a while. Or keep on doing the ordinary things – burying bodies – until the sun rises again.

But for us, believers in the resurrection, we know that the sun will rise again. And so we wait – not without pain but not without hope either – for the Son to come back to us. As he will.

COLLECT

Almighty Lord and everlasting God,
we beseech you to direct, sanctify and govern
    both our hearts and bodies
in the ways of your laws
    and the works of your commandments;
that through your most mighty protection, both here and ever,
we may be preserved in body and soul;
through our Lord and Saviour Jesus Christ,
who is alive and reigns with you,
in the unity of the Holy Spirit,
one God, now and for ever.

Psalm **37***
1 Samuel 17.1-30
Luke 23.56b – 24.12

Luke 23.56b – 24.12

'… these words seemed to them an idle tale' (24.11)

It is the combination of the extraordinary and the ordinary that makes the accounts of the resurrection such fun and so plausible.

The women have been doing ordinary 'women things' (in first-century terms). They have worked out how to get back to the tomb on their own. They have prepared the funeral ointments. They have rested. But then they see a vision of two 'men' whose appearance is like a flash of lightning. They are helped to believe and to understand that Jesus is no longer dead, but has been raised and is among the living. Extraordinary beyond the most extraordinary.

But when the women try to tell the eleven and the rest, they are, as usual, not believed. Their words and beliefs are 'nonsense'. I wonder how often these women had been derided for talking 'nonsense'. Luke is at his sharpest here, exposing blatant misogyny.

The resurrection is extraordinary and I think we are depriving ourselves if we do not live with a sense of its extraordinariness. But the large majority of life is ordinary: planning, waiting, trying, working with fallible human beings. We deceive ourselves if we imagine life to be all resurrection. But we are impoverished if we encounter no resurrection. Thank God that the women believed their 'idle tales' enough for us to catch glimpses of the resurrection, then and now.

Lord God,
your Son left the riches of heaven
and became poor for our sake:
when we prosper save us from pride,
when we are needy save us from despair,
that we may trust in you alone;
through Jesus Christ our Lord.

COLLECT

215

Friday 3 August

Luke 24.13-35

'Oh, how foolish you are …' (v.25)

Do you feel the mutual exasperation in this story? When the disciples meet the risen Jesus, they cannot believe that he does not know the news. Indeed, they are so surprised that they have to stop walking to be able to tell him. But the risen Jesus is even more direct back. 'Aaagh' might be a good translation of 'Oh!' (v.25). He then describes them as being 'without understanding', 'obtuse', 'dull', 'slow'. 'Dumb' might be a good colloquial translation. He is not mincing his words.

I am grateful that we have glimpses of the exasperation of Jesus, including the risen Jesus. As a theological educator and a parish priest, I experience lots of exasperation! And students and parishioners get exasperated too. Sometimes we are just slow to 'get it'. And while I do not excuse either my own bad temper or pomposity, a little plain speaking together might help the Church to be a more honest as well as a more effective institution …

But Jesus does not leave it there. The loving patience is the under-girding value and he works with these dopey disciples till they begin to 'get it' and then there is that unforgettable moment of recognition and reconciliation.

Plain-talking and deep loving don't have to be opposites. 'Speaking the truth in love' can be a cover for verbal abuse. Or it can be a moment of mutual love in Christ.

COLLECT

Almighty Lord and everlasting God,
we beseech you to direct, sanctify and govern
　　both our hearts and bodies
in the ways of your laws
　　and the works of your commandments;
that through your most mighty protection, both here and ever,
we may be preserved in body and soul;
through our Lord and Saviour Jesus Christ,
who is alive and reigns with you,
in the unity of the Holy Spirit,
one God, now and for ever.

Psalms 41, **42**, 43
1 Samuel 17.55 – 18.16
Luke 24.36-end

Luke 24.36-end

'Touch me ...' (v.39)

Whatever he was, the risen Jesus was not a ghost. Luke describes Jesus eating 'broiled fish'. (My concordance said 'roast or grilled fish', which sounds so much more appetizing!) And Luke and John (1 John 1.1) use the same word for touch – *psēlaphaō* – which my concordance also translates as 'handle' or even 'grope'! There is something embarrassingly tangible about the resurrection. Why?

Because this is resurrection, not the liberation of the spirit from the body. Part of what the resurrection seems to suggest is that the conquering of death by God in Christ includes the redemption of the material order. This is not the same as its preservation. The risen Jesus has a very odd 'body' by our normal standards, but he has a body. Conquering death does not mean leaving embodied reality behind, rather the triumph over death is total. All is raised, albeit transformed.

I think this is good news. It is good news because much of the time, this world is beautiful. I do not want its beauty to perish. I do not want to lose 'me', and how can I conceive of 'me' except in a personal form? I do not want to lose those 'I have loved and lost a little while'. I want to meet them as persons.

None of this is, however, surprising. What else would we expect from a God whose love for us counts even the hairs on our head, as Luke so vividly taught us?

Lord God,
your Son left the riches of heaven
and became poor for our sake:
when we prosper save us from pride,
when we are needy save us from despair,
that we may trust in you alone;
through Jesus Christ our Lord.

COLLECT

217

Monday 6 August

The Transfiguration of Our Lord

Psalms 27, 150
Ecclesiasticus 48.1-10
or I Kings 19.1-16
I John 3.1-3

1 Kings 19.1-16

'… a sound of sheer silence ' (v.12)

The modern Church seems to be being offered two clichés. Either that faith has to be minutely and definitely expressed, so that there is no room for doubt or error. Or that faith is too uncertain to be defined and so cannot be – except that it is obviously true that it is too uncertain to be defined … The story of Elijah takes us to the heart of how it is to be human in the face of God.

Elijah does not doubt the existence of God. He appears to be doubting his own effectiveness in God's service and perhaps even God's commitment to him. He is utterly spent – defeated even. He is so worn out, he just wants to die.

God does not come to him with a 'statement of faith'. Nor does God overwhelm him. God just comes to him. The encounter is indescribable – NRSV says 'the sound of sheer silence' – but Elijah knows it is God who has come to him. This is not noisy faith or thin faith. Rather it is an authentic encounter with God in this world, but one that is beyond words.

And what is the first thing that God does? Not a telling off. Not a theological statement. No. God provides colleagues. Which, of course, is what worn-out and depressed Elijah needs most of all.

Authentic encounter with God will be indescribable, but it will have tangible consequences.

COLLECT

Father in heaven,
whose Son Jesus Christ was wonderfully transfigured
before chosen witnesses upon the holy mountain,
and spoke of the exodus he would accomplish at Jerusalem:
give us strength so to hear his voice and bear our cross
that in the world to come we may see him as he is;
who is alive and reigns with you,
in the unity of the Holy Spirit,
one God, now and for ever.

Acts 1.15-end

'… and the lot fell on Matthias' (v.26)

Who? When I was a theological college tutor and we kept the 'red letter days', Matthias would come around regularly and it became a sport among the staff to categorize our Matthias Day homilies. They covered a range from 'God can use anyone, even you' to 'even God's unknown servants have a worthy ministry'. To be honest, without dabbling into early Church legends, there was not much more to be said about Matthias.

But he had a job to do. He had the right qualifications. He met the 'person spec'. And we trust that he got on and did his job properly. It is just the case that not all ministry for Christ is glamorous. I serve in a 900-year-old church. I am just the latest in a long line of faithful (mostly) parish priests who have served Christ here. Not long after I am gone, I will be forgotten. And I have some nice jobs to do while I am here, and some tough ones. For the moment, the 'lot has fallen' on me here. That is just how it is in God's economy.

When I start getting stressed or pompous – and the two are not so far apart – it may be because in my own mind I have exaggerated my role. I am serving here, now, for a little while. I will then be gone. The Church will go on because it is God's.

Almighty God,
who sent your Holy Spirit
to be the life and light of your Church:
open our hearts to the riches of your grace,
that we may bring forth the fruit of the Spirit
in love and joy and peace;
through Jesus Christ your Son our Lord,
who is alive and reigns with you,
in the unity of the Holy Spirit,
one God, now and for ever.

COLLECT

Wednesday 8 August

Acts 2.1-21

'…each of us, in our own native language' (v.8)

Have you ever sat in a Pentecost service and wondered about the list of nationalities, especially if the reader has struggled to pronounce some of them? The reading begins with the huge excitement of the pouring out of the Holy Spirit and ends with Peter's great converting sermon. And in the middle we have a list of names …

It is in fact an intriguing list of names. These people come from all across the eastern Roman empire, as far as Rome itself, but also from outside the empire; Medes and Parthians were too fierce to be conquered by Rome. And it looks as if, as well as Jews and proselytes (gentiles converting to Judaism) (v.10), there were people with other ethnic and religious identities. 'Arabs' – from where? And we know that Paul had strong views about 'Cretans' (Titus 1.12-13)! This is a very mixed bunch.

And that of course is the obvious point. The gospel is for everyone: citizens of the empire and the uncivilized; respected people from ancient cultures and the dodgy nouveau riche; people from the visible Church and those beyond it. I wonder how we might communicate this staggering breadth of relevance and how this shatters the boundaries by which our churches so often live? Perhaps we could re-write Acts 2:

'How is that we hear the Good News, each of us in our own language – black and white, chav and toff, Unionist and Nationalist, African and American, French and English?'

COLLECT

Almighty God,
who sent your Holy Spirit
to be the life and light of your Church:
open our hearts to the riches of your grace,
that we may bring forth the fruit of the Spirit
in love and joy and peace;
through Jesus Christ your Son our Lord,
who is alive and reigns with you,
in the unity of the Holy Spirit,
one God, now and for ever.

Thursday 9 August

Acts 2.22-36

*'… this man, handed over to you according to the definite plan …
of God' (v.23)*

Divine providence – God's activity in the world – not a popular subject in modern theology, but alive and kicking in the parish! How are we to speak wisdom with folk who have the faith to believe God is at work in their lives but who also have a yearning for a definiteness that may be 'unfaith'?

Is the point of providence that it is difficult to see God at work at the time because God works *under* and *through* and *with* human life, not over it? In this passage, Luke portrays Peter preaching a hard sermon to his Jewish listeners. He does not let them off the hook of crucifying Christ. (We must note that such passages have a terrible later history in the life of the Church and for Jewish people.) But, for Peter, this is also, simultaneously, God's action. The two are interwoven together inextricably, but only one is clearly visible at the time.

Faith is sometimes just that – faith: trust, blind trust, inarticulate trust. No 'sight' to speak of. That is hard, and it does not stop us asking rigorous theological questions about the providence and absence of God, and about human free will. But faith as gut trust is ok.

I find myself thinking of Cowper's poignant hymn, 'God moves in a mysterious way'. A hymn written by someone whose life was deeply scarred by depression. Yet he wrote: 'God is his own interpreter, and he will make it plain.'

Gracious Father,
revive your Church in our day,
and make her holy, strong and faithful,
for your glory's sake
in Jesus Christ our Lord.

COLLECT

221

Acts 2.37-end

'They devoted themselves ...' (v.42)

This is what the Church looks like. Isn't it? Or is it choral evensong? Luke certainly intends us to see this as a description of the ideal church: mass conversion marked by public repentance and baptism; devotion to learning the faith, prayer and eucharist; miracles; communal living. Indeed, during periods of renewal, the Church does often look like this. This was true of the radical sects in seventeenth-century England. But it was also, in a different way, true of early Franciscanism. It has been true of some parts of the modern Church. Should the Church always be striving for this degree of enthusiasm and commitment?

It is certainly the case that some of us might be cautious about the claims to the miraculous and wary of the style of leadership that can be characteristic of this mode of Church. This level of spiritual temperature can foster self-deception and hypocrisy. It also seems not to be sustainable. This energy burns itself out. And there is a deep and deeply Christian wisdom in the slow rhythms of the Anglican Church; patient growth in communal holiness.

But, perhaps – especially in a period when we can see with our own eyes the consequences of two generations when the Church of England has often failed to recruit new members, and when the old ways of being Church are under immense strain – a bit of Lucan passion might not go amiss?

COLLECT

Almighty God,
who sent your Holy Spirit
to be the life and light of your Church:
open our hearts to the riches of your grace,
that we may bring forth the fruit of the Spirit
in love and joy and peace;
through Jesus Christ your Son our Lord,
who is alive and reigns with you,
in the unity of the Holy Spirit,
one God, now and for ever.

Psalm **68**
1 Samuel 23
Acts 3.1-10

Acts 3.1-10

'I have no silver or gold, but what I have I give you' (v.6)

There is a beautiful simplicity about this story, especially Peter's humble offering: 'I have no money, but I can share with you what I have: faith in Jesus Christ.'

Even after twenty years of ordained ministry, I still find myself agonizing about some of the simplest of questions. When I am doing a pastoral visit – funeral, sick, christening – should I pray out loud with the people? From one perspective, it is self-evident. What are we bringing to that pastoral encounter, if it is not our faith in the love of God, expressed in prayer? And yet, I often find myself not praying (though in self-defence, I always say that we are praying for them at church), because of the embarrassment they show when asked about prayer.

And what do I pray at the sick bed? Do I pray for healing with the same simplicity as Peter in Acts? Sometimes. But sometimes it does not feel right to pray for healing in this simple and dramatic way. And I don't think it is just my lack of faith.

However, reading this passage again has made me think. Why am I as a Christian minister here, now, in this home? And am I being tempted to offer all sorts of other things, other than faith in Christ? For any of us, when we are with people in need, what do we offer them? Gifts? Kindness? Faith?

Gracious Father,
revive your Church in our day,
and make her holy, strong and faithful,
for your glory's sake
in Jesus Christ our Lord.

COLLECT

Monday 13 August

Acts 3.11-end

'... all the prophets ... also predicted these days' (v.24)

Peter – a Jewish man – describes his fellow Jews as having 'killed the author of life'. With the spectre of Christian anti-Jewishness near to us modern readers, it is important to see how this speech by a Jew to Jews is framed. First, it takes place in the Jewish temple, at which Peter himself is still a worshipper. So this is not a straightforward rejection of Jewish religion; it is an attempt to find a new way of inhabiting it.

Modern Christians cannot worship in the temple now, and neither can modern Jews. It's no longer there. But there is a second 'location' for Peter's challenging speech where Jews and Christians *can* still find themselves meeting, and that is Scripture. In his speech, Peter affirms this shared body of Scripture, just as in his actions he affirms the temple. And his appeal to non-Christian Jews is to join Christian Jews in going back to Scripture in the light of the new things that have happened in Christ. 'Repenting' and 'refreshing' should partly take the form of looking again at what Moses taught, as well as at 'all the prophets'. And this is set against a profound reaffirmation of God's covenant with the Jewish people. Peter looks to the covenant that is enshrined in Scripture as a site of blessing, and to the ongoing work of returning to Scripture, from which Christians just as much as Jews are never exempted, as a practice whereby that blessing is received.

If we want a lesson from Peter's speech to the men of Israel, perhaps it is that *all* of us should allow *every* new historical experience to send us back to the sacred words we inherit, for we can never master or exhaust them.

Let your merciful ears, O Lord,
be open to the prayers of your humble servants;
and that they may obtain their petitions
make them to ask such things as shall please you;
through Jesus Christ your Son our Lord,
who is alive and reigns with you,
in the unity of the Holy Spirit,
one God, now and for ever.

Psalm **73**
1 Samuel 26
Acts 4.1-12

Acts 4.1-12

'There is no other name under heaven ...
by which we must be saved' (v.12)

'What's in a name?', says Juliet to Romeo. In the darkness of the garden, these two teenagers struggle to negotiate the terrible legacy of the names they bear. They long for a safe space in which their names won't *matter*. But there, of course, is the tragedy. There *isn't* any escape from their names. They are from families at terrible enmity with each other, and their love is forbidden. Histories and feuds and social conditioning – forces over which they have absolutely no control – play themselves out in their names, whether they like it or not. What's in a name? The answer seems to be: a lot.

The book of Acts asks us to consider the positive power of a name. Peter and John announce to the Sanhedrin that they exist and act *in the name* of Jesus Christ. They locate themselves *within* this name, as if it, too, were some kind of force-field. And that is not a stupid suggestion on their part. Peter and John have found the name of Jesus Christ changing the course of their lives, and in some deep sense beginning to define them. They have taken the name of Christians – it triggers fellowship and it also triggers hatred. Either way, they will not deny the name with which they are now associated, and that is because of their fundamental belief that amidst all the names that there are and will be in the world, there is no other name that has a field of force great enough and *capacious* enough to unite all people in itself. It is the name that will overcome the world's divisions precisely because it does not strive for its own self-promotion – unlike Montague, unlike Capulet. It is the name of the Crucified One.

Lord of heaven and earth,
as Jesus taught his disciples to be persistent in prayer,
give us patience and courage never to lose hope,
but always to bring our prayers before you;
through Jesus Christ our Lord.

COLLECT

Wednesday 15 August

The Blessed Virgin Mary

Psalms 98, 138, 147.1-12
Isaiah 7.10-15
Luke 11.27-28

Isaiah 7.10-15

'... the Lord himself will give you a sign' (v.14)

We cannot know the unknowable God directly. And we cannot know the unknowable God in the way that we know created things, for God is not one thing among others as creaturely things are. So we can know God only through signs.

What is a sign of God? It is a creature that in a gracious way is enabled to say something about its unknowable Creator. Such signs are created things that *refer beyond themselves* to God; that become transparent to the 'depth' of God who is the ground of all things. We should not disparage or underestimate these signs. They are real, and necessary, and God-given.

Here, the prophet Isaiah overrides the false coyness of Ahaz (who says he does not want a sign). The sign in this case is something God *wants* to give; it is an act of grace, without which something important would remain forever unknown. And what is the sign? It is a young woman's womb made full, followed by a wonderful birth. This birth signals the God who creates out of nothing; the God for whom virgin space is an occasion for unique, mysterious, unfathomable generativity. We do not have the experience of any such thing in the created world with which to compare God's action. But in this sign given to Ahaz, and to us, we are brought into relation with the mystery of a God who is beyond that causal chain by which every created thing is always linked to another created thing; a God who can bring about new being in the way he brought about *all* being: as pure gift and bounteous surprise. This is a God we can really hope in. That is the message of this sign.

COLLECT

Almighty God,
who looked upon the lowliness of the Blessed Virgin Mary
and chose her to be the mother of your only Son:
grant that we who are redeemed by his blood
may share with her in the glory of your eternal kingdom;
through Jesus Christ your Son our Lord,
who is alive and reigns with you,
in the unity of the Holy Spirit,
one God, now and for ever.

Psalm **78.1-39***
1 Samuel 31
Acts 4.32 – 5.11

Acts 4.32 – 5.11

'You did not lie to us but to God!' (5.4)

The Church in the immediate aftermath of Pentecost is a new creation. And within it there is an Eden-like stewardship of created goods; one that is exercised for the benefit of all, and that is free from the fundamentally competitive exercise of proprietary rights. Instead of individual ownership there is a collective possession that is *communicative*. United as they are in the Spirit, the Christians use their goods as a means of communicating with each other: communicating blessing; being in relationship; giving, receiving and forgiving together.

But in this new Eden, there are a new Adam and Eve who are tempted all over again, and (like Adam and Eve) receive a terrible sentence of death. The offence of Ananias and Sapphira can be seen as a repeat of Adam and Eve's sin. They covet something for themselves. They take it. And then they hide what they have done. They lie to God. Theirs is an offence against communion; a betrayal of the communication that is the life-blood of the newly created people of God. They sin against the Holy Spirit.

Martin Luther once argued that not giving to the poor when you do actually have the resources to help them is no different from stealing. This story from Acts says something similar about the dangers of viewing one's goods not as the collective resource of the Church but as one's own private store. In this vision, withholding something (what we might call a 'sin of omission') is not ultimately any different from active theft (a 'sin of commission'). It is a sobering thought, which might energize us to examine our own inclinations to do what we think is an acceptable minimum ...

Let your merciful ears, O Lord,
be open to the prayers of your humble servants;
and that they may obtain their petitions
make them to ask such things as shall please you;
through Jesus Christ your Son our Lord,
who is alive and reigns with you,
in the unity of the Holy Spirit,
one God, now and for ever.

COLLECT

Friday 17 August

Acts 5.12-26

'Go ... and tell the people the whole message about this life' (v.20)

Simon Peter once said to Jesus, 'Lord, to whom shall we go?; you have the words of eternal life'. Now, those 'words of life' are his own to speak. The angel who releases him and the other apostles from prison encourages them to speak these words with confidence.

What we witness here is the transposition of Jesus Christ's form into the lives and actions of his disciples. It has been said that Christianity was founded on the loss of a body – first at the empty tomb and then in the empty sky, towards which the frightened apostles stood looking after the ascension. But that does not account for the extraordinary way in which the resurrection and ascension of Jesus make possible, through the Spirit, a *new* series of 'embodiments' of Jesus. It is as though he is at work in the voices and hands and even through the shadows of his apostles (healing shadows need bodies to cast them, after all). The apostles do all the things Jesus did. They proclaim his message. They heal – and even restore to life. They are arrested. They are, in a manner of speaking, 'entombed' in prison. And they rise from the tomb and continue to minister.

Peter has come a long way from his early, uncertain, and dependent relation to Jesus. The promise of Jesus that 'he who hears you hears me', and 'he who receives you receives me' has come to miraculous fruition. We hear Jesus *in* the person of the ones sent out to carry his word of life. Do we dare to seek such christoformity in our own lives and in the life of the Church?

Let your merciful ears, O Lord,
be open to the prayers of your humble servants;
and that they may obtain their petitions
make them to ask such things as shall please you;
through Jesus Christ your Son our Lord,
who is alive and reigns with you,
in the unity of the Holy Spirit,
one God, now and for ever.

Acts 5.27-end

'... if this plan or undertaking is of human origin, it will fail' (v.38)

Gamaliel was one of the most senior figures in the highest Jewish court in Jerusalem at the time when the apostles were preaching. The Mishnah would later present him as one of the greatest Jewish teachers ever. In this momentous encounter before the Sanhedrin, Gamaliel plays a crucial role in safeguarding the Christian mission. He argues for the life of the apostles, and is successful. The good news of Christ that is being preached by Peter and his fellows meets the deep wisdom of this Jewish teacher of the law, and they do not combust. Rather, Gamaliel draws on the law and on his own experience to come to a judgement with which Jesus himself would have been quite at home: 'You will know them by their fruits' (Matthew 7.16).

It is a judgement in service of life, and a judgement made in humility, for the key aspect of it is that it refers the dispute between the Christian and the non-Christian to God's greater purposes. The other members of the Sanhedrin, so it seems, do not regard a process of patient discernment as a desirable option. Gamaliel operates with a sense of the provisionality of human judgements, and the fact that their authority is derived from a higher source.

Moses once received wise advice from outside his own religious tradition. His father-in-law, Jethro, was not an Israelite but a Midianite priest, yet at a crucial time he advised Moses how best to judge the people. In this passage, we see a gift to the fragile Christian Church from a source that is outside it (and it was not Gamaliel's only gift to the Church, for he was also a teacher of the man who would become Paul the Apostle). What might *we* receive from Gamaliel's example?

Lord of heaven and earth,
as Jesus taught his disciples to be persistent in prayer,
give us patience and courage never to lose hope,
but always to bring our prayers before you;
through Jesus Christ our Lord.

COLLECT

Monday 20 August

Acts 6

'... his face was like the face of an angel' (v.15)

Angels have got lots to teach us – important things; things about the dynamism of God's action in the world. The silliness of medieval debates about angels has become almost proverbial – not least that notorious debate about whether you could fit angels on the head of a pin. And the reason that debate sounds silly in the travestied form in which we've come to know it is because it seems to talk about angels simply as *things*. Or to put it another way, it reduces angels to the status of *nouns* – noun-like things: things you can in principle prod and manipulate. Angels are much better described as God's *verbs*: modes of God's action, his purposing, his *doing*. For the dynamism of God – in history, and the created order, and the lives of individual human beings – is effective when he wills to achieve something. Angels are, to put it another way, a mode of God's effectiveness. Their being is a sort of doing – an expression of God's doing.

The account of the ordination of the first deacons is a great occasion for thinking about God's verbs: not just noun-like *persons*, but the uses God makes of them when he *acts through them*. It's a great occasion for thinking about the sendings of God; the working out of God's purposes in manifold ways, not least through the people commissioned within God's Church to do particular things. As we are presented with the first deacons by the book of Acts, we do not just meet a row of proddable, noun-like human beings: Philip, and Prochorus, and Nicanor, and Timon, and Parmenas, and Nicolaus, and Stephen. We see divine verbs. We see God's doing – his activity in them, his faithfulness and love, his sending and his making fruitful.

C O L L E C T

O God, you declare your almighty power
most chiefly in showing mercy and pity:
mercifully grant to us such a measure of your grace,
that we, running the way of your commandments,
may receive your gracious promises,
and be made partakers of your heavenly treasure;
through Jesus Christ your Son our Lord,
who is alive and reigns with you,
in the unity of the Holy Spirit,
one God, now and for ever.

Psalms 87, **89.1-18**
2 Samuel 5.1-12
Acts 7.1-16

Tuesday 21 August

Acts 7.1-16

*'He did not give him any of it as a heritage,
not even a foot's length' (v.5)*

Stephen's great speech to the high priest, which will be a sort of recapitulation of all the great events of salvation history, begins with the figure of Abraham being told to 'go out' from his land. Abraham appears to be for Stephen what he will be for Paul: a model of faith. A model of what it means to live not by present securities – one's possessions and land and offspring – but by a promise. It is, we may imagine, a model that Stephen too finds himself valuing as he stands arrested and in danger of his life. His only resource is the promise of God's faithfulness.

In one way, and very obviously, his speech is all about being disinherited. The identity of the Christian – like the identity of the patriarchs Abraham, and Isaac and Jacob, and like the identities of all the Hebrew slaves in Egypt – is an identity forged through an experience of suffering, departure, displacement, relinquishment. It is about leaving familiar places for strange places – not once, but over and over again. Stephen, and all the new converts to the Way, have undertaken just this sort of journey in their various respective decisions to follow Jesus Christ.

But at the same time, and paradoxically, this embrace of dispossession also *gives* them an inheritance. They are given the epic story which Stephen recounts as a story that they can call their *own* story. They are given the inheritance of a place among the divinely disinherited – the inheritance of fellowship with the patriarchs, and with the people of the Exodus. And with this, they too are given a promise to which no other promise is equal.

God of glory,
the end of our searching,
help us to lay aside
all that prevents us from seeking your kingdom,
and to give all that we have
to gain the pearl beyond all price,
through our Saviour Jesus Christ.

COLLECT

Wednesday 22 August

Psalm **119.105-128**
2 Samuel 6.1-19
Acts 7.17-43

Acts 7.17-43

'[Moses] received living oracles to give to us' (v.38)

Do we find ourselves taken aback to find Genesis and Exodus given a pretty straight retelling in New Testament texts like this one? We shouldn't. It shows their permanent importance for the Church.

Stephen appeals to the Torah – the five books of the Pentateuch, which are the container of the Jewish law. He concentrates most on the parts of the law that have the form of narrative – narratives that he is convinced contain promises to Christ's followers and not only to traditional Jews. If there is a use of the law from which Stephen is distancing himself, his appeal to it here nonetheless indicates that he believes it has unavoidable and vital importance for Christians. The Christian path he has chosen does not entail the law's 'replacement'. It invites a discovery within the law of the law's own 'moreness': of aspects of the law as yet underexplored.

Law has always been central for a 'we' which is Jewish. But the 'we' for whom Stephen re-narrates Torah is the Church, and it is soon going to include non-Jewish Christians as well as Jewish. Part of what all new Christians will inherit by their entry into the chosen people will precisely be the history of Israel, supremely embodied in their Scriptures. Paul will make explicit what is implicit in the inclusion of Stephen's speech in the New Testament canon: new Christians who are not Jews join the company of those who have long had the law as their custodian. New gentile Christians *gain* a relationship to the law by virtue of their joining of this community: they gain a history in which the law plays a central part. If they do not join Jews in inheriting the law as legal code, they nevertheless join them in relating to it as *Scripture*.

COLLECT

O God, you declare your almighty power
most chiefly in showing mercy and pity:
mercifully grant to us such a measure of your grace,
that we, running the way of your commandments,
may receive your gracious promises,
and be made partakers of your heavenly treasure;
through Jesus Christ your Son our Lord,
who is alive and reigns with you,
in the unity of the Holy Spirit,
one God, now and for ever.

Psalms 90, **92**
2 Samuel 7.1-17
Acts 7.44-53

Acts 7.44-53

'... houses made by human hands' (v.48)

The straw that breaks the camel's back: Stephen's speech culminates in a direct attack on the temple and the 'stiff-necked' people who maintain it. In the course of these few verses, there is a subtle transition from talking about '*our* fathers' to talking about '*your* fathers'. A common identity seems to give way, tragically, to an oppositional one, and the enraged response of Stephen's hearers confirms that this transition has taken place from their side too.

The critique of the temple may be one of the most Christ-like things Stephen says in the course of his entire speech. Indeed, what finally gets him killed may be just the thing that got Jesus killed. Jesus' apparent claim that he would destroy the temple also provoked horrified reactions in *his* hearers. But at the same time, both Jesus and Stephen really only take their place within an intra-Jewish debate about the rights and wrongs of having a human monarch and a massive and permanent temple. The Feast of Tabernacles builds into Jewish life a yearly reminder of the impermanence of all human constructions (including the erstwhile temple) by briefly evoking desert living; a reminder that one can be closer to God when dispossessed of such things. Stephen's words draw on Old Testament texts to make the same point. God is greater than the dwellings we try to make for him with our hands. Following the true God means being trained to be dispossessed repeatedly of the constructions we make *of*, and *for*, that God – and sometimes to be dispossessed of our very selves, by having the 'temples' that are our bodies destroyed. We may angrily refuse to learn this dispossession. Or we may embrace it, and find again the God of heaven who is beyond our decorated ceilings.

God of glory,
the end of our searching,
help us to lay aside
all that prevents us from seeking your kingdom,
and to give all that we have
to gain the pearl beyond all price,
through our Saviour Jesus Christ.

COLLECT

Friday 24 August

Bartholomew the Apostle

Psalms 86, 117
Genesis 28.10-17
John 1.43-end

John 1.43-end

'You will see heaven opened and the angels of God ascending and descending on the Son of Man' (v.51)

Jesus' words here are an interpretation of the episode of Jacob's ladder in Genesis 28. For his first disciples, a new kind of vision is opening up, as a new kind of vision opened up for Jacob in the desert. Jesus claims that he himself is a new ladder on whom the angels will ascend and descend. In him, there is a wonderful exchange between earth and heaven. He is not Jacob dreaming the ladder (Jacob's place is occupied by the new visionaries, and in particular that otherwise rather obscure disciple Nathanael). Rather, he is the ladder itself. What can this mean? It means that, like Jacob's ladder, Jesus is graced in such a way that the divine light appears there ('In him was life; and the life was the light of men', John 1.4). He is an occasion for the disclosure of a particular kind of truth, the deepest truth.

There is a curious additional aspect to John 1's relationship to Genesis 28. As a prelude to his sleep and his vision, Jacob takes a stone for a pillow, and before the revelation of the ladder in verse 51 of John's Gospel there is also the setting up of a stone: Simon is renamed Cephas, which means 'a stone'. In Genesis, the stone is associated very closely with the ladder – it becomes holy by association with the ladder. Jacob anoints the stone, and it is thenceforth the marker of a holy place. In John, Peter is 'set up' as the stone on which, it is promised, the *Church* (Christ's Body) will be established. And along with Peter, the other apostles – one of whom we especially remember today – are chosen, placed and anointed to witness to the divine light's appearance. Christ the ladder rests upon them, and they point heavenward.

COLLECT

Almighty and everlasting God,
who gave to your apostle Bartholomew grace
    truly to believe and to preach your word:
grant that your Church
may love that word which he believed
and may faithfully preach and receive the same;
through Jesus Christ your Son our Lord,
who is alive and reigns with you,
in the unity of the Holy Spirit,
one God, now and for ever.

Psalms 96, **97**, 100
2 Samuel 9
Acts 8.4-25

Acts 8.4-25

'May your silver perish with you ...' (v.20)

As modern global citizens, if we are paid in money or in any of the global market's products, it seems that we will inevitably be subjected to its rule. And one of its powerful tendencies is to break down all our activities into measurable units, so that they can be costed against the comparable activities of other people all over the world.

In a world of performance indicators, and input/output ratios, it is difficult to know what to do with 'non-quantifiable' elements of life. A shared day of rest, for example – once valued highly for the solidarity it represented, for being a collective acknowledgement of the Sabbath grace that makes possible all our work – can seem a bit of a puzzle. Surely someone, somewhere will have to pay for it? We instinctively try to find a place for such non-quantifiable 'commodities' in the system of exchange. And that is just what Simon the Magician does here. For him, magic has been good business – he knows you can put a price on healing – and he is intrigued that Philip comes to Samaria with signs and healings for which he does not charge. And then he witnesses the gifts of the Holy Spirit being bestowed on new converts by the apostles, and his first response is to want to buy them for himself too. Peter's rebuke is severe.

Our world risks the same rebuke, with its conviction that markets are the real repository of value and of truth. Christians who come together as a Church co-operate with God's work of bringing about a new world order, by refusing to live by the market's values alone, and by placing their vocational centre of gravity in another framework of value and worship. Their witness is to God's free grace.

O God, you declare your almighty power
most chiefly in showing mercy and pity:
mercifully grant to us such a measure of your grace,
that we, running the way of your commandments,
may receive your gracious promises,
and be made partakers of your heavenly treasure;
through Jesus Christ your Son our Lord,
who is alive and reigns with you,
in the unity of the Holy Spirit,
one God, now and for ever.

COLLECT

235

Monday 27 August

Acts 8.26-end

'What is to prevent me from being baptized?' (v.36)

The eunuch described in this text presents something of a paradox. A castrated man, he held a post of great importance at the court of the Ethiopian queen, a common enough appointment in Mediterranean countries. But despite his high standing, the Jewish law made it absolutely clear that his castration barred him from full participation in the covenant community (Deuteronomy 23.1). It is in Luke's resolution of this tension that we see his preferential option for the excluded, the poor and the powerless.

For Israel, this incident enters uncharted territory, but Philip is one whose spiritual senses are finely tuned to God's guidance. The Spirit is working powerfully through him, as the miraculous signs detailed earlier bear witness (Acts 8.5-7). Historically, the eunuch's conversion indicates that God is now challenging Israel to allow the boundaries to be moved beyond the confines of those indicated in the law. But we, too, are being challenged here: to deepen our listening, not simply in order to discern the inner promptings of the Spirit, but that we may also be able to perceive where God is challenging our own fiercely defended boundaries.

How well are we able to see when God is attempting to 'move the goalposts'? And how willing are we to let him move them, and cooperate with him in the process?

COLLECT

Almighty and everlasting God,
you are always more ready to hear than we to pray
and to give more than either we desire or deserve:
pour down upon us the abundance of your mercy,
forgiving us those things of which our conscience is afraid
and giving us those good things which we are not worthy to ask
but through the merits and mediation
of Jesus Christ your Son our Lord,
who is alive and reigns with you,
in the unity of the Holy Spirit,
one God, now and for ever.

Psalm **106*** (or 103)
2 Samuel 12.1-25
Acts 9.1-19a

Acts 9.1-19a

'Lord, I have heard from many about this man ...' (v. 13)

At the same time that Philip was baptizing the eunuch, Saul was intensifying his persecution of the followers of the Way. The familiar account in today's text tells of his sudden awakening in the very midst of his increasing harassment of the believers. Struck blind by the experience, he is led to Damascus by his companions.

With Saul's conversion, the Israelites are taken even deeper into unknown territory, and their Jewish inheritance is being enlarged beyond their imagining. Ananias, knowing Saul's reputation only too well, is here put terrifyingly on the spot. God commands him to go and minister to Saul, because Saul is to have a unique role in the extension of God's kingdom. In trust and trepidation, Ananias obeys.

Had they been asked, Ananias' friends must surely have said he was mad! There is something slightly unsettling here about the nature of guidance. When seeking the way forward, we are wisely advised to take soundings, testing our impressions against the thoughts of those whose spiritual judgement we trust. But the risk is that we proceed only when we are as sure as we can be that things will work out. Occasionally, however, there are times, as here, when we have no such outer assurances – when we have nothing to guide us but the compelling voice of God within.

God of constant mercy,
who sent your Son to save us:
remind us of your goodness,
increase your grace within us,
that our thankfulness may grow,
through Jesus Christ our Lord.

COLLECT

237

Wednesday 29 August

Psalms 110, 111, 112
2 Samuel 15.1-12
Acts 9.19b-31

Acts 9.19b-31

'... the Jews plotted to kill him, but their plot became known to Saul' (vv.23-24)

Reading today's passage, I find my mind fast-forwarding 1,500 years to St John of the Cross, the sixteenth-century Carmelite friar and mystic. In 1567, he was enlisted by his older contemporary St Teresa of Avila in her reforming of the Carmelite order. Ten years later, he was imprisoned in the monastery at Toledo by those Carmelites violently opposed to the changes. John's eventual escape took place in the dark of night, down a rope of knotted blankets.

John's experience carries strong resonances of Saul's imprisonment by his erstwhile friends and allies. Despite Saul's conversion, the atmosphere still crackles with fear: the fear of the Jerusalem believers, because they did not believe Saul's change was genuine; the Jews' fear at the loss of their greatest advocate, and their consequent plot to kill him. Saul the predator has become Saul the prey, and the Jews are now his bitterest enemies. His escape, too, is by night.

We should not be surprised. The urge to kill what we perceive as hostile, or what we do not understand, is as old as humanity itself. But there are more ways of killing than physical murder.

What do you perceive as threats within your own life and experience? What – or who – would you prefer to 'kill', rather than have to confront an uncomfortable truth about yourself?

COLLECT

Almighty and everlasting God,
you are always more ready to hear than we to pray
and to give more than either we desire or deserve:
pour down upon us the abundance of your mercy,
forgiving us those things of which our conscience is afraid
and giving us those good things which we are not worthy to ask
but through the merits and mediation
of Jesus Christ your Son our Lord,
who is alive and reigns with you,
in the unity of the Holy Spirit,
one God, now and for ever.

Psalms 113, **115**
2 Samuel 15.13-end
Acts 9.32-end

Acts 9.32-end

'Aeneas, Jesus Christ heals you; get up and make your bed!' (v.34)

In 1984, the famous evangelical Anglican priest David Watson died of cancer at the young age of fifty. Once the diagnosis was known, much earnest prayer was offered, in the confidence that God would heal so that David's powerful evangelistic work could continue. When he died, therefore, there were desperate attempts in some quarters to account for why so much fervent prayer had not been answered. One suggestion was that, despite appearances, David's faith must not have been strong enough. Another, even more outlandish, was that his grandmother used to read tea leaves.

We do not know why David Watson died when he did, and why some are healed physically and others not. That this is so, reminds us that when we pray for healing, we are offering ourselves as channels for God to work in ways of which we cannot be fully aware. One of the 'reasons' for the healings in today's passage seems to be in order to encourage the continuing growth of the Church: both the healing of Aeneas and the raising to life of the widow Tabitha are followed by a surge in the Church's numbers.

Yes, we are called to pray in confidence and trust, but God's ways are not our ways, and the outcome must always lie within the mystery of his purposes.

God of constant mercy,
who sent your Son to save us:
remind us of your goodness,
increase your grace within us,
that our thankfulness may grow,
through Jesus Christ our Lord.

COLLECT

239

Friday 31 August

Acts 10.1-16

'Get up, Peter; kill and eat' (v.13)

There is something mildly reassuring about the fact that even an apostle as key to God's purposes as Peter seemed to need God's messages to him reinforced in triplicate. Before the crucifixion, Jesus had warned Peter that before the cock crew (Luke 22.34), he would deny him three times; and, after the resurrection, Jesus asked him three times if he loved him (John 21,15-17). And here, Peter's daytime vision shows him 'something like a large sheet' being lowered from heaven, containing all kinds of creatures, clean and unclean. And Peter takes the vision, three times, at face value: when urged to 'kill and eat' he indignantly refuses, even though he recognizes the voice as the Lord's.

It is important to remember that, at this point, Peter has no idea what the vision means. He simply responds instinctively, in accordance with his upbringing as a good Jew. For him, enlightenment will not be long in coming, but this is not always the case with the intimations from God that come to us. His communications may well be enigmatic, cryptic – and may not yield to immediate interpretation.

When this is so, we need to resist the temptation hurriedly to resolve the tension; we need rather to rest within the experience of 'unknowing' until the veil is lifted and the meaning is revealed.

COLLECT

Almighty and everlasting God,
you are always more ready to hear than we to pray
and to give more than either we desire or deserve:
pour down upon us the abundance of your mercy,
forgiving us those things of which our conscience is afraid
and giving us those good things which we are not worthy to ask
but through the merits and mediation
of Jesus Christ your Son our Lord,
who is alive and reigns with you,
in the unity of the Holy Spirit,
one God, now and for ever.

Psalms 120, **121**, 122
2 Samuel 17.1-23
Acts 10.17-33

Saturday 1 September

Acts 10.17-33

'Stand up; I am only a mortal' (v.26)

In today's reading, we witness the pivotal event for which Peter's vision has been the preparation: his meeting with Cornelius, who will be the first uncircumcised gentile to be admitted into the Christian faith as a result of Peter's preaching. The speed at which events move to this point is breathtaking, and the interventions of the Spirit in guiding Peter are urgent. Cornelius' men appear while Peter is still puzzling over the meaning of his three-fold vision, but the invitation they bring, together with the Spirit's prompting, enable him to make the necessary connections.

Cornelius' reaction on meeting Peter is to fall down at his feet and worship him, but Peter is quick to remind Cornelius that he, too, is only human. This was a vital realization: it would have been all too easy for Peter to be seduced by the miracles being worked through him, and to believe that they were somehow due to his own gifts and ability. Perhaps Peter's need for triple reinforcement was used by God to remind him that he had feet of clay, and that, in his own strength, the outcome had previously been a sorry failure.

There is to be no cult of personality here; the salvation being wrought is to be a miraculous work of God, not of some kind of superman.

God of constant mercy,
who sent your Son to save us:
remind us of your goodness,
increase your grace within us,
that our thankfulness may grow,
through Jesus Christ our Lord.

COLLECT

Monday 3 September

Acts 10.34-end

'... I truly understand that God shows no partiality' (v.34)

With today's reading comes the climax to which all the events of the last couple of chapters have been leading. Peter tells Cornelius and his household the good news of salvation, and the effect is instantaneous. 'The Holy Spirit fell upon all who heard the word' (v.44) with the gift of tongues and praise of God.

The rejoicing was not universal, however. Without the benefit of Peter's vision, the believers who accompanied him to Cornelius' house still needed some convincing. They were 'astounded' at what was happening – and their indignation leaps at us off the page. But Peter's challenge to them is direct and unflinching: 'Can anyone withhold the water for baptizing these people who have received the Holy Spirit just as we have?' (v. 47).

How often have we heard the words, 'Your God is too small'? The first Christian believers had to learn that the loving embrace of the God who had revealed himself to them so powerfully in the risen Christ extended far beyond the boundaries of the nation of Israel. In what ways is our God 'too small'? Who are the groups that we would exclude, and place beyond his loving embrace? These words still have resonance today, as God constantly eludes the limits that we, in our fear and weakness, try to place on him.

COLLECT

Almighty God,
who called your Church to bear witness
that you were in Christ reconciling the world to yourself:
help us to proclaim the good news of your love,
that all who hear it may be drawn to you;
through him who was lifted up on the cross,
and reigns with you in the unity of the Holy Spirit,
one God, now and for ever.

Tuesday 4 September

Acts 11.1-18

'Why did you go to uncircumcised men and eat with them?' (v.3)

Peter returns to Jerusalem, to find that the news of what happened with Cornelius has reached the believers there. Again, he is met with indignant incomprehension, and we can sense Peter's weariness as he begins to justify his actions yet again. What follows is a summary of the events we have been reflecting on these past few days, explained patiently 'step by step' as Peter attempts to take his hearers with him. At the end, his challenge to the Jerusalem believers is the same as that he posed to his travelling companions: 'If then God gave them the same gift that he gave us when we believed in the Lord Jesus Christ, who was I that I could hinder God?' (v.17).

And that question reduces Peter's critics first to silence and then to praise. Perhaps for us, too, there is wisdom in this sequence of response. Where the things of God are concerned, there is a limit to what we can achieve in personal or corporate understanding simply through argument and debate. We need to be silent so we may listen deeply for those truths of God that lie deeper than words; to wait for the gentle promptings of the Spirit so easily quenched by our noisy self-certainty. And from the depths of that silence, we cannot help but praise.

Almighty God,
you search us and know us:
may we rely on you in strength
and rest on you in weakness,
now and in all our days;
through Jesus Christ our Lord.

COLLECT

Wednesday 5 September

Acts 11.19-end

'... according to their ability, each would send relief to the believers living in Judea' (v.29)

After the intensity and close focus on the activities of Peter, the scene now broadens out to encompass events occurring over a wider canvas. Cornelius and his household are not the only non-Jewish converts: with the preaching in Antioch of some of those who had been scattered as a result of the persecution that followed Stephen's martyrdom, the gospel is making further inroads into the gentile world. By this time, the Church in Jerusalem accept and understand the way the Spirit is moving, and they send Barnabas to Antioch to strengthen and encourage the new believers. And it is now that Saul re-enters the picture: Barnabas brings him from Tarsus to Antioch and together they spend a year strengthening the Church there.

A constant theme running through all these narratives is that the good news of Jesus is never just for the individual alone. The love of God must constantly reach out, seeking to bring others within the circle of its light and life. And even the firmly established Church fellowship must keep its eyes turned outwards, alert to the needs of others.

When news of a severe famine reaches the Church in Antioch, they determine to send relief, according to their means, to the believers in Judea. And it is Barnabas and Saul who are entrusted with the mission.

COLLECT

Almighty God,
who called your Church to bear witness
that you were in Christ reconciling the world to yourself:
help us to proclaim the good news of your love,
that all who hear it may be drawn to you;
through him who was lifted up on the cross,
and reigns with you in the unity of the Holy Spirit,
one God, now and for ever.

Psalms **143**, 146
2 Samuel 19.24-end
Acts 12.1-17

Thursday 6 September

Acts 12.1-17

*'While Peter was kept in prison, the church prayed fervently
to God for him' (v.5)*

The rapid spread of the Church has its inevitable political effect, and Herod lays 'violent hands' on some of the believers. James the brother of John is killed, with Peter arrested and thrown into prison to await, presumably, the same fate. The night before Herod intends to act, Peter has another heavenly encounter; but this time it is no vision (v.9). Freed from his chains and guided by an angel past the sleeping guards to the lane outside the prison, Peter makes his way to the house of Mary, the mother of John Mark.

It is here that the tension yields to a touch of the Ealing comedies. The believers are praying, presumably for Peter and his plight, when he knocks at the gate. As the astonished maid in her consternation leaves Peter standing there, still knocking, the believers tell her she is mad. When Peter manages to convince them that it truly is him and not his 'angel', he urges them to tell the other believers what has happened.

Prayer is dynamite. Whether the results are dramatically in tune with what we ask for, or whether, as is more often the case, the response is more indirect, the act of praying connects us deeply and mysteriously with a God who always works in our lives for our good.

Almighty God,
you search us and know us:
may we rely on you in strength
and rest on you in weakness,
now and in all our days;
through Jesus Christ our Lord.

COLLECT

Friday 7 September

Acts 12.18-end

'... he was eaten by worms and died' (v.23)

Ealing comedy rapidly gives way to Hammer House of Horror – Luke graphically portrays the gruesome end of Herod's political machinations, as he becomes a victim of his own pride and hubris. There has been no escape, either, for Peter's hapless guards, put to death by Herod for not preventing his escape from prison. The weight of divine judgement hangs heavily in the air, cutting through a corrupt and unjust system that refuses to accept or acknowledge the claims of God. But despite the political and social upheavals, 'the word of God continued to advance and gain adherents' (v.24).

'God is working his purpose out, as year succeeds to year' state the words of a familiar hymn. But as we live under constant threat of terrorist attack in a world as turbulent and war-torn as ever, it is difficult to see beyond the surface appearance of things and hold on to that truth in faith. But the triumphant message here is that, despite all appearances to the contrary, the redeeming love of Christ, working in and through world events and personal circumstances, is unquenchable.

In the words of the same hymn: 'nearer and nearer draws the time, the time that shall surely be; when the earth shall be filled with the glory of God as the waters cover the sea.'

COLLECT

Almighty God,
who called your Church to bear witness
that you were in Christ reconciling the world to yourself:
help us to proclaim the good news of your love,
that all who hear it may be drawn to you;
through him who was lifted up on the cross,
and reigns with you in the unity of the Holy Spirit,
one God, now and for ever.

Saturday 8 September

Acts 13.1-12

*'... will you not stop making crooked the straight paths
of the Lord?' (v.10)*

God's work continues, and in Antioch the missionary pairing of Barnabas and Saul (hereafter Paul) is set apart by the Spirit for further work. At Salamis, they encounter devious opposition to their message when the Jewish magician Elymas attempts to turn the pro-consul Sergius Paulus away from the faith.

What follows is fascinating because of its resonances to a recent dramatic experience in Paul's own life. In place of 'Saul, Saul, why do you persecute me? (9.4), Paul challenges Elymas, 'You son of the devil ... will you not stop making crooked the straight paths of the Lord?' (v.10). Saul got up from the ground but was blind, and was not able to see again for three days. Here, he pronounces that Elymas, too, will be blind for a time (v.11). When Saul was blinded, his companions on the road 'led him by the hand and brought him to Damascus' (9.8), while Elymas 'went about groping for someone to lead him by the hand' (v.11).

This is the only time we meet Elymas, so it is impossible to know whether these resonances are deliberate, and that what we are witnessing here is Elymas' conversion. As Paul knew only too well, drastic situations call for drastic measures, and in the mercy of God, nothing is impossible.

Almighty God,
you search us and know us:
may we rely on you in strength
and rest on you in weakness,
now and in all our days;
through Jesus Christ our Lord.

COLLECT

Ordinary Time

Ordinary Time

Monday 10 September

Psalms 1, 2, 3
1 Kings 1.5-31
Acts 13.13-43

Acts 13.13-43

'So Paul stood up and with a gesture began to speak' (v.16)

This is a breathtaking overview of salvation history from Paul. You can tell he was trained in the Tarsus school by Gamaliel, that great Mediterranean Jewish scholar. You can also tell that all of this training and all of this command of the story of God's redeeming grace through Jewish history was itself utterly transformed and reinterpreted by Paul's experience of the risen Christ on the road to Damascus. Paul now sees that his dramatic encounter with God in resurrection life was, in fact, the life of God, who had created the journey of the people of Israel. This life had been moving through all of the history of the world and, in particular, in and through the consciousness and destiny of the ancestors of Israel. This life was present in their liberation from Egypt, in their wilderness time in the desert, in their settlement of Canaan, in the judges and kings – and now decisively and ultimately forthtold by John in the arrival of a saviour once and for all. This has to be good news. There can be no greater goodness than the goodness that this news comes to bring.

The resurrection of Jesus is all about the overcoming of the powers of sin and death. It is all about freedom from 'all those sins', meaning their death-dealing power, 'for God did not give us a spirit of cowardice, but rather a spirit of power and of love and of self-discipline' (2 Timothy 1.7).

COLLECT

Almighty God,
whose only Son has opened for us
a new and living way into your presence:
give us pure hearts and steadfast wills
to worship you in spirit and in truth;
through Jesus Christ your Son our Lord,
who is alive and reigns with you,
in the unity of the Holy Spirit,
one God, now and for ever.

Psalms **5**, 6 (8)
1 Kings 1.32 – 2.4; 2.10-12
Acts 13.44 – 14.7

Acts 13.44 – 14.7

'... a great number of both Jews and Greeks became believers' (14.1)

Can a new wine be contained in old wine skins? This incident is one of a number where we see the bursting of old wine skins with the strength and quality of new wine.

Some members of the Jewish community in Antioch, in Pisidia, loudly challenged and opposed Paul and Barnabas. This is because they had proclaimed the forgiveness of sins and the freedom Jesus brings to those who have faith. This freedom, they said, was not possible by the law of Moses, because God was doing a work that would not be believed under the old dispensation. New wine needs new wine skins to contain it at all for the sharing. And so Paul and Barnabas turn to the gentile community 'to be a light for the gentiles so that you may bring salvation to the ends of the earth'. This was a form of new wine skins for the new wine of the gospel of freedom from sin.

Some devout Jewish converts also became new wine bearers. However, this dynamic also occurred in a number of places where the apostles visited around the Mediterranean. The gospel grew in Greek communities, no longer confined to the smaller Jewish converts of the local synagogues where it was first preached. It was to become a message for the whole world. This is new wine for everyone and could be savoured everywhere because of the joy and the Holy Spirit that filled these disciples.

Merciful God,
your Son came to save us
and bore our sins on the cross:
may we trust in your mercy
and know your love,
rejoicing in the righteousness
that is ours through Jesus Christ our Lord.

COLLECT

Wednesday 12 September

Psalm **119.1-32**
1 Kings 3
Acts 14.8-end

Acts 14.8-end

'We are mortals just like you, and we bring you good news' (v.15)

Words like 'rise up and walk' immediately remind us of a command that Jesus gave to a crippled man. But here in this text, they come from Paul and have the same effect. 'The man sprang up and began to walk' (v.10). This event must have been so convincing that the priest of Zeus, mobilized by the crowds who had seen the healing, made a classic pagan response. Barnabas and Paul were given the names of gods and they were approached with pagan sacrifices. They tear their clothes and rush out into the crowd shouting '... we are mortals just like you'. They instinctively and strongly centre themselves in the God who made the heaven and the earth and the sea and all that is in them, who does good to humankind with rain from the heavens and fruitful seasons, which fill the people with food and their hearts with joy.

This is the secret to the 'power' of Paul and Barnabas in these chapters. This power is not their own; they are simply agents of the power. They would lose their power if they located it in themselves. They themselves are cracked vessels and Paul eventually dies a very mortal death. We ourselves are all vulnerable, limited and mortal, clay vessels, but we carry within us a power that transforms the world. It is not about us, it is about the power that is the grace and goodness of God in the world.

COLLECT

Almighty God,
whose only Son has opened for us
a new and living way into your presence:
give us pure hearts and steadfast wills
to worship you in spirit and in truth;
through Jesus Christ your Son our Lord,
who is alive and reigns with you,
in the unity of the Holy Spirit,
one God, now and for ever.

Thursday 13 September

Acts 15.1-21

'... he has made no distinction between them and us' (v.9)

Thank goodness that we find, in this portion of Acts, a detailed example of the liberating power of the gospel within the ordinary limitations and myopia of human group dynamics. Every Christian committee, council, Synod, organized gathering of any kind that has ever had to make a significant or fundamental decision has its inspiration and its hope in this event. The underlying issue is, as always, how inclusive is the grace of God? In this case, can uncircumcised Greek men and their families be included within the sacred realities of the new covenant? Do they need the outward and visible sign of the culture of Jewish men? Who is the gospel for and on what terms?

The apostles, Peter, Barnabas and Paul, functioning as bishops for the newly born Church, witnessed to the good news as it transformed the gentile community. Peter said God had cleansed the hearts of the gentiles by faith and, in so doing, had no distinction between Jews and gentiles. It was the cleansing of the heart by faith, not the outward marks that incorporated people in the saving grace of Christ. The power of the gospel is evidenced in what comes out of a person, not what is done upon them.

After much patient listening, conversation and prayer, the Holy Spirit caused a remarkable experience of God's big picture to fill the souls of everyone present. Where do we need this experience, here and now?

Merciful God,
your Son came to save us
and bore our sins on the cross:
may we trust in your mercy
and know your love,
rejoicing in the righteousness
that is ours through Jesus Christ our Lord.

COLLECT

251

Friday 14 September

Holy Cross Day

Psalms 2, 8, 146
Genesis 3.1-15
John 12.27-36a

John 12.27-36a

'... the kind of death he was to die.' (v.33)

You sometimes get the impression that it is Jesus' death alone that reconciles us to God, when listening to Christian teaching. In John's Gospel, the focus is not only on the death of Jesus and its reconciling effect, but also on Jesus' relationship with God throughout the incarnation. Jesus' birth, life, teaching, healing, actions, all express his utterly transparent love relationship with God, and this continues on into his death and resurrection. All of these realities witness to a reconciling grace through the presence of divine love in Jesus, which makes Jesus and his Father one throughout.

Jesus' death, anticipated here in this reading, is the consummation of everything that went before and is utterly true to it all. And so the cross finds its place in the centre of his being as it is within the heart of God. God's love is a cross-shaped love, a cross-shaped hope. This is the love and the hope that created the universe, the world and everything in it. This is the truth in the centre of everything: 'God so loved the world' (John 3.16). Sacred, self-giving love, seen on the cross, is simply a window into the way God lives and moves all of the time. God is full of love like this and constantly pours it out like this.

This love overcomes the shadows and malice of the world the way it did on Easter morning, all of the time. This is the love at the centre of your being as a Christian.

COLLECT

Almighty God,
who in the passion of your blessed Son
made an instrument of painful death
to be for us the means of life and peace:
grant us so to glory in the cross of Christ
that we may gladly suffer for his sake;
who is alive and reigns with you,
in the unity of the Holy Spirit,
one God, now and for ever.

Psalms 20, 21, **23**
1 Kings 8.1-30
Acts 15.36 – 16.5

Saturday 15 September

Acts 15.36 – 16.5

'The disagreement became so sharp that they parted company' (15.39)

It is an enormous relief to know that sharp disagreement was there at the beginning of the Church. Deep seismic tensions have been a characteristic of Church community dynamics ever since. Some of the issues are so profound that the Church has split down the middle. Even previously strong friendships have been fractured. It was Pusey who said, when thinking of the departure of his old friend and colleague, Newman, for the Roman Catholic Church, that 'it is what is unholy on both sides which keeps us apart'.

These divisions and partings of the way are particularly painful because Christ called us to be one, and we believe that his cross and resurrection have overcome the enmity between us, as well as the distance between us and God. So the sharp disagreement between Barnabas and Paul over John called Mark is a huge challenge to the integrity of the gospel itself. The resolution here is the creation of different parties going two different ways. However, we see from the rest of the account in Acts that this parting of the ways did not finally outmanoeuvre the cause of the gospel in the Mediterranean. Paul and Silas head for Derbe and Lystra and finally, unexpectedly, are called to Greece: the beginning of the Western Church. Barnabas and Mark sail to Cyprus, strengthening the mission in the central Mediterranean.

This parting did not damage mission overall and did not produce a different gospel. God is bigger than our differences.

Almighty God,
whose only Son has opened for us
a new and living way into your presence:
give us pure hearts and steadfast wills
to worship you in spirit and in truth;
through Jesus Christ your Son our Lord,
who is alive and reigns with you,
in the unity of the Holy Spirit,
one God, now and for ever.

COLLECT

253

Monday 17 September

Acts 16.6-24

'During the night Paul had a vision ...' (v.9)

It has sometimes been said 'if you want to hear God laugh, tell God your five-year plan!' In this story, we see the human-laid plans of Paul and Barnabas and John Mark, as well as their relationships, for a while, dribble into the sand. Then Paul attempts a very reasonable strategy – in human terms – to go into Bithynia, a very strategic Roman province. But the spirit of Jesus did not allow the party to proceed. Instead, during the night, down in Troas, Paul has a vision of a man calling him to come to Macedonia and help. This calling to proclaim the good news, in part of Greece, is not what Paul had in mind originally at all. And yet this divine inspiration, which altered Paul's plan and gave him a totally new vision, saw the gospel move into the borders of Western Europe for the first time. From this move, came the first churches of the West. From this base, western Christianity was born.

Had Paul proceeded up into Bithynia, not taking the vision seriously as a call from God, he may well have become bogged down in a very unproductive and beleaguered context. A move up into north-east central Asia, at that point, may have been the wrong move at the wrong time.

We are called to discern our Christian instincts when we are given visions on this earthly pilgrimage. We are not a compass unto ourselves.

COLLECT

God, who in generous mercy sent the Holy Spirit
    upon your Church in the burning fire of your love:
grant that your people may be fervent
    in the fellowship of the gospel
that, always abiding in you,
they may be found steadfast in faith and active in service;
through Jesus Christ your Son our Lord,
who is alive and reigns with you,
in the unity of the Holy Spirit,
one God, now and for ever.

Acts 16.25-end

'Sirs, what must I do to be saved?' (v.30)

From the shaking of the foundations, literally, comes the making of the foundations of a tiny cell church in Philippi. This area is still known for its regular and significant earthquakes. The earthquake here is a liberation of timing. Paul and Silas' freedom, suddenly opening up, also resulted in the liberation of their jailer and his household through baptism. All were shaken to their core; all were thrown together by the crisis and forged into that bond of Christian brotherhood and sisterhood. They all end up in Lydia's home who, through a similar miracle of timing, had been given an open heart to Paul's message in the days before, resulting in the baptism of her and all of her household. Her house is big enough to offer hospitality and undoubtedly became the first house church in Europe.

It has long been thought that Lydia's means as a businesswoman, and the roominess of her house as a host, provided the ideal conditions for the brothers and sisters to gather, including Paul, Silas and the jailer's family. Add to this mix the slave girl whom Paul and Silas had also liberated into Christ, under equally shaky conditions. She is freed from her slavery to her owners and also from her slavery to the fates of divination and fortune telling.

What a combination of class, gender, age and background! What diversity and unity! Just the precedent the newly founded Church would need to grow in freedom and truth.

Lord God,
defend your Church from all false teaching
and give to your people knowledge of your truth,
that we may enjoy eternal life
in Jesus Christ our Lord.

COLLECT

255

Wednesday 19 September

Psalm **34**
I Kings 10.1-25
Acts 17.1-15

Acts 17.1-15

'[Paul] argued with them from the scriptures' (v.2)

It is sometimes tempting to think that 'the truth' can be settled by trying to win an agreement over the exact terms of the authority of Scripture. A right understanding of Christian teaching or a faithful response to the truth of the gospel are not guaranteed by scholarly debates over the Bible or its meaning. The Bible also affirms this. There is no substitute for an authentic celebration of the gospel, embodied in the life of the Christian community. The real question is not *who* is right, but *what* is right? What is right in gospel terms is what happens when Christ is recognized in the centre of the room. By relating to the person, the wisdom and the grace of God in Christ, we then find our own relating between each other to be in proportion and in Christ. It is this kind of community life together that can truly draw all people toward Christ in faith.

In our passage today, the conflict between Paul and his critics is not actually over his interpretation of the Hebrew Scriptures but over Paul's faith position that the Messiah of God is the risen Jesus to whom the hope of the Scriptures is orientated. The real defence and proof of Paul's faith will not be established by proof texting from the scriptures, but ultimately by the Christ-shaped hope that was in him, personally and visibly. Paul is saved through hope, and this hope is the hope of everyone.

COLLECT

God, who in generous mercy sent the Holy Spirit
    upon your Church in the burning fire of your love:
grant that your people may be fervent
    in the fellowship of the gospel
that, always abiding in you,
they may be found steadfast in faith and active in service;
through Jesus Christ your Son our Lord,
who is alive and reigns with you,
in the unity of the Holy Spirit,
one God, now and for ever.

Thursday 20 September

Acts 17.16-end

*'... some scoffed; but others said, "We will hear you again
about this"' (v.32)*

This is one of the longest and most artful presentations of the gospel
in the New Testament. Paul has studied the context, he has reflected
on what matters most to the people, he has researched their
writings. Because of his point of difference, because of his courage
and persistence, he has made his presence felt in Athens. Crucially,
he is *asked to share* his message rather than making a forced entry.

He begins, appropriately, with God the creator of all things and all
peoples. Then he talks of the fundamental unity of all humankind in
God, the maker. Then he talks of the human search for God, the
source, in every human being, even though God is not far from any
one of us, in whom 'we live and move and have our being'. Then he
proclaims the living God who is present in all, rather than locked
into particular things. Then he proclaims the right judgement of the
world that comes in the justice and mercy of Christ, whose
resurrection has overcome the power of sin and death.

This way of presenting the gospel was so powerful that some of the
sophisticated – and probably somewhat cynical – intellectual
Athenians want to know more. Some also believe and join the body
of Christ. We can do well to learn from this powerful and eloquent
proclamation of the liberating good news of God in Christ. It is, after
all, the actual story of God in life.

Lord God,
defend your Church from all false teaching
and give to your people knowledge of your truth,
that we may enjoy eternal life
in Jesus Christ our Lord.

COLLECT

Friday 21 September

Matthew, Apostle and Evangelist

Psalms 49, 117
I Kings 19.15-end
2 Timothy 3.14-end

2 Timothy 3.14-17

'All scripture is inspired by God ...' (v.16)

This is the clearest statement we have in the whole of the Bible of what the sacred writings of Holy Scripture are actually for. The text says that the Scriptures are 'God-breathed'. This does not mean that the author of the particular Scriptures is simply inspired as an individual from within themselves, but is receiving sacred enlightenment and wisdom from God, from the mind of God.

Of course, this God-breathed insight is received in the mind of the particular author and takes its shape within that particular consciousness. The grammar is not God's dictation, but the message is. The purpose of the sacredness of the writing is for the end of 'making wise for salvation'. The whole point is that the sacred writings are for the great good of the disciples, to educate the Christian community to live the gospel. The emphasis here is on living, acting, making the word flesh, as it were, rather than quibbling over intricate details within the structure of the word, as interesting and significant as these are.

We might pray that what we read with our eyes, we may believe in our hearts, and that what we believe in our hearts, we may show forth in our lives. The point is not that we might simply tell others about the word, but that we might 'show' others the word. Ultimately, Christ is the Word and the written word of God in the Bible is a witness to this living Word.

COLLECT

O Almighty God,
whose blessed Son called Matthew the tax collector
to be an apostle and evangelist:
give us grace to forsake the selfish pursuit of gain
    and the possessive love of riches
that we may follow in the way of your Son Jesus Christ,
who is alive and reigns with you,
in the unity of the Holy Spirit,
one God, now and for ever.

Psalms 41, **42**, 43
I Kings 12.1-24
Acts 18.22 – 19.7

Acts 18.22 – 19.7

'Priscilla and Aquila ... took him aside and explained the Way of God to him more accurately' (18.26)

We are baptized by the Holy Spirit who makes the risen Jesus present within us and in the midst of our community. It is not Jesus alone but rather God as Father, Son and Holy Spirit who gathers the new baptized Christian up into the love field of the life of the holy and undivided Trinity. We find ourselves within the life of the triune God by being 'in Christ'. God as Creator made us and all things; God in Jesus redeemed us by his grace; God the Holy Spirit makes our faith-life 'happen'.

Apollos' approach had not offered baptism in Christ or the power of the Holy Spirit. This is why, even though Apollos was eloquent and well-educated in the Scriptures, he needed to be challenged with the fullness of the life of the God-head.

A rich and whole understanding of our faith is possible only if there is some sense of its being held in common by a wide variety of people who source their collective wisdom from the same sacred texts of the Bible. Apollos needed Priscilla and Aquila. It is interesting to note that here within this catholicity, a Christian woman forms an equal partnership with her husband and in the local congregation, as well as offering a lead. Apollos needed the benefit of the God-given wisdom of a woman in partnership.

God, who in generous mercy sent the Holy Spirit
upon your Church in the burning fire of your love:
grant that your people may be fervent
in the fellowship of the gospel
that, always abiding in you,
they may be found steadfast in faith and active in service;
through Jesus Christ your Son our Lord,
who is alive and reigns with you,
in the unity of the Holy Spirit,
one God, now and for ever.

COLLECT

259

Monday 24 September

Acts 19.8-20

'... collected their books and burned them publicly' (v.19)

What are we to make of this 'bonfire of the vanities'?

There are some remarkable things happening in this passage and much to admire. Paul opens his gospel up to debate and scrutiny among religious experts in the synagogue, and philosophers in the debating hall. He contends for the gospel as public truth, not some niche-marketed lifestyle option and is ready to take up the challenges that entails. Even his miracles obliquely witness to Paul's engagement with ordinary life. The 'handkerchiefs' and 'aprons' are really the sweatbands and craftsman's apron that went with his trade as a tentmaker. But a claim for public truth involves public controversy, and so we come to the book burning. Of course for those who freely chose to burn their magical books, this was an act of liberation, a clean break with the past, witnessing that the perfect love Paul preached had indeed – in some cases, literally – 'cast out fear'. Yet we cannot read this without remembering Milton's warning:

'Unless wariness be used, as good almost kill a man as kill a good book; who kills a man kills a reasonable creature, God's image; but he who destroys a good book, kills reason itself, kills the image of God, as it were, in the eye.'

In a world where bigots burn their enemies' sacred texts to provoke war and hatred, we had better be wary along with Milton, than be quite so gung-ho with Luke.

O Lord, we beseech you mercifully to hear the prayers
　　of your people who call upon you;
and grant that they may both perceive and know
　　what things they ought to do,
and also may have grace and power faithfully to fulfil them;
through Jesus Christ your Son our Lord,
who is alive and reigns with you,
in the unity of the Holy Spirit,
one God, now and for ever.

Psalms **48**, 52
I Kings 13.11-end
Acts 19.21-end

Acts 19.21-end

'... I must also see Rome' (v.21)

This verse is the key to the whole drama with which Acts concludes, and the worldwide Church begins: Paul's resolution first to go to Jerusalem and his recognition that, afterwards, his road inevitably leads to Rome. For these are not just lines on a map. The lines of tension that run between Jerusalem and Rome run through hearts and minds as well as fields and hills. Jerusalem and Rome are not only the two opposed power-points in the psycho-geography of Paul's world, they are still nodal points in the religious sensibility of our world.

Paul's journey between two ancient capitals is also a journey along those lines of tension between a whole series of apparently polar opposites: Jew and gentile, faith and philosophy, monoculture and multiculture, transcendent and immanent, imageless and manifest, exclusive and inclusive. But Paul's gospel, his ministry of reconciliation, was precisely to show that these contraries are complementary. In this pioneering mission, he was inevitably misunderstood as each of these separated 'poles' saw and despised in him its opposite. So, in the temple of Artemis, he is despised as the monotheist abolisher of images, and in the parallel and complementary riot scene in the temple of Yahweh, he is accused of idolatry. But, in both places, Paul was manifesting Christ, the reconciler, the God-man who holds all these tensions together in one person and has thereby released a new energy and power of love into the world.

Lord of creation,
whose glory is around and within us:
open our eyes to your wonders,
that we may serve you with reverence
and know your peace at our lives' end,
through Jesus Christ our Lord.

COLLECT

Wednesday 26 September

Psalm **119.57-80**
1 Kings 17
Acts 20.1-16

Acts 20.1-16

'... began to sink off into a deep sleep while Paul talked still longer' (v.9)

This passage is one of the first accounts we have of worship in the early church and already someone has fallen asleep! It's an unfair reading, of course, but the inclusion of this episode, which might be seen as unflattering to Paul, yet reads so clearly as an eye-witness account, makes me feel the whole narrative of Acts is trustworthy. Indeed, verse 5 gives us one of those unguarded moments when Luke slips into the first person narrative and we realize he is reading from his own journal of these events.

What do we make of this episode now, apart from taking comfort in the thought that sometimes even Paul could be less than riveting? Well, the presence of the 'lad' itself seems telling; we get the sense of a mixed gathering of all ages, and all sorts and conditions – so this is 'all-age worship'. Because 'the breaking of bread' is mentioned twice in this passage, it may be that the service described here included both an '*Agape*' (or 'love-feast') and also a Eucharist. So these Christians were sharing an evening meal, but they were also celebrating the mystery of their communion with one another and with Christ. The conviviality of 'café church' and the solemnity of the holy mysteries both had a place for them in the same service! Once again Paul seems to be reconciling 'opposites' that we have chosen to divide.

COLLECT

O Lord, we beseech you mercifully to hear the prayers
    of your people who call upon you;
and grant that they may both perceive and know
    what things they ought to do,
and also may have grace and power faithfully to fulfil them;
through Jesus Christ your Son our Lord,
who is alive and reigns with you,
in the unity of the Holy Spirit,
one God, now and for ever.

Psalms 56, **57** (63*)
1 Kings 18.1-20
Acts 20.17-end

Thursday 27 September

Acts 20.17-end

*'And now I commend you to God and to the message
of his grace' (v.32)*

What an extraordinary act of letting go this is. Think of all the love
and effort that Paul had poured into the church at Ephesus, all he
had suffered in his efforts to build them up. Most people would
want to hang on to their achievements tightly with both hands.
Most of us in Paul's position – especially given his fears and
premonitions about the 'fierce wolves' that might come in his
absence – would be over-controlling and overprotective, keeping
our fingers on the levers of power, 'for the sake of the vulnerable'.
But Paul just lets it all go and is free to walk away. He lets it all go
because he knows he can let it go into God. Here is a pastor who is
confident that God can occasionally manage without him!

Not many vicars have to leave a parish because they are 'under arrest
and bound for certain suffering', but people have to leave parishes
and churches nevertheless, leaving behind half-finished tasks,
delegating, letting go … If we could be as trusting as this, as ready
as Paul is just to drop everything and everyone into the hands of
God, then we might not only make parting easier, but we might
also carry our cares more lightly in the first instance, knowing that
they were always shared with and ready to be returned to the God
whose grace is sufficient for us all.

Lord of creation,
whose glory is around and within us:
open our eyes to your wonders,
that we may serve you with reverence
and know your peace at our lives' end,
through Jesus Christ our Lord.

COLLECT

263

Friday 28 September

Acts 21.1-16

'Through the Spirit they told Paul not to go on to Jerusalem' (v.4)

As Paul fulfils his calling and turns towards Jerusalem, there is a sense of mounting dread and danger, but also of intense clarity, the sense of something fore-ordained, yet freely chosen, something glimpsed over a horizon at last becoming manifest. There are strong parallels with the turning point in the Gospels where Jesus sets his face towards Jerusalem and, bewildered, frightened, still protesting, the disciples stumble after. The closer Paul gets to his destination, the more dire the warnings become – and yet the clearer Paul's sense of vocation. And to answer that calling, Paul has to gainsay dear friends and fellow Christians who claim to be speaking in the name of the Lord and under direct guidance of the Holy Spirit. This necessary disagreement, and contradiction, reduces him to tears, and he exclaims 'What are you doing, weeping and breaking my heart?' (v.13).

So much of our life together as Anglicans now has just this heartbreaking combination of deep spiritual kinship and fundamental disagreement, of disciples who have journeyed together each feeling called to take a separate path. But here, at least, the disagreeing parties had the grace to let each other follow conscience and say 'The Lord's will be done' (v.14).

COLLECT

O Lord, we beseech you mercifully to hear the prayers
    of your people who call upon you;
and grant that they may both perceive and know
    what things they ought to do,
and also may have grace and power faithfully to fulfil them;
through Jesus Christ your Son our Lord,
who is alive and reigns with you,
in the unity of the Holy Spirit,
one God, now and for ever.

Saturday 29 September

Michael and All Angels

Acts 12.1-11

'Peter went out and followed him' (v.9)

The thought of St Michael and All Angels conjures up images of cosmic powers, 'supernal energies, in their unguessed-at modes of being,' to borrow a phrase of English poet John Heath-Stubbs. But, here, we see the angelic manifest in the midst of the ordinary: the close confines of the prison and the plain pavements of the high street, though there is still something dreamlike and mysterious in the whole sequence – the sudden summons, the chains simply falling off and the door swinging silently open of its own accord. Peter naturally thought he was dreaming until he saw that the waking result of this dream-sequence was real and practical liberation.

Whatever happened outwardly and visibly in those pre-dawn hours in Jerusalem, there is no doubt that this story, the story of an awakening, a summons, a loosing of chains and a new freedom, unfolds a sequence that has repeatedly transformed lives from that day to this. For example, every detail of this story informs the inscape of Charles Wesley's soul, his own story, as he tells it in a hymn that rings true for so many who sing it now:

'Long my imprisoned spirit lay
Fast bound in sin and nature's night;
Thine eye diffused a quickening ray,
I woke, the dungeon flamed with light;
My chains fell off, my heart was free,
I rose, went forth and followed Thee.'

Everlasting God,
you have ordained and constituted
the ministries of angels and mortals in a wonderful order:
grant that as your holy angels always serve you in heaven,
so, at your command,
they may help and defend us on earth;
through Jesus Christ your Son our Lord,
who is alive and reigns with you,
in the unity of the Holy Spirit,
one God, now and for ever.

Acts 21.37 – 22.21

'Saul, Saul, why are you persecuting me?' (22.7)

The words of the risen Christ are extraordinary and contain the key to all Paul's subsequent teaching about the Church, about our life in Christ, and his life in us. For Christ does not say 'Why are you persecuting my followers, or my friends?' but 'Why are you persecuting *me*?'

Years later, Matthew was to record the saying, 'just as you did it to one of the least of these who are members of my family, you did it to me' (Matthew 25:40), but Paul saw it all in an instant on the road to Damascus. And it had to be that road and no other. For it was outside the Damascus gate that Paul had stood by and consented to the shedding of Stephen's blood. He must have ridden past that spot, the memories of that horrific death still fresh, the ground darkened with blood.

When the scales fall from his eyes in Damascus, he sees not just Ananias, a devout man whom he had intended to persecute, but he also sees a part of the Body of Christ, and from then on everywhere, in the poor and ragged followers of the way, even in himself, the poorest and most ragged of them all, he sees the risen Christ, the glory of God in a human being fully alive.

COLLECT

Almighty God,
you have made us for yourself,
and our hearts are restless till they find their rest in you:
pour your love into our hearts and draw us to yourself,
and so bring us at last to your heavenly city
where we shall see you face to face;
through Jesus Christ your Son our Lord,
who is alive and reigns with you,
in the unity of the Holy Spirit,
one God, now and for ever.

Acts 22.22 – 23.11

'Is it legal for you to flog a Roman citizen who is uncondemned?'
(22.25)

Is it lawful for you to water-board a detainee who is uncondemned? If torture is illegal or distasteful to you, will you have him rendered to some other country where your friends can do it for you?

The whole sequence of events in these chapters poses serious questions about how we handle those who are accused of sedition and stirring up religious hatred, for these are the very things of which Paul stood accused. It also raises questions about the accountability of our enforcers. It's remarkable what an immediate protection Paul's legal status as a Roman afforded him, 'Immediately those who were about to examine him drew back from him' (v.29).

They withdrew because they knew there would be consequences for them if they abused Paul, for they belonged to a legal system where even the most high-handed of officers could not act with impunity. Paul is a 'suspect' in the eyes of both religious and secular establishments. It is chastening for those of us who belong to a religious establishment to observe that here, in our own Scriptures, it is the secular establishment that is shown to have acted with greater justice.

Gracious God,
you call us to fullness of life:
deliver us from unbelief
and banish our anxieties
with the liberating love of Jesus Christ our Lord.

COLLECT

Wednesday 3 October

Acts 23.12-end

'Now the son of Paul's sister heard about the ambush' (v.16)

Oh no, Uncle Paul's in trouble again!

The sudden appearance of Paul's young nephew comes as quite a shock. We are used to seeing Paul as a colossal, iconic figure, a foundational theologian, a mover and shaker on the wide stage of history. We don't think of him as a man with an anxious and bewildered family. His Tarsus kindred must have been so proud that he'd gone to Jerusalem to study with the great Gamaliel. Perhaps his nephew had come to Jerusalem to follow in his distinguished uncle's footsteps? Instead, he found himself caught up in a bitter conflict that divided, perhaps imperilled, his whole family. For the Sanhedrin were persecuting Paul with the special bitterness they reserved for one of their own, as indeed Paul had done in his turn. If his nephew was aware of the plot, it may be because he was expected to approve, or even be part of it. For the plotters, this was in some sense an 'honour killing'; Paul had betrayed his fellow Pharisees by joining a heretical sect, and such a betrayal might well be seen as a stain on his family name.

What risks this young man took to visit his uncle and then reveal the plot to the authorities, what divided loyalties he may have felt. The families of those we incarcerate must go through the same thing every day.

Almighty God,
you have made us for yourself,
and our hearts are restless till they find their rest in you:
pour your love into our hearts and draw us to yourself,
and so bring us at last to your heavenly city
where we shall see you face to face;
through Jesus Christ your Son our Lord,
who is alive and reigns with you,
in the unity of the Holy Spirit,
one God, now and for ever.

Psalm **78.1-39***
2 Kings 1.2-17
Acts 24.1-23

Acts 24.1-23

'But this I confess unto thee, that after the way which they call heresy, so worship I the God of my fathers' (v.14 KJV)

The King James Version, whose 400th anniversary we celebrate this year, dares to use the 'H' word, transliterating the Greek: 'heresy'. The NRSV shies away with the euphemism 'a sect'. So Paul, the common source and acknowledged authority for all the writers on every side of every Church divide who have ever called one another 'heretic', is himself accused of heresy!

One might have hoped that this episode would have given every subsequent controversialist pause before they drew breath to anathematize one another. Indeed, Paul's very phrasing – 'that way which *they call heresy*' – draws our attention to the fact that 'heresy' is always an adversarial, and not an objective, definition. That is not to say that there isn't an ultimate truth, and that some people will turn out to have been right and others wrong. But it is to say that all our present definitions are necessarily partial and partisan, and that now, in this present life, we need a certain humility before the truth, a certain courtesy towards one another. For now, as Paul says in another place, 'our knowledge is imperfect', and until the glass through which we are all peering at the mystery is a little less dark, it behoves us to suspend our judgement.

Gracious God,
you call us to fullness of life:
deliver us from unbelief
and banish our anxieties
with the liberating love of Jesus Christ our Lord.

COLLECT

Psalm **55**
2 Kings 2.1-18
Acts 24.24 – 25.12

Acts 24.24 – 25.12

'You have appealed to the emperor; to the emperor you will go'
(25.12)

'What is truth? said jesting Pilate, and would not stay for an answer' – so Francis Bacon, the English Renaissance philosopher, opens his famous essay 'On Truth'. But the case of Felix is stranger still. He is drawn to Paul and troubled by him – he doesn't seem to know himself whether he wants redemption, entertainment, or a backhander! Perhaps he wants all three at once, his motives as mixed as ours. Paul's gospel would have been as good news for Felix and Drusilla as for anyone, but their moment comes and goes. Felix's corruptions and intrigues finally catch up with him and his own prisoner outlasts him. So the whole process begins again with Festus – the trials and retrials – when Paul makes his dramatic move.

Paul's appeal to Caesar was not so much a 'Get out of Jail' card as a 'Get into a Different Jail' card, and naturally our response to this momentous decision is coloured by our knowledge of Paul's eventual martyrdom in Rome. Nevertheless, Luke is at pains to demonstrate the Roman system working well, within its limits, and also to hint that more is at work in these events than the routines of a secular administration; the man with a message that would turn the Roman world upside down was being enabled to speak that message in the heart of Rome itself.

COLLECT

Almighty God,
you have made us for yourself,
and our hearts are restless till they find their rest in you:
pour your love into our hearts and draw us to yourself,
and so bring us at last to your heavenly city
where we shall see you face to face;
through Jesus Christ your Son our Lord,
who is alive and reigns with you,
in the unity of the Holy Spirit,
one God, now and for ever.

Acts 25.13-end

'I would like to hear the man myself' (v.22)

'... you will be dragged before governors and kings because of me, as a testimony to them and the gentiles' (Matthew 10.18).

Christ's predictions, recorded in Matthew chapter 10, come true, one by one, in Acts. Paul has already been delivered up to councils and flogged in synagogues (Matthew 10.17) and has shown before the Sanhedrin that he could indeed be 'wise as serpents' and 'innocent as doves' (Matthew 10.16), and now he comes before the governor and the king.

The appearance of King Agrippa and Bernice in all their finery is one of the great set pieces in Acts, and, like so much in Luke's skilful narrative, the description is laced with all kinds of subversive irony. Agrippa and Bernice take their place 'with great pomp' says Luke, for he knows, as does everyone else, that the 'king' is a mere puppet, and it is his host, the mere 'governor', who is actually in charge. Luke lays it on even thicker: the purple-clad royalty, flanked with the assembled phalanxes of high-ranking officials, the 'military tribunes and prominent men of the city' (v.23), all of them, having everything, yet possessing nothing – and then Paul stands before them, a tent-maker in chains, 'treated as an impostor and yet true, as unknown, and yet well-known, ... poor, yet making many rich; having nothing, yet possessing everything' (2 Corinthians 6.9-10).

Gracious God,
you call us to fullness of life:
deliver us from unbelief
and banish our anxieties
with the liberating love of Jesus Christ our Lord.

COLLECT

Monday 8 October

Acts 26.1-23

*'I will rescue you from your people and from the gentiles –
to whom I am sending you' (v.17)*

In Paul's speech before Agrippa and Festus, we have a sense, much as we have in the scenes of Christ before Pilate, that it is the prisoner who is in charge, the man in chains who is the active free agent, and the supposedly free captors who are chained and constrained by their circumstances. The series of ironic reversals in this scene is crowned by Paul's use of the word *apostello*, for he tells Agrippa that Christ appeared to him and said: *ego apostello se* 'I am sending you' (v.17).

For Paul the meaning of the word apostle had already been radically subverted. An emissary of the Sanhedrin with letters of authority was formally known as an 'apostolos'. It was as an apostle of the Sanhedrin that he had set out for Damascus, as an apostle of Christ that he arrived. Festus was also, in one sense, an apostle. It was with delegated authority as an 'apostle of Caesar' that he had summoned Paul. But now he discovers that these roles are reversed. He thought he was summoning Paul, but Paul was summoning him; he thought he had been sent to deliver Paul up to the judgement of Caesar, but Paul has been sent to deliver him up to the judgement of Christ. Festus and Agrippa wanted to face Paul with the consequences of his choices; instead, he faces them with the consequences of theirs.

COLLECT

Almighty and everlasting God,
increase in us your gift of faith
that, forsaking what lies behind
and reaching out to that which is before,
we may run the way of your commandments
and win the crown of everlasting joy;
through Jesus Christ your Son our Lord,
who is alive and reigns with you,
in the unity of the Holy Spirit,
one God, now and for ever.

Acts 26.24-end

'Are you so quickly persuading me to become a Christian?' (v.28)

Here we see, in the reactions of Festus and Agrippa, the two classic strategies for avoiding an uncomfortable truth: explaining away and walking away. Instead of actually responding to the rationality of Paul's arguments, Festus explains it all away with a diagnosis of madness, 'I am afraid to listen to him so I will label him "mad", and since he is now "mad", I needn't listen to him.' This is, of course, the very stratagem used to chilling effect in many totalitarian regimes, where rational opposition is medicalized, dissidents are put in mental hospitals and sedated, or worse – but perhaps we do the same to our cost. For many years, we postponed attention to the arguments of environmentalists, dismissing them as a 'lunatic fringe'. Now we hear too late.

Agrippa, who is more deeply moved and knows he might be on the brink of a real change, just makes an exit so that his attention might be diverted. Our culture is almost entirely driven by the need for diversion and evasion, so that now we don't need to get up and leave the room lest a train of thought might challenge all we are; we have only to flip a channel or click a hyperlink.

God, our judge and saviour,
teach us to be open to your truth
and to trust in your love,
that we may live each day
with confidence in the salvation which is given
through Jesus Christ our Lord.

COLLECT

Acts 27.1-26

*'Julius treated Paul kindly, and allowed him to go to his friends
to be cared for' (v.3)*

This is an example of kindness and empathy on the part of those who have power to make a difference. Since Paul's theology allowed that Christ might be worshipped even as an 'unknown god', so here we see the pagan Julius, serving Christ, though he little knows it, as he meets the needs of one of the least of those who belong to Christ. The other striking thing about this verse is that it gives another instance of the way in which, wherever he goes, in all the scattered ports of the Mediterranean, Paul meets with friends and receives hospitality. It gives depth and substance both to his constant urging in the letters that we should practise hospitality and be 'kindly affectioned' (Romans 12.10 AV) one to another and also his genuine thanksgiving for the Christians in all the scattered communities to which he writes. Almost every letter he writes begins with a thanksgiving for its recipients, even and especially those letters that reveal he has doctrinal differences with his correspondents.

Julius was to have a chance, in this gentle start to their journey, to see what deep affection and respect Paul inspired; in the second part of the voyage, he would discover just how strong and dependable a companion Paul could be when things got rough.

COLLECT

Almighty and everlasting God,
increase in us your gift of faith
that, forsaking what lies behind
and reaching out to that which is before,
we may run the way of your commandments
and win the crown of everlasting joy;
through Jesus Christ your Son our Lord,
who is alive and reigns with you,
in the unity of the Holy Spirit,
one God, now and for ever.

274

Psalms **90**, 92
2 Kings 9.17-end
Acts 27.27-end

Acts 27.27-end

'... none of you will lose a hair from your heads' (v.34)

This account of a storm at sea is strangely reminiscent of the book of Jonah, evoking a series of parallels and reversals. Both Jonah and Paul are prophets of God embarked on a voyage in which the safety of the whole crew is bound up with their own. For both of them, obedience to God (delayed, in Jonah's case) ultimately brings safety to their companions. Paul – apparently a prisoner, but really free – travels in God's care to the city God has chosen. Jonah – apparently free, but really God's escaped prisoner – flees from God's chosen city, only to be found and turned around by his master. Both men assure their fellow travellers that they are safe and that God has mercy on those who do not know him as well as those who serve him. But, whereas Jonah's disobedience to Yahweh was the cause of the storm, Paul's obedience to Christ is the guarantee that his companions will survive the storm.

Christ had, of course, offered the sign of Jonah as the sign of his resurrection and his mission. This shipwreck to come, with Paul and the crew cast into the sea and then brought safe on to land, is both a historical event and an emblem of that death and resurrection. In the midst of the storm, Paul breaks bread and makes Eucharist for Jesus, the true Jonah who cast himself overboard that we might all be saved.

God, our judge and saviour,
teach us to be open to your truth
and to trust in your love,
that we may live each day
with confidence in the salvation which is given
through Jesus Christ our Lord.

COLLECT

Friday 12 October

Acts 28.1-16

'… they changed their minds and began to say that he was a god'
(v.6)

This turn of events on Malta is a striking example of how we either demonize or deify people, and how these twin projections of our own 'stuff' are related. We will always demonize the person we have deified when they fail to deliver the heavenly goods. Unfortunately, these projections onto others cast a long shadow across our history. In his poem 'Epitaph for Anton Schmidt', Tom Gunn, the Anglo-American poet, praises the clear-sightedness of a German soldier who found a way of helping the Jews he was supposed to be exterminating:

> 'I know he had unusual eyes,
> Whose power no orders could determine,
> Not to mistake the men he saw,
> As others did, for gods or vermin.'

Paul too had a clarified vision, for the scales had fallen from his eyes: '… we look not at what can be seen', he said, 'but at what cannot be seen; for what can be seen is temporary, but what cannot be seen is eternal' (2 Corinthians 4.18). And what he saw, in all the children of God, was a hidden glory that all creation is longing to see revealed.

COLLECT

Almighty and everlasting God,
increase in us your gift of faith
that, forsaking what lies behind
and reaching out to that which is before,
we may run the way of your commandments
and win the crown of everlasting joy;
through Jesus Christ your Son our Lord,
who is alive and reigns with you,
in the unity of the Holy Spirit,
one God, now and for ever.

Acts 28.17-end

'He … welcomed all who came to him' (v.30)

So Paul arrives in Rome, and there is both a great sense of completion, of things falling into place, and yet also of tragic incompleteness, a wound in the being of his mission, a wound which he probes and searches deeply in the eleventh chapter of his letter to the Romans. Almost Paul's first action is to call together the leaders of the Jewish community. He is well aware of his apostolate to the gentiles, but his heart is as open as ever to his own people, and it seems that none of the disappointments, the furies and the lynching he has received so far has defeated the faith, the hope, or the love he wants to share. Even when he admits temporary defeat in his efforts to share the gospel, he does it in words from Isaiah, words that were on Jesus' lips and words which, taken rightly, are as much a promise of final recognition as a rebuke for temporary blindness.

Luke the gentile narrator wants to rush to the message that the gentiles will listen, but Paul the Jew, hurt and exasperated as he is, knows that the old olive tree belongs as much to God as the new graft. Even here in the centre of the gentile world, he knows that Christ is for all – Jew as well as gentile, slave as well as free.

God, our judge and saviour,
teach us to be open to your truth
and to trust in your love,
that we may live each day
with confidence in the salvation which is given
through Jesus Christ our Lord.

COLLECT

277

Monday 15 October

Philippians 1.1-11

'I am confident … that the one who began a good work among you will bring it to completion' (v.6)

'Be patient, God hasn't finished with me yet!' ran the slogan on the T-Shirt of an annoyingly noisy teenager on the campsite of a Christian arts festival – and so my words of rebuke were stopped in my throat, and I sighed and thought 'Fair enough'.

Paul's gospel of a dynamic, ongoing work of God, an unfolding through time of the eternally given implications of incarnation and resurrection, goes even further than the observation that all of us are, in one way or another, 'works in progress'. We are all in his view, 'partakers of grace' and channels through which the reconciling love released into the world by Christ may abound as more and more people consciously participate 'in Christ'. This ongoing, dynamic reconfiguring in Christ of all we thought we knew is already implicit in Paul's greeting to the Philippians: 'Grace to you and peace' (v.2). 'Grace' (*'charis'*) is the characteristic greeting of the gentile, Greek-speaking world, and 'Peace' (*'eirene'*, *'shalom'*) is the special greeting of the eastern peoples. Philippi lay on the mountain pass between Asia and Europe, and Paul wants the Philippians to become reconcilers and connecters 'in Christ', mutually exchanging, between Jew and gentile, these once-exclusive blessings.

COLLECT

O God, forasmuch as without you
we are not able to please you;
mercifully grant that your Holy Spirit
may in all things direct and rule our hearts;
through Jesus Christ your Son our Lord,
who is alive and reigns with you,
in the unity of the Holy Spirit,
one God, now and for ever.

Philippians 1.12-end

'I want you to know, beloved, that what has happened to me has actually helped to spread the gospel' (v.12)

'My passion his action' wrote John Donne, the great preacher and poet, reflecting on the grace at work in his apparent helplessness, as he lay ill. In a single phrase, Paul here reveals just such a paradox and reversal, a new reading of the whole story of his arrest in Jerusalem and his being carried as a prisoner to Rome. Outwardly and officially, from the point of view of the various authorities involved in Paul's incarceration and deportation to Rome, the 'advance' of a pernicious doctrine is being halted, and a ringleader is being taken out of circulation.

Luke's narrative in Acts reveals a different truth. Paul's journey to Rome is the triumphant progress of a royal ambassador; kings are summoned to his presence; and he is given a guard and escort and greeted with joy as he travels down the Appian Way to the heart of Rome. And now, in Rome at the climax of that journey, Paul reveals that he has access to the whole Praetorian Guard and, through them, to the household of Caesar. Things could not have been better arranged!

In our present darkness, it is hard to find the providence hidden in the midst of our happenstance, but this letter gives us good grounds for trying.

Faithful Lord,
whose steadfast love never ceases
and whose mercies never come to an end:
grant us the grace to trust you
and to receive the gifts of your love,
new every morning,
in Jesus Christ our Lord.

COLLECT

Wednesday 17 October

Philippians 2.1-13

'Let the same mind be in you that was in Christ Jesus' (v.5)

It is good to be reminded that the context for this golden passage of 'Christology' is an appeal to a divided church for humility towards one another, an appeal for a unity that will come only from a mutual kenosis, from our own ways of self-emptying. So much has been said, and will be said, about incarnation here, about what is unique to Christ in this hymn to the divine humility, about the way the incarnation reveals the heart of God's self-giving Love. But to contemplate kenosis in the mind of Christ is not for Paul a theological speculation but an active participation. 'We have the mind of Christ' – it is possible for our mutual love to continue that divine momentum away from self and towards the other.

As we stare across the divide between conservative and liberal, tradition and fresh expression, North and South, can we find enough encouragement in what we share, enough compassion and sympathy, enough consolation from the Love we all acknowledge, to stop clinging to an identity that depends on being against some heretical 'other', and become instead parts of the bridge that Love wants to build between us?

COLLECT

O God, forasmuch as without you
we are not able to please you;
mercifully grant that your Holy Spirit
may in all things direct and rule our hearts;
through Jesus Christ your Son our Lord,
who is alive and reigns with you,
in the unity of the Holy Spirit,
one God, now and for ever.

Psalms 145, 146
Isaiah 55
Luke 1.1-4

Isaiah 55

'See, you shall call nations that you do not know' (v.5)

It's easy to see why this passage of Isaiah was chosen for the day we remember Luke the Evangelist, who was also Luke the gentile. His very conversion and participation in the gospel is a fulfilment of this prophecy, and his further role in Acts as the companion and chronicler of Paul in his mission to the gentiles fulfils Isaiah's prophecy even further.

But Isaiah 55 reveals a yet deeper connection with the vision of Luke's Gospel. A free offer of refreshment to the thirsty, and bread, wine and milk to the poor (v.1), a call for the return of the strays and the prodigals to a God who will abundantly pardon (v.7), a vision of a final and inclusive joy in which the very trees and hedgerows participate (vv.12-13) – these elements of Isaiah's prophecy are all the leading marks of Luke's Gospel, and might be summed up in the revelation that God's generosity is not limited by the short reach of our stunted imagination, 'for as the heavens are higher than the earth, so are my ways higher than your ways, and my thoughts than your thoughts' (v.9).

Almighty God,
you called Luke the physician,
whose praise is in the gospel,
to be an evangelist and physician of the soul:
by the grace of the Spirit
and through the wholesome medicine of the gospel,
give your Church the same love and power to heal;
through Jesus Christ your Son our Lord,
who is alive and reigns with you,
in the unity of the Holy Spirit,
one God, now and for ever.

COLLECT

281

Psalm **139**
2 Kings 19.20-36
Philippians 3.1 – 4.1

Philippians 3.1 – 4.1

'For his sake I have suffered the loss of all things, and I regard them as rubbish, in order that I may gain Christ' (3.8)

'That's me in the corner
That's me in the spotlight
Losing my Religion.'

So sang REM in their definitively mournful 90s hit, but here St Paul is not so much mournfully losing his religion as gleefully throwing it away! For what he 'regards as rubbish' in this passage is not discarded sin or error, but discarded religious achievement and status. Every distinguishing mark and sign of election, excellence and distinction is cast aside in order that he may begin again with Christ. And he wants to begin at the same point on the scale, the zero point, as every other needy human being. This is indeed kenosis in practice (see p. 280): a debonair detachment from the very status and respectability that, for so many, is the unacknowledged goal of religious life. 'No one can claim already to have heard the gospel', said Karl Barth, the great Swiss reformed theologian, in one of his startling aphorisms, for even faith can turn into an ego-inflating work when we cling to the status it confers.

To grasp the one who has grasped us, we must let go of everything else, even and especially our religious achievements and reputation.

COLLECT

O God, forasmuch as without you
we are not able to please you;
mercifully grant that your Holy Spirit
may in all things direct and rule our hearts;
through Jesus Christ your Son our Lord,
who is alive and reigns with you,
in the unity of the Holy Spirit,
one God, now and for ever.

Saturday 20 October

Philippians 4.2-end

'... help these women because they have struggled beside me in the work of the gospel' (v.3)

It may be that a temporary disagreement between two leading women in the Philippian church was the occasion for this entire letter. It is certain that, from Paul's initial encounter with Lydia onwards, women played a leading role in the founding and growth of that church, and it is abundantly clear that Paul regarded them as partners in the gospel, not simply home-makers and hostesses.

Scholars suggest that women in Macedonia had a great deal more power and leverage in society than they did in, for example, Corinth, and it is extraordinary, given his background, that this was an aspect of Macedonian culture with which Paul seemed perfectly comfortable. Once more, the kenosis of Christ is ongoing in his Body the Church, for Paul has emptied out and cast aside his own pharisaical culture in order to know Christ. Not Christ the remembered Jewish man, but Christ alive, living and loving in these two gentile women. For, whatever their present disagreement, Paul knows that their final agreement will be 'in the Lord', for they are as surely 'in Christ' as he is and we are.

Perhaps only when we are prepared to 'forget what lies behind and strain forward to what lies ahead' (Philippians 3.13) as radically and readily as Paul did, will we, too, in our divided communion, eventually find our agreement in Christ.

Faithful Lord,
whose steadfast love never ceases
and whose mercies never come to an end:
grant us the grace to trust you
and to receive the gifts of your love,
new every morning,
in Jesus Christ our Lord.

COLLECT

Monday 22 October

Psalms 123, 124, 125, **126**
2 Kings 21.1-18
1 Timothy 1.1-17

1 Timothy 1.1-17

*'... love that comes from a pure heart, a good conscience,
and sincere faith' (v.5)*

The first letter to Timothy written by the apostle Paul – or someone writing in his name – is known as a pastoral letter. It deals with matters relating to Timothy's ministry and the life of the young church. Then and now, such concerns often appear inward-looking and somewhat esoteric. In this letter, Timothy is reminded of the purpose in it all.

Don't preach just to impress, or teach to be clever; instead, seek love, purity and faith (vv.3-7).

Don't use your moral standards to make you and others feel superior; instead help others to turn around and find God's forgiveness (vv.8-11).

Don't let your faith make you proud; remember that it's all down to God's amazing grace and mercy (vv.12-17).

It is easy for church to become a debating society where finer points of faith are discussed endlessly. Too often, church is a club for those who keep the rules and where status and position are all important. Today's reading reminds us that church is, at its heart, a community for all who find in God's love a wide welcome; to all who are discovering in God's mercy and forgiveness the strength and opportunity to live faithful and good lives.

COLLECT

God, the giver of life,
whose Holy Spirit wells up within your Church:
by the Spirit's gifts equip us to live the gospel of Christ
    and make us eager to do your will,
that we may share with the whole creation the joys of eternal life;
through Jesus Christ your Son our Lord,
who is alive and reigns with you,
in the unity of the Holy Spirit,
one God, now and for ever.

Psalms **132**, 133
2 Kings 22.1 – 23.3
1 Timothy 1.18 – end of 2

1 Timothy 1.18 – end of 2

'… so that we may lead a quiet and peaceable life
in all godliness and dignity' (2.2)

There are a few tricky bits in this passage. The writer might come across to us as someone who wants to exclude people from church, who doesn't want to rock the boat politically and who wants to put women in their ('silent' and 'submissive') place. Have we, in the twenty-first century, got anything to learn from such sentiments?

We might note that the reason for these injunctions is belief in a God who 'desires everyone to be saved and come to the knowledge of the truth' (v.4). So, Christians should pray, with thankfulness, for all people, not just a select few (v.1). So, prayer for rulers is in order to enable Christians to live lives that will point others to God (v.2). So, the behaviour of men and women in church should be marked by reverence and godliness, not argument and ostentation (vv.8-15) because the church is called to be a sign of God's love.

Today, that modesty and godliness will look different. Today, we have opportunities to engage politically, not just to pray.

The key question of today's passage, however, remains: how do we live in the world, and organize ourselves within the Church, so that it becomes more likely (rather than less likely) that others will see and discover the love that God has for them?

God, our light and our salvation:
illuminate our lives,
that we may see your goodness in the land of the living,
and looking on your beauty
may be changed into the likeness of Jesus Christ our Lord.

COLLECT

Psalm **119.153-end**
2 Kings 23.4-25
1 Timothy 3

1 Timothy 3

'Now a bishop must be above reproach' (v.2)

As we seek to adapt to a rapidly changing society and life becomes more complex, it might be argued that our leaders need, above all, to be managers – people who can manage change, who can develop strategy and deliver growth. It is interesting to note that the writer of 1 Timothy, in a time of no less flux and uncertainty, argues that the essential quality to be looked for is character.

Character is seen in one's personal qualities (vv.2,3) and in one's relationships both with family and friends (vv.4,5) and with those who are outside one's immediate circle (v.7). This is true for bishops, or maybe more simply pastors, and also those who serve alongside them as deacons (vv.8-13).

The Christian faith is rooted in the incarnation of Christ – the grace and truth of God, the character of God, 'revealed in flesh' (v.16). So it is in our lives, in our character, however falteringly and faintly, that the character of God is revealed.

We rightly celebrate our skills, our abilities and gifts – the things we can do and do well. We need also to consider our character – those qualities by which we are known to those around us. What do people see? Who do they see revealed in our life?

COLLECT

God, the giver of life,
whose Holy Spirit wells up within your Church:
by the Spirit's gifts equip us to live the gospel of Christ
and make us eager to do your will,
that we may share with the whole creation the joys of eternal life;
through Jesus Christ your Son our Lord,
who is alive and reigns with you,
in the unity of the Holy Spirit,
one God, now and for ever.

Psalms **143**, 146
2 Kings 23.36 – 24.17
1 Timothy 4

Thursday 25 October

1 Timothy 4

'... godliness is valuable in every way' (v.8)

Even a brief look at the different faiths in the world, and the different expressions within a single faith, illustrates vastly contrasting ideas of godliness. These are often rooted in quite different understandings of God and God's engagement with the world.

For some, like the ones described here (v.3), godliness is seen in withdrawal from the world in search of spiritual purity. For some, as described here (v.7), godliness is seen in knowing particular god-given truths hidden from others. Such godliness is exclusive and often unattractive; it seems to be rooted in a sense that God really doesn't like the world, let alone love it.

For the writer, godliness reflects the goodness of God and the goodness of God's creation (v.4); godliness is fed by hope and faith in a God who embraces all people (v.10). Godliness is seen in a life lived openly with integrity, where speech matches conduct (v.12). Such godliness is more likely to be attractive and welcoming.

Take time to reflect on your understanding of God and of God's love for the world. What sort of 'godliness' might reflect this understanding with authenticity and joy? How might you grow in a godliness that is open and attractive?

God, our light and our salvation:
illuminate our lives,
that we may see your goodness in the land of the living,
and looking on your beauty
may be changed into the likeness of Jesus Christ our Lord.

COLLECT

Friday 26 October

1 Timothy 5.1-16

*'… whoever does not provide for relatives …
has denied the faith' (v.8)*

As a student, I remember reading a book about the life of Henry Martyn, a renowned missionary to India and Persia in the early years of the nineteenth century. The book was called *My Love Must Wait*. Martyn chose to leave behind his fiancée when he sailed for India in 1805; he died on his way home in present-day Turkey in 1812. His story moved me.

Does God require us to deny ourselves human love in order to find his love? Sometimes it might be so. But it is also true that God calls us into love and into relationship, not just with him, but also with one another.

The young Christian community that Timothy led was seeking to explore how this might work out in practice. The advice he receives is practical and full of realism. Show respect to all (v.5). Care first for those in real need (v.9). Don't let people use their faith as an excuse for not caring for their relatives (v.8).

Our faith does not relieve us of responsibilities; it's not permission to escape. Our faith invites us to get involved, to take responsibility, to care and to provide. God calls us to love and to be loved, and to find great delight in that.

COLLECT

God, the giver of life,
whose Holy Spirit wells up within your Church:
by the Spirit's gifts equip us to live the gospel of Christ
    and make us eager to do your will,
that we may share with the whole creation the joys of eternal life;
through Jesus Christ your Son our Lord,
who is alive and reigns with you,
in the unity of the Holy Spirit,
one God, now and for ever.

Psalm 147
2 Kings 25.22-end
1 Timothy 5.17-end

1 Timothy 5.17-end

*'… keep these instructions without prejudice,
doing nothing on the basis of partiality' (v.21)*

We all meet people we naturally warm to; there are people we like more than others, there are those who like us and with whom we gel. Whether at work or in the Church, or even within our families, it happens. It's important we recognize this, especially if we, like Timothy, are in a leadership role. It is greatly damaging to a community or organization if there is seen to be favouritism or partiality. It is destructive and destabilizing.

Some like to favour themselves or those close to them. Timothy's problem may well have been the opposite. He is encouraged not to deny himself the joy (and the medicine) of a little wine (v.23). We can be hard and unfair in our treatment of others; we can also be hard and unfair in our treatment of ourselves.

Take a bit of time to reflect on your relationships in the communities in which you belong. Are you unfair on some? Is there an element of partiality in the way you engage with people?

Take a bit of time to reflect on the way you treat yourself. Are you unfair on yourself? What might be a way in which by being generous with yourself you are better able also to love and care for others?

God, our light and our salvation:
illuminate our lives,
that we may see your goodness in the land of the living,
and looking on your beauty
may be changed into the likeness of Jesus Christ our Lord.

COLLECT

Monday 29 October

Psalms 1, 2, 3
Judith 4
or Exodus 22.21-27, 23.1-17
I Timothy 6.1-10

Exodus 22.21-27, 23.1-17

*'… if your neighbour cries out to me, I will listen,
for I am compassionate' (22.27)*

One of the great challenges to people of faith is the reality that it frequently appears that God doesn't hear the cries of those in need. All too often, there is little evidence that God responds to those who call to him for help, for food, for justice. In today's passage, we are told that God does hear, and that he listens and that he is compassionate.

What the passage also says is that God expects his people – *us* – to act. In fact, the only divine actions described are not the promise of help for the poor but the threat of judgement on his people for their indifference and inactivity.

So the real challenge to people of faith when faced with the apparently unheard cries of those in need is to act. The challenge is to welcome the stranger (22.21), to care for the needy (22.22), to refuse to take advantage of those who are defenceless and vulnerable (22.25-27).

The real challenge is not to struggle to go on *believing*, but to strive to go on *doing* something – so to do justly and so to love mercy that we discover that we are walking humbly with our God (Micah 6.8).

COLLECT

Blessed Lord,
who caused all holy Scriptures to be written for our learning:
help us so to hear them,
to read, mark, learn and inwardly digest them
that, through patience, and the comfort of your holy word,
we may embrace and for ever hold fast
    the hope of everlasting life,
which you have given us in our Saviour Jesus Christ,
who is alive and reigns with you,
in the unity of the Holy Spirit,
one God, now and for ever.

Psalms **5**, 6 (8)
Judith 5.1 – 6.4
or Exodus 29.38 – 30.16
1 Timothy 6.11-end

Exodus 29.38 – 30.16

'I will dwell among the Israelites, and I will be their God' (29.45)

> 'The Lord is here,
> His Spirit is with us'

It's a regular and familiar response; but how do we know that God is among us; how do we recognise his presence?

Exodus details instructions for a range of rituals – linked to the culture of the day – in Israel's worship of God. A lamb, together with flour, oil and wine to be offered to a generous God. Sweet smelling incense to be burned before a holy God. A coin given by each person to a redeeming God. Signs that point to the character of God and also to the presence of God (vv.42,45,46)

Ritual can often seem to emphasize – not least in its ceremony and grandeur – the transcendence of God. It often reminds us of the otherness of God. Yet, it can also – through its intimacy, through colour and image, through sound and smell – speak powerfully of God's immanence, his constant presence throughout the universe, his closeness.

What helps you to glimpse the mystery and otherness of God in your life today? The glory of worship? The glory of creation?

What is it that helps you glimpse the presence and nearness of God? The gift of love and friendship? The gift of Christ in the breaking of the bread?

Merciful God,
teach us to be faithful in change and uncertainty,
that trusting in your word
and obeying your will
we may enter the unfailing joy of Jesus Christ our Lord.

COLLECT

Wednesday 31 October

Psalm 119.1-32
Judith 6.10 – 7.7 or Leviticus 8
2 Timothy 1.1-14

Leviticus 8

*'Then Moses brought Aaron and his sons forward,
and washed them with water' (v.6)*

It's quite a chapter to read today – detailed and graphic. Not, perhaps, to be read while eating your breakfast. Fine priestly robes. Oil to anoint both priest and altar. Bull and rams sacrificed, sin offering, burnt offering and ordination offering. Smoke and smell, blood and flesh – a ritual, performed with meticulous care, that engaged and gripped its participants. It might make our ordination services appear somewhat bland and brief.

Yet it begins simply, with washing. Quite a contrast to the colour, the intensity, the noise and smell of all that followed. Yet, perhaps in its simplicity, just as powerful.

Water, as in baptism, is a symbol of life, of refreshment, of cleansing and a symbol of new birth. It celebrates the God who gives life and sustains life in creation. It speaks of the God who forgives and renews, who gives joy and rest. It invites us to draw near to the God who brings new life through death.

Aaron and his sons began a life as priests as they came forward and were washed. Our worship and our life in Christ begin, and continue each day, as we receive the forgiveness, the joy, the refreshment of God. What might the cleansing, life-giving love of God help you to begin today?

COLLECT

Blessed Lord,
who caused all holy Scriptures to be written for our learning:
help us so to hear them,
to read, mark, learn and inwardly digest them
that, through patience, and the comfort of your holy word,
we may embrace and for ever hold fast
     the hope of everlasting life,
which you have given us in our Saviour Jesus Christ,
who is alive and reigns with you,
in the unity of the Holy Spirit,
one God, now and for ever.

Psalms 15, 84, 149
Isaiah 35
Luke 9.18-27

Thursday 1 November

All Saints' Day

Isaiah 35

*'For waters shall break forth in the wilderness,
and streams in the desert' (v.6)*

We take a break from Exodus and Leviticus today to celebrate All Saints Day. The prophet Isaiah paints a picture of transformation – a transformation of people and a transformation of the land.

Those with weak hands, feeble knees and fearful hearts are called to be strong (vv.3,4). The blind, the deaf, the lame and the speechless find sight and hearing, leap and sing (vv.5,6). It's a great image for All Saints Day. These are the people of God, the Saints of God, those who know in their lives the amazing transformation of God. Those who know his strength, his healing and joy.

Yet there is a further transformation in Isaiah's vision – the transformation of the desert. As God brings life and strength to his people, so he brings water to the desert (vv.6,7). As his transformed people walk the way, life is brought to the land through which they pass.

The Saints of God are not simply those who know God's transforming power in their own lives; they are those who through their love and prayers, their life and action, bring that transformation to the communities and the world in which they live. Celebrate your sainthood today in gratitude and by living a transformed and transforming life.

Almighty God,
you have knit together your elect
in one communion and fellowship
in the mystical body of your Son Christ our Lord:
grant us grace so to follow your blessed saints
in all virtuous and godly living
that we may come to those inexpressible joys
that you have prepared for those who truly love you;
through Jesus Christ your Son our Lord,
who is alive and reigns with you,
in the unity of the Holy Spirit,
one God, now and for ever.

COLLECT

Friday 2 November

Psalms 17, **19**
Judith 8.9-end
or Leviticus 16.2-24
2 Timothy 2.14-end

Leviticus 16.2-24

'… so that it may be sent away into the wilderness to Azazel' (v.10)

William Holman Hunt is probably most well known for his painting 'The Light of the World' – Christ standing outside a closed door patiently waiting for it to be opened. He painted an equally powerful and poignant picture called 'The Scapegoat'. He travelled to Palestine to paint the picture and chose to place the goat in what he described as 'a scene of beautifully arranged horrible wilderness', on the shore of the Dead Sea. It is as desolate and desperate a scene as you can imagine.

The priest, Aaron, laid his hands on the goat and sent it off by itself to the desert, the goat symbolically carrying away the sins of the people. Burnt offerings and sin offerings can seem quite strange to us, but scapegoats we do understand. We do it all the time. Those who commit particularly horrendous crimes, idols who come crashing down, minority groups, officials on whose watch something goes wrong; we are often quick to find scapegoats who take into the desert not just their wrong-doing but ours as well.

We believe that Christ, himself a scapegoat for the fears and anger of others, 'bore our sins away'. We have no need, therefore, to send others into the desert carrying our anger, our fear and our sins.

COLLECT

Blessed Lord,
who caused all holy Scriptures to be written for our learning:
help us so to hear them,
to read, mark, learn and inwardly digest them
that, through patience, and the comfort of your holy word,
we may embrace and for ever hold fast
　　the hope of everlasting life,
which you have given us in our Saviour Jesus Christ,
who is alive and reigns with you,
in the unity of the Holy Spirit,
one God, now and for ever.

Psalms 20, 21, **23**
Judith 9 *or* Leviticus 17
2 Timothy 3

Saturday 3 November

Leviticus 17

'For the life of every creature – its blood is its life' (v.14)

It's easy to see how blood has often been seen not just as a symbol of life, but as life itself. As blood flows round our bodies, so we live; as blood drains away, so we die. The commandments in this reading about the shedding of the blood of animals and the injunction against eating blood can be understood in this context. The blood of the animal is its life, and it is to be returned to the earth (v.13) and not consumed by another.

We see blood differently. We are probably happy to eat products containing blood. (We may even enjoy black pudding!) But if the blood of animals is no longer 'sacred' to us, how do we view their lives? What is our attitude to the lives of the animals that provide food or companionship for us? Are they merely commodities to meet our needs? How do we view the lives of all creatures struggling to survive in a resource-hungry world and an exploited environment? What is being lost to us?

Take a bit of time today to consider the sacredness of 'the life of every creature'. What can you do to treasure, respect and revere that life?

Merciful God,
teach us to be faithful in change and uncertainty,
that trusting in your word
and obeying your will
we may enter the unfailing joy of Jesus Christ our Lord.

COLLECT

Monday 5 November

Psalms **2**, 146 *or* 27, **30**
Daniel 1
Revelation 1

Daniel 1

'... vegetables to eat and water to drink' (v.12)

Private discipline is the foundation for public influence. Daniel and his friends are to be counsellors of kings and administrators of a kingdom. Their wisdom is acquired through years of disciplined study of language and literature as they learn to live in exile in Babylon. Yet there is something more that marks them out as different.

A major theme of the book of Daniel is how to live as a community in a strange land. How can you remain true to all that you believe in, yet genuinely live well and serve a different society? How can you grow the inner strength you will need to be able to make the key choices when they come? These choices will determine whether you are absorbed into the larger culture or can transform it from within.

The key inner disciplines for Daniel are private prayer (which runs as a thread through the book) and voluntary abstinence from the king's rich food. They are choices that grow into habits that, in turn, shape character. They are about the inner chamber, not the public realm. They are practices shared among a small group of colleagues who are determined to be different.

Where are the secret inner disciplines that are shaping your public life?

COLLECT

Almighty and eternal God,
you have kindled the flame of love in the hearts of the saints:
grant to us the same faith and power of love,
that, as we rejoice in their triumphs,
we may be sustained by their example and fellowship;
through Jesus Christ your Son our Lord,
who is alive and reigns with you,
in the unity of the Holy Spirit,
one God, now and for ever.

Tuesday 6 November

Daniel 2.1-24

'... revealed ... in a vision' (v.19)

Daniel's first crisis is about vegetables, but the second is a matter of life and death. The challenge Nebuchadnezzar poses his advisers takes them beyond every human resource and wisdom. How is it possible to draw out an interpretation when you have no hint about the dream itself?

When he comes face to face with death, Daniel does not panic, nor does he submit. He prays and calls on his friends to seek mercy from the God of heaven. There is a lesson here for times of crisis.

But that lesson goes further still. The book of Daniel is written to teach us that human wisdom has value, but is not enough. There is a need still for revelation directly from God. Even the wise and powerful need that revelation and understanding. That revelation comes to us in the quietness, in private, in the night. It shines like a searchlight in the darkness and shows us new paths we had never considered.

There is no way to receive that revelation, the life-changing word, except by prayer and attention. As you come in prayer this day to the living God, remember that he is the one who reveals deep and hidden things, who knows what is in the darkness. Learn to hear his word again.

God of glory,
touch our lips with the fire of your Spirit,
that we with all creation
may rejoice to sing your praise;
through Jesus Christ our Lord.

COLLECT

297

Wednesday 7 November

Daniel 2.25-end

'... a kingdom that shall never be destroyed' (v.44)

Receiving God's revelation tests the character of the prophet. Daniel takes care to make clear that what he is about to share is not human wisdom but God's own revelation. Daniel himself is simply the messenger. Prophecy is not some kind of ecstatic alternative to wisdom but a necessary accompaniment to human learning. It demands exactly the same humility and strength of character, forged through the same disciplines. It demands the same skill in communication.

The dream and its interpretation help Nebuchadnezzar and readers in every generation to see their place in human history and divine providence. Human kingdoms rise and fall. Some are like gold, or silver, bronze or iron mixed with clay. Even the most glorious and most powerful will come to an end. But there is a kingdom greater than any human reign, a kingdom not made with human hands, set up by the God of heaven, which shall never be destroyed.

In this kingdom season, we look back over two thousand years since Jesus came proclaiming that the kingdom of heaven is at hand. We look back and survey a multitude of kingdoms rising and falling, some of bronze and some of clay. Still God's kingdom stands through every change. And still we pray: your kingdom come.

Almighty and eternal God,
you have kindled the flame of love in the hearts of the saints:
grant to us the same faith and power of love,
that, as we rejoice in their triumphs,
we may be sustained by their example and fellowship;
through Jesus Christ your Son our Lord,
who is alive and reigns with you,
in the unity of the Holy Spirit,
one God, now and for ever.

Psalms 11, **15**, 148 *or* **37***
Daniel 3.1-18
Revelation 3.1-13

Daniel 3.1-18

'... we will not serve your gods' (v.18)

We belong to the kingdom of heaven, yet we live out our lives in one of the kingdoms of this world.

One of the greatest gifts God's people need in every generation is discernment. Living in the world requires compromise, but there are some occasions where we need to stand firm. Which are they?

For Shadrach, Meshach and Abednego, to worship an idol breaks the first and second commandments and is an absolute. Every time the music plays, everyone must bow down to the idol. There is no way around the king's decree except quiet disobedience. The three may have escaped were it not for 'certain Chaldeans' who are clearly jealous of their prominence. Anti-Semitism and prejudice against those who hold themselves different from the community around them are woven through the passage.

Nebuchadnezzar's view (which was the view of the Romans many years later) is that religious obedience and conformity are the key to a united kingdom. The view of the exiles (and the later Christians in the Roman empire) is that it is possible to be loyal to a political system and yet have a higher and greater allegiance to God.

What are the areas today where our allegiance would be tested and we would refuse to bow down?

> God of glory,
> touch our lips with the fire of your Spirit,
> that we with all creation
> may rejoice to sing your praise;
> through Jesus Christ our Lord.

COLLECT

Friday 9 November

Daniel 3.19-end

'... four men unbound, walking in the middle of the fire' (v.25)

Children love the story of the escape from the fiery furnace and the second great deliverance story that will follow as Daniel escapes the lions' den. It is told with great drama. The king is so filled with rage his face is distorted. The furnace is heated seven times more than is customary. Even the guards who throw the bound companions into the fire are consumed.

But Shadrach, Meshach and Abednego live through the ordeal. Even in the midst of the hottest of fires, they cannot be burned (Isaiah 43.2). Nebuchadnezzar looks and sees not three but four men walking in the midst of the flames. One who has the appearance of a god is with them even in their intense suffering and trial, the great crisis of their lives. They walk unharmed from the flames.

From the first readers of Daniel to the present day, the other group who have found immense comfort in this story are those who experience the fire of crisis, of persecution and suffering for their faith. They know, as we know, that in this life the pain is often real. God does not always afford his saints miraculous deliverance. Yet we know, as we walk through fire, his presence in our trials and the hope of a still greater salvation beyond death itself.

COLLECT

Almighty and eternal God,
you have kindled the flame of love in the hearts of the saints:
grant to us the same faith and power of love,
that, as we rejoice in their triumphs,
we may be sustained by their example and fellowship;
through Jesus Christ your Son our Lord,
who is alive and reigns with you,
in the unity of the Holy Spirit,
one God, now and for ever.

Daniel 4.1-18

'I saw a dream that frightened me' (v.5)

Nebuchadnezzar sets his wise men a second task. On the surface it seems easier than the first (where they had to describe the dream and interpret it). Yet still they stumble. As Nebuchadnezzar relates his vision, the responsibility of telling the king what it means is passed quickly up the line until it reaches Daniel.

Here the actual interpretation of the dream is not difficult. We know by now that Nebuchadnezzar himself is likely to be the subject of any vision he has. Surely the king himself is clearly the tree. The meaning of the vision is that he will be struck down in some way.

Imagine the conversation. Do you want to tell him that? Not me. How about you? No fear. Let's pass it up the line. It is one thing to be bearers of a message that is good news but another to bring a word that is less welcome.

Daniel's great quality in this passage is once again his integrity. He has the courage to speak truth to power: the essential quality in any senior advisor to government as in any pastor, counsellor or preacher. It is surprisingly easy to tell people only what they want to hear. It takes huge courage to grow in the habit of speaking the truth. Yet, without the truth, there is ultimately no comfort.

God of glory,
touch our lips with the fire of your Spirit,
that we with all creation
may rejoice to sing your praise;
through Jesus Christ our Lord.

COLLECT

Monday 12 November

Daniel 4.19-end

'... his kingdom endures' (v.34)

Here are more lessons about kings and kingdoms for this season. The metaphor of the tall tree recurs in the prophets as an image for the proud kingdom that has grown too full of itself. It is used both of God's people and of foreign nations.

In Daniel, the subject is a foreign ruler and one who has taken God's people captive. Nebuchadnezzar has grown too full of himself and his own greatness. His kingdom is taken away from him and he must live for a while like a beast until he has learned that the Most High has sovereignty over the kingdom of mortals.

Nebuchadnezzar learns his lesson and is restored. He gives thanks to the King of heaven. Yet there are other lessons here for the people of God. God's kingdom extends way beyond those we think of as the people of God – whether those people are the Jews in the Old Testament or the Christian Church in the time after Pentecost. God is at work wherever people will work with him.

In our daily work this week, where might we suppose God is active, revealing himself to those who have power through dreams in the night, through encounters with God's prophets? Are our eyes open to see more of what God is doing as the kingdom is established?

COLLECT

Almighty Father,
whose will is to restore all things
in your beloved Son, the King of all:
govern the hearts and minds of those in authority,
and bring the families of the nations,
divided and torn apart by the ravages of sin,
to be subject to his just and gentle rule;
who is alive and reigns with you,
in the unity of the Holy Spirit,
one God, now and for ever.

Tuesday 13 November

Daniel 5.1-12

'... let Daniel be called' (v.12)

The fourth great crisis of Daniel's life comes when he is in some kind of temporary retirement and largely forgotten by the court.

The story of King Belshazzar's feast is a classic story of pride followed by destruction. The height of sacrilege is reached when the holy vessels from the temple are brought into the feast when the king and his companions are drunk and, by implication, carousing. The early readers of the book of Daniel knew what sacrilege meant as they saw the rebuilt temple and the holy customs of the Jewish people brought into contempt.

As the king and his concubines praise the gods of wood and stone, a hand appears and traces words no one can understand on the plaster. The king is filled with fear. Once again the cry goes out for someone of insight, able to read the writing on the wall. The person who reads it must have wisdom to read a foreign tongue, prophetic insight to interpret the words in their context and the courage, once again, to offer words of rebuke and judgement to a king.

There is only one in Babylon who has this rare combination of gifts. They send for Daniel.

And if they had sent for you or me to bring the word of God to Belshazzar, what would we have said?

God, our refuge and strength,
bring near the day when wars shall cease
and poverty and pain shall end,
that earth may know the peace of heaven
through Jesus Christ our Lord.

COLLECT

Wednesday 14 November

Psalms **23**, 25 *or* **119.57-80**
Daniel 5.13-end
Revelation 7.1-4, 9-end

Daniel 5.13-end

'Mene, mene, tekel, parsin' (v.25)

Power has gone to Belshazzar's head. He seems to focus only on its outward trappings: parties, glamour and feasting. All the Bible knows of his reign is that he gave a feast and drank from the temple vessels.

Once again, Daniel is called upon to speak the truth to a king. There must have been others who could read the Aramaic script and translate it. Once translated, the meaning is not so obscure. Was it really so difficult to work out the meaning?

The words spoken to Belshazzar by Daniel are a warning not only to Nebuchadnezzar's son but to those in every generation called to exercise power. Leadership is not about status and magnifying yourself before others. Leadership is a sacred trust to govern for the good of all. A vital part of such leadership is acknowledging the higher authority of God and his sovereignty over the kingdom of mortals.

Christians who exercise any kind of power need to heed this warning for themselves as well as offer it to others. We are also drawn in this kingdom season to contrast Belshazzar's kingship with the kingship of Jesus Christ, who came, as a king should, not to be served but to serve, and who has left us a more lasting and most holy feast.

COLLECT

Almighty Father,
whose will is to restore all things
in your beloved Son, the King of all:
govern the hearts and minds of those in authority,
and bring the families of the nations,
divided and torn apart by the ravages of sin,
to be subject to his just and gentle rule;
who is alive and reigns with you,
in the unity of the Holy Spirit,
one God, now and for ever.

Daniel 6

'... to pray to his God and praise him' (v.10)

The fifth and final crisis in Daniel's life comes when he is at the very height of his powers. Throughout his life, he has chosen the paths of integrity and has found ways both to be faithful to God and to serve at the highest levels in the civil service of Babylon. He is highly skilled in his task and no fault whatsoever can be found in his life or work. All of this is no small achievement.

However, this does not mean he has no enemies. In the plotting of the court, there are many who seek his downfall. The plan is hatched.

Every day of his adult life, Daniel has gone to his upper chamber, opened the windows toward Jerusalem and offered prayer and praise to God. This is the heart of his inner discipline, of his integrity and his ability to serve both God and the state without compromise for so long and so well. The trap is sprung. Daniel is cast into the lions' den, yet miraculously delivered. God's kingdom is affirmed even by Darius (v.26). It is a kingdom of dominion yet also salvation.

How much does your prayer life mean to you? In which inner, secret place is your integrity forged day by day?

God, our refuge and strength,
bring near the day when wars shall cease
and poverty and pain shall end,
that earth may know the peace of heaven
through Jesus Christ our Lord.

COLLECT

Friday 16 November

Daniel 7.1-14

'To him was given dominion and glory and kingship' (v.14)

The book of Daniel changes from story to vision at the beginning of chapter 7 (although the section of the book written in Aramaic rather than Hebrew extends from 2.4 to the end of this chapter). We are now in the genre of apocalyptic: visions and messages revealed from heaven. Revelation is the New Testament book that echoes much of Daniel, but there is a significant apocalyptic literature outside the Bible, some in the Apocrypha.

Today's reading has the vision; tomorrow's the interpretation through the words of an attendant. The vision is in three parts: a vision of four beasts (corresponding to four great empires and echoing Daniel 2) in verses 1 to 8; a vision of the Ancient of Days and the heavenly court in verses 9 to 11; and a vision of 'one like a human being' (v.13).

The chapter is written to strengthen God's people in times of great persecution. Behind the most terrible of human events lies another much deeper reality, which we can lose sight of in our suffering or the press of daily life. The most powerful kingdom is transitory, yet there is a kingdom founded by God that will never be destroyed. Every human kingdom is a shadow and a pale reflection of God's kingdom, which is both present and still to come in all its fullness.

COLLECT

Almighty Father,
whose will is to restore all things
in your beloved Son, the King of all:
govern the hearts and minds of those in authority,
and bring the families of the nations,
divided and torn apart by the ravages of sin,
to be subject to his just and gentle rule;
who is alive and reigns with you,
in the unity of the Holy Spirit,
one God, now and for ever.

Saturday 17 November

Daniel 7.15-end

'... their kingdom shall be an everlasting kingdom' (v.27)

The interpretation of Daniel's vision focuses on the four kingdoms and especially the fourth beast. Scholars believe the text refers here to a particular king, Antiochus Epiphanes, who led a vicious persecution of the Jewish people in Palestine in 175 BC. This part of Daniel was given originally to strengthen God's people during the time of the great persecution, but has been read in every generation and every part of the world where God's people are oppressed by a hostile regime.

The four great pagan kingdoms of the vision are represented by beasts. They are normally taken to signify the empires of Babylonia, Media, Persia and Greece. However, in contrast, God's kingdom is entrusted to one who is 'like a human being' (NRSV) or, more conventionally, 'like a Son of Man'. This phrase is borrowed from Psalm 8 and the prophet Ezekiel (AV). It is taken up, of course, by Jesus in the Gospels as one of the key ways in which the Lord describes himself. In using the phrase of himself, Jesus is drawing attention both to his own humanity and to the truth that he is the divinely appointed Christ, or king, whose kingship is one that shall never be destroyed.

As we journey through this kingdom season and reflect on a turbulent world, we remember both the humanity and the greatness of God's anointed king.

God, our refuge and strength,
bring near the day when wars shall cease
and poverty and pain shall end,
that earth may know the peace of heaven
through Jesus Christ our Lord.

COLLECT

307

Monday 19 November

Psalms **46, 47** *or* **71**
Daniel 8.1-14
Revelation 10

Daniel 8.1-14

'... a vision appeared to me, Daniel' (v.1)

It's probably true to say that the visions related in the book of Daniel don't always make immediate sense. Here, at the beginning of chapter 8, we are introduced to a ram with two horns. The identity of the ram isn't revealed until verse 20 (so we must wait until tomorrow), but this animal is clearly bent on domination as it butts its way west, north and south. Then a goat with an even larger horn appears on the scene. A battle of wills ensues – and then we're told about yet more horns. It feels a bit like a nightmare where everything is distorted and nothing makes sense.

As we will see tomorrow, Daniel is to continue reflecting on his vision until he understands its meaning. He can't shake it off and forget all about it, as he might a bad dream. He is to wrestle with the things he has seen until they begin to make sense.

We live in an age where everything must be understood *immediately* – we're not very good at mystery. And yet wisdom comes not from immediate knowledge, but from pondering and reflecting on all that we see and hear and experience as we journey through life.

Just because we might not immediately understand what God wants of us, doesn't mean we should give up seeking.

COLLECT

Heavenly Father,
whose blessed Son was revealed
    to destroy the works of the devil
and to make us the children of God and heirs of eternal life:
grant that we, having this hope,
may purify ourselves even as he is pure;
that when he shall appear in power and great glory
we may be made like him in his eternal and glorious kingdom;
where he is alive and reigns with you,
in the unity of the Holy Spirit,
one God, now and for ever.

Psalms 48, **52** *or* **73**
Daniel 8.15-end
Revelation 11.1-14

Daniel 8.15-end

'... then I arose and went about the king's business' (v.27)

Daniel's vision continues, and the identities of the ram, the goat and the little horn are revealed as the Medo-Persian, Greek and Roman empires. In other words, the future world powers. Daniel foresees, with horror, the stamping-out of his people's religion, together with the desecration of the temple at Jerusalem and the slaughter of hundreds of his people. And this is to be a lengthy persecution.

Little wonder, then, that Daniel takes to his bed. He has seen what lies ahead and it fills him with dread. Depression sets in and he is paralysed by darkness and despair. Daniel could, at that moment, have given up. Faced with all that the future holds, he could easily have decided that there was little point in carrying on. Instead, after a couple of days, he draws on every inch of his spiritual, physical and psychological resources and gets back to work.

Sometimes, when we look ahead, the future can seem very bleak indeed. Sometimes, it can feel as if there is little point in carrying on when all that we are trying to achieve is met with negativity or even outright hostility. Daniel shows us what it means to be a true disciple. God's work must go on; God's kingdom must be built, even if we ourselves may never see the fruit of our labours.

'O Jesus, I have promised to serve thee to the end.'

Heavenly Lord,
you long for the world's salvation:
stir us from apathy,
restrain us from excess
and revive in us new hope
that all creation will one day be healed
in Jesus Christ our Lord.

COLLECT

Wednesday 21 November

Psalms **56**, 57 *or* **77**
Daniel 9.1-19
Revelation 11.15-end

Daniel 9.1-19

'O Lord, hear; O Lord, forgive;
O Lord, listen and act and do not delay!' (v.19)

Daniel has been studying the book of Jeremiah. He realizes that the period prophesied for the exile is a limited period – 70 years – and then comes the promise of restoration. He falls to his knees in prayer – and records his words for us to read today so that we can see that the restoration of God's people comes about not only as the fulfilment of prophecy, but also in answer to heartfelt and intimate and searching prayer. God calls us to relationship in prayer.

Daniel draws strength, reassurance and courage from his understanding of God's covenant with his people. He knows, in his heart of hearts, that, no matter how far God's people have strayed from him and no matter how much they have thought that they can get along just fine without him, God will not let them go. Daniel's heartfelt prayer stems both from his gratitude to God for such depth of love and commitment – and from a crushing sorrow for the failure of his people to live up to God's promises. Both gratitude to God for his love and sorrow for the ways in which we have marred his love in us should be features of our prayer as we receive Holy Communion – the sign of God's new covenant to us, brought about through Jesus' death and resurrection.

Daniel's prayer can be summarized in the 15 words quoted above from verse 19. Not a bad prayer for us to memorize today to use in times of urgent need, when an 'arrow prayer' is all that time or circumstance will allow.

COLLECT

Heavenly Father,
whose blessed Son was revealed
    to destroy the works of the devil
and to make us the children of God and heirs of eternal life:
grant that we, having this hope,
may purify ourselves even as he is pure;
that when he shall appear in power and great glory
we may be made like him in his eternal and glorious kingdom;
where he is alive and reigns with you,
in the unity of the Holy Spirit,
one God, now and for ever.

Psalms 61, **62** *or or* **78.1-39***
Daniel 9.20-end
Revelation 12

Thursday 22 November

Daniel 9.20-end

'... at the time of the evening sacrifice' (v.21)

There are many interpretations of Daniel's vision of 'the 70 weeks'. It would seem that there is no general agreement about its contents, and that perhaps we shouldn't trouble ourselves too much about its exact meaning, other than to note the promise of an 'anointed prince'. What we may feel to be of significance is hidden away almost as a throwaway remark at the end of verse 21. Daniel receives the vision – and the reassurance of God's love for him – at the time of the evening sacrifice.

Decades have passed since Daniel was present in the temple in Jerusalem for the evening sacrifice. And yet the pattern of prayer practised at the temple was so ingrained in him that he kept to its rhythm, even though separated from Jerusalem by considerable distance and time.

How ingrained in us are our patterns of prayer? How long would they sustain us if circumstances caused us to be cut off from prayer book, Bible and communal worship? Have we lost something by our failure to learn by heart passages from the Psalms, much-loved prayers, 'purple passages' from the Scriptures, verses of stirring and sustaining hymns?

Taking our cue from Daniel, perhaps today might be the day to begin – a verse at a time, a prayer at a time – until we have our own treasury to draw upon in times of joy or sorrow.

Heavenly Lord,
you long for the world's salvation:
stir us from apathy,
restrain us from excess
and revive in us new hope
that all creation will one day be healed
in Jesus Christ our Lord.

COLLECT

Friday 23 November

Daniel 10.1 – 11.1

'… your words have been heard' (10.12)

The final three chapters of the book of Daniel contain another vision followed by a prophecy. But, tellingly, they begin by informing us that we are now in the third year of the reign of King Cyrus of Persia. This raises the question, why is Daniel still in Babylon?

We know from the book of Ezra that, by this time, Cyrus had already decreed that the exiles could return to Jerusalem, and work on the rebuilding of the temple could begin. This is the moment for which Daniel has been watching and waiting and longing. So why wasn't he in the first wave of those who returned?

Daniel must have known in his heart of hearts that his place was there in Babylon. He must have understood that his task was not to be among the great leaders of this new chapter in the history of God's people. Ezra and Nehemiah would be at the forefront of the rebuilding of the temple. Daniel's role is now to be much quieter, and seemingly unspectacular. He is to stay put. And to pray.

It's important for us to be sensitive to when a particular task, given to us by God, is complete. God needs us to be able to step back when it's time for someone else to take up the mantle. To do so may demand of us grace, patience and understanding. But to hang on in there, when we need gracefully to retire, is to risk frustrating God's plans.

COLLECT

Heavenly Father,
whose blessed Son was revealed
    to destroy the works of the devil
and to make us the children of God and heirs of eternal life:
grant that we, having this hope,
may purify ourselves even as he is pure;
that when he shall appear in power and great glory
we may be made like him in his eternal and glorious kingdom;
where he is alive and reigns with you,
in the unity of the Holy Spirit,
one God, now and for ever.

Saturday 24 November

Daniel 12

'But you, go your way, and rest' (v.13)

In this final chapter, Daniel is given a picture of the end times. Many elements of the prophecy are 'sealed until the time of the end' (v.4) and so we will not know or understand them until then. We are, however, given a clear hope of personal resurrection (v.2) and a picture of some form of judgement. Those who are wise will shine like stars amid a darker world of ongoing sin and evil (v.4), and many will be 'running back and forth' searching for spiritual sustenance while rejecting those who can truly feed them.

If we're struggling to understand the passage, it's reassuring to note that Daniel also is confused (v.8). But look at what is said to him. 'Go your way, Daniel, for the words are to remain secret and sealed until the time of the end' (v.9).

There is no need for Daniel to understand every single word that is spoken to him. There is no way that he – or we – can fully understand God's words or God's ways. Our task is simply to listen, to act on what we do understand, and then to trust that God is working his purposes out as year succeeds to year. We must simply remain true to him, as he is to us, even when we have no idea where we're going and what God is up to.

And then we, like Daniel, will be able to receive God's reassurance: 'But you, go your way, and rest; you shall rise for your reward at the end of the days' (v.13).

Heavenly Lord,
you long for the world's salvation:
stir us from apathy,
restrain us from excess
and revive in us new hope
that all creation will one day be healed
in Jesus Christ our Lord.

COLLECT

Monday 26 November

Isaiah 40.1-11

'Comfort, O comfort my people' (v.1)

We have celebrated Christ the King, and now we turn our eyes towards Advent and Christmas, and the prophecies that foretell the King's arrival. This beautiful passage from Isaiah will be far from unfamiliar, and the haunting strains of Handel's *Messiah* may well be echoing in our minds.

We're in the land of Babylon. God's people have been here in exile for so long that they have almost given up on ever being able to return. Through their minds – on more than one occasion – must have passed the worrying conclusion that God must, after all, have given up on them, forgotten them, left them to wallow in their disobedience and despair.

And then a lone voice cries out. 'Comfort my people!' He hasn't forgotten them after all! He seemed so far away and yet he's been there all the time, silently watching over them, carefully waiting for the right time to reveal the promise of his glory. The good shepherd is coming, tenderly gathering his lambs in his arms. Here comes one who will give his own life for his flock.

Sometimes, God feels very far away. Sometimes, we can't hear his voice and he never seems to hear our prayer. Today's passage speaks clearly to us. Don't despair. God is never far away. At the right time and in the right place, he will make himself known.

COLLECT

Eternal Father,
whose Son Jesus Christ ascended to the throne of heaven
    that he might rule over all things as Lord and King:
keep the Church in the unity of the Spirit
and in the bond of peace,
and bring the whole created order to worship at his feet;
who is alive and reigns with you,
in the unity of the Holy Spirit,
one God, now and for ever.

Tuesday 27 November

Isaiah 40.12-26

'It is he … who stretches out the heavens like a curtain' (v.22)

Put yourself, for a moment, in the shoes of a second-generation exile. Babylon is all you have ever known. Those who remember Jerusalem and its mighty temple have passed away. You've listened to the words of the prophets telling you of something better, but life really isn't too bad in Babylon. You've put down roots, set up business. Life is comfortable. Why, then, would you even consider setting out on a long and arduous journey, leaving most of what you own behind – all on the say-so of a rumour of a promise from God? The temptation to forget all about it, and stay put, must have been very great indeed.

'Wake up!' cries the prophet, and his cry echoes down the centuries to us today. Have you forgotten just how great is our God? No one and nothing is his equal. He is the creator of all that is seen and unseen. Our so-called enemies are his puppets, his playthings. This is no wooden idol we worship – but a mighty, powerful God, who just happens to be as gentle as a shepherd. There really isn't anything that God and you together can't handle.

If Isaiah were writing a popular paperback, he might well have got there first with the title: 'Feel the fear – and do it anyway'.

God the Father,
help us to hear the call of Christ the King
and to follow in his service,
whose kingdom has no end;
for he reigns with you and the Holy Spirit,
one God, one glory.

COLLECT

Wednesday 28 November

Isaiah 40.27 – 41.7

*'... but those who wait for the Lord ...
shall mount up with wings like eagles' (40.31)*

Before going on to put the heathen nations on trial in chapter 41, the end of chapter 40 shows God, through Isaiah, taking the opportunity to put a spanner in the works. There are to be no excuses for remaining in Babylon. Second best simply won't do for God's people. They have a destiny to fulfil.

In the same way, those same words challenge us, God's weak and weary children, never to be content with living second-rate lives. We may be very comfortable where we are. But is it where God wants us to be? And if, in our heart of hearts, we know it is not, God will have an answer to every excuse we care to invent, if we will sit in his presence long enough to listen.

We're frightened of change? Then our God is too small – as shown in the magnificent passage we read yesterday. We don't think we have the energy to do something different? Then God will give us something of his inexhaustible energy and strength. With God beside us we can 'mount up with wings like eagles ... run and not be weary ... walk and not faint.'

So what is today's excuse for remaining comfortable? And what does our indefatigable and resourceful God say in reply?

COLLECT

Eternal Father,
whose Son Jesus Christ ascended to the throne of heaven
    that he might rule over all things as Lord and King:
keep the Church in the unity of the Spirit
and in the bond of peace,
and bring the whole created order to worship at his feet;
who is alive and reigns with you,
in the unity of the Holy Spirit,
one God, now and for ever.

Psalms **125**, 126, 127, 128
or 90, **92**
Isaiah 41.8-20
Revelation 16.12-end

Isaiah 41.8-20

'Do not fear, you worm Jacob, you insect Israel!' (v.14)

Sometimes it does no harm to be called a worm. Especially when the name-caller is God. When we get too big for our boots, think that we don't need any help from our Creator, then perhaps it does us good to be reminded by the architect of the universe of our comparative size.

Alternatively, 'worm' might well have been an accurate description of how the people of Israel felt about themselves at that particular point in their history. At least, since you can't get much lower than a worm, the only way must be up. God wants to boost the self-esteem of his children who, browbeaten by so many years in exile, have forgotten their calling.

And this passage reminds them just what it is they are called to be – God's chosen servant – with the corresponding promise, 'I have chosen you … do not fear' (vv.9-10). Their task is to make God's name known; to make God real to those around them.

The servant theme needs little introduction to those of us who worship the 'servant king'. We know what we are called to do. We know who we are called to be. We simply need the confidence to confront the strident voices that say that there is no place for God in our so-called secular world and, casting our perceived worm-like status aside, set out to love and serve that same world into submission.

God the Father,
help us to hear the call of Christ the King
and to follow in his service,
whose kingdom has no end;
for he reigns with you and the Holy Spirit,
one God, one glory.

COLLECT

Friday 30 November

Andrew the Apostle

Psalms 47, 147.1-12
Ezekiel 47.1-12
or Ecclesiasticus 14.20-end
John 12.20-32

John 12.20-32

'... where I am, there will my servant be also' (v.26)

Some Greeks wish to see Jesus. They have heard about him and want to see him for themselves – and learn something from his disturbing, yet truth-filled, teachings. They approach Philip. He shares a Greek heritage and bears a Greek name. He's the easiest of Jesus' followers to approach. Philip consults with Andrew, and together they go to find Jesus.

At first, Jesus seems to have ignored the request of the gentiles. He begins instead a discourse about wheat and fruit. But, indirectly, he's supplying Andrew and Philip – and us in turn – with a direct answer for those who want to see him.

Jesus is to lose his life, for only then will he gain it, in the same way that a grain of seed must seemingly die in the hard winter soil before rising up to greet the arrival of spring. Those who follow Jesus are called to follow him – to lose their lives, and to live not for themselves but for him. To follow Jesus wherever he may lead. To live out his teachings whatever it may cost.

The Greeks will see Jesus – through the faithful witness of Philip and of Andrew. Those around us may see Jesus – if we, too, are willing to put aside our own wants and desires, and instead live out the life Jesus has modelled, and lived and died, for us.

COLLECT

Almighty God,
who gave such grace to your apostle Saint Andrew
that he readily obeyed the call of your Son Jesus Christ
    and brought his brother with him:
call us by your holy word,
and give us grace to follow you without delay
    and to tell the good news of your kingdom;
through Jesus Christ your Son our Lord,
who is alive and reigns with you,
in the unity of the Holy Spirit,
one God, now and for ever.

Psalms **145** *or* 96, **97**, 100
Isaiah 42.10-17
Revelation 18

Saturday 1 December

Isaiah 42.10-17

'Sing to the Lord a new song' (v.10)

It's well worth starting today's passage back at verse 1, because, in celebrating Andrew the Apostle yesterday, we missed some crucial verses introducing the new servant. This servant is distinctly the Messiah whose task is to bring justice and to teach God's law to the gentiles with gentle, courteous grace.

This is a new hope and a new promise for those all too used to 'singing the Lord's song in a strange land'. They are to sing a *new* song – one that will be sung to the very ends of the earth.

Do you sing? Not just in formal worship, but on your own, in the car, around the house? Do you have a storehouse of hymns, psalms and worship songs ready to strengthen and encourage you when you're down? Are you able to 'sing the Lord's song in a strange land' – when tired, discouraged, ill or afraid? And do you have the words of praise to sing when taking the name of God out into your daily work?

Music has a way of soothing and encouraging, which, combined with the words of songs and hymns, can lift us into proclaiming God's goodness even when we don't feel we're up to the task. It's been said that the one who sings prays twice.

'Forth in thy name, O Lord, I go; my daily labour to pursue ...'

Eternal Father,
whose Son Jesus Christ ascended to the throne of heaven
that he might rule over all things as Lord and King:
keep the Church in the unity of the Spirit
and in the bond of peace,
and bring the whole created order to worship at his feet;
who is alive and reigns with you,
in the unity of the Holy Spirit,
one God, now and for ever.

COLLECT

Reflections for Daily Prayer: Advent 2012 to the eve of Advent 2013

Reflections for Daily Prayer returns for the 2012–13 church year with another range of illustrious contributors! Confirmed writers so far include Stephen Cotterell, Steven Croft, Andrew Davison, Martyn Percy, John Pritchard, Christina Rees, Angela Tilby and Jane Williams.

£16.99 • 312 pages
ISBN 978 0 7151 4249 3
Available May 2012

Reflections for Daily Prayer: Lent and Holy Week 2012

Do you enjoy reading *Reflections for Daily Prayer* and wish you could share its benefits with others? This shortened edition of *Reflections* is ideal for group or church use during Lent, or for anyone seeking a daily devotional guide to the most holy season of the Christian year. It is also an ideal taster for those wanting to begin a regular pattern of prayer and reading.

Please note this book reproduces the material for Lent and Holy Week found in the volume you are now holding.

£3.99 • 48 pages
ISBN 978 0 7151 4248 6
Available November 2011

Order now at www.chpublishing.co.uk
or via **Norwich Books and Music**
Telephone **(01603) 785923**
E-mail **orders@norwichbooksandmusic.co.uk**

Resources for Daily Prayer

Common Worship: Daily Prayer

The official daily office of the Church of England, *Common Worship: Daily Prayer* is a rich collection of devotional material that will enable those wanting to enrich their quiet times to develop a regular pattern of prayer.

It includes:

- Prayer During the Day
- Forms of Penitence
- Morning and Evening Prayer
- Night Prayer (Compline)
- Collects and Refrains
- Canticles
- Complete Psalter

896 pages • with 6 ribbons • 202 x 125mm

Hardback	978 0 7151 2073 6	**£22.50**
Soft cased	978 0 7151 2178 8	**£30.00**
Bonded leather	978 0 7151 2100 9	**£45.00**